THE CHANGE IMPERATIVE

CREATING THE NEXT GENERATION NGO

THE CHANGE IMPERATIVE

CREATING THE NEXT GENERATION NGO

Paul Ronalds

 Kumarian Press

A Division of Lynne Rienner Publishers, Inc. • Boulder & London

Published in the United States of America in 2014 by
Kumarian Press
A division of Lynne Rienner Publishers, Inc.
1800 30th Street, Boulder, Colorado 80301
www.kpbooks.com
www.rienner.com

and in the United Kingdom by
Kumarian Press
A division of Lynne Rienner Publishers, Inc.
3 Henrietta Street, Covent Garden, London WC2E 8LU

The cover image is by Dion Jampijinpa Brown, a young, emerging Australian
indigenous artist. It is an "Emu Dreaming" story. World Vision Australia runs a
social enterprise in Sydney, called Birrung Gallery, that sells indigenous
artwork such as this. It is also working with this artist's community, Yuendumu,
on an early childhood program in central Australia.

Library of Congress Cataloging-in-Publication Data
Ronalds, Paul, 1971–
The change imperative: creating the next generation NGO / Paul Ronalds.
    p. cm.
Includes bibliographical references and index.
ISBN 978-1-56549-326-1 (cloth: alk. paper)
ISBN 978-1-56549-325-4 (pbk. : alk. paper)
1. Non-governmental organizations. 2. International organization. I. Title.
JZ4841.R66 2010
341.2—dc22

                                    2010006973

British Cataloguing in Publication Data
A Cataloguing in Publication record for this book
is available from the British Library.

Printed and bound in the United States of America

(∞)   The paper used in this publication meets the requirements
       of the American National Standard for Permanence of
       Paper for Printed Library Materials Z39.48-1992.

    5   4   3   2

To my children, Piper, Asher, and Bailey, and the world they will inherit

Contents

List of Illustrations

Figures

Tables

Case Studies

Abbreviations and Acronyms

ACFID	Australian Council for International Development
ADF	Australian Defence Force
ALNAP	Active Learning Network for Accountability
ALPS	Accountability, Learning, and Planning System
AMREF	African Medical Research Foundation
AMR	Annual Ministerial Reviews
APRODEV	Association of Protestant Development Agencies in Europe
BRAC	Bangladesh Rural Advancement Committee
CARE	Cooperative for Assistance and Relief Everywhere
CCCD	Child-Centered Community Development
CCM	Country Coordinating Mechanisms
CER	Certified Emission Reduction
CERF	Central Emergency Response Fund
CIVICUS	World Alliance for Citizen Participation
CONCORD	European Confederation of NGOs for Aid and Development
CRC	Convention on the Rights of the Child
DAC	Development Assistance Committee
DATA	Debt, AIDS, Trade, Africa
DCF	Development Cooperation Forum
DFID	Department for International Development, United Kingdom
ECOSOC	Economic and Social Council (of the United Nations)
EITI	Extractive Industries Transparency Initiative
EU	European Union
FAO	Food and Agriculture Organization
GFATM	Global Fund to Fight AIDS, Tuberculosis, and Malaria
G7	Group of seven industrial countries—Canada, France, Germany, Italy, Japan, the United Kingdom, and the United States
G8	Group of eight industrial countries—Canada, France, Germany, Italy, Japan, Russia, the United Kingdom, and the United States
GAVI	Global Alliance for Vaccination and Immunization
GNI	Gross National Income

GNP	Gross National Product
GRI	Global Reporting Initiative
HAP	Humanitarian Accountability Partnership
HRW	Human Rights Watch
IASC	Inter-Agency Standing Committee
IAWG	Inter-Agency Working Group
ICBL	International Campaign to Ban Landmines
ICRC	International Committee of the Red Cross
ICC	International Criminal Court
IFFIm	International Finance Facility for Immunization
IFRC	International Federation of the Red Cross
IGO	International Governmental Organization
ILO	International Labor Organization
IMF	International Monetary Fund
ISO	International Organization for Standardization
INGO	International Nongovernmental Organization
LEAP	Learning Through Evaluation, Accountability, and Planning
MAI	Multilateral Agreement on Investment
MDGs	Millennium Development Goals
MSF	Médecins Sans Frontières or Doctors Without Boarders
NGDO	Nongovernmental Development Organization
NGO	Nongovernmental Organization
OCHA	Office for Coordination of Humanitarian Assistance
ODA	Official Development Assistance
ODI	Overseas Development Institute
OECD	Organization for Economic Cooperation and Development
OXFAM	Oxford Committee for Famine Relief
PRC	Partnership Representative Council (of World Vision)
R2P	Responsibility to Protect
TCPR	Triennial Comprehensive Policy Review
TNC	Transnational Corporation
UN	United Nations
UNCTAD	United Nations Conference on Trade and Development
UNDP	United Nations Development Program
UNFCCC	United Nations Framework Convention on Climate Change
UNHCR	United Nations High Commissioner for Refugees
USAID	United States Agency for International Development
WEF	World Economic Forum
WFP	World Food Program
WHO	World Health Organization
WTO	World Trade Organization
WVA	World Vision Australia
WVI	World Vision International
WWF	World Wildlife Fund

Preface

Our current global governance system is broken, and our political climate, despite the international optimism created by the election of Barack Obama, remains bleak, dominated by popular expediency, cynicism, and partisan one-upmanship. On the other hand, the problems we face as a planet have never been greater: global poverty, environmental degradation and climate change, terrorism, runaway population growth, and global financial instability to name just a few. As a result, I agree with Jeffrey Sachs (2008, 4) who said, "In the twenty-first century our global society will flourish or perish according to our ability to find common ground across the world on a set of shared objectives and on the practical means to achieve them."

While ultimately they can be no more than part of the solution, civil society and in particular nongovernment organizations (NGOs) with international influence can play a critical role in helping us find this common ground.

That is why I have written this book. I believe that international nongovernment organizations (INGOs) have a fundamental part to play in helping us solve many of the transnational problems we face in a globalized world. However, I am also deeply worried about whether they are up to the task. Despite the magnitude of the problems they are seeking to help solve and the changes occurring around them, my experience suggests many INGOs are not sufficiently prepared for the future.

Of course, the task faced by managers of INGOs is somewhat daunting. There are many people who question whether INGOs have any legitimate role to play in helping to solve global problems. There are growing questions from critics about INGOs' accountability, efficiency, and effectiveness. Further, the enormous growth that many INGOs have experienced in recent years has stretched their basic processes, systems, and policies to the breaking point. Add to this mix an increasing number of natural disasters, rising food insecurity, greater politicization of aid, and a less-than-conducive global economic environment and you may begin to see the magnitude of the challenges INGO leaders face.

As a result, the primary audience for this book is leaders of INGOs. My hope is that it will assist them in reflecting more creatively about their changing strategic context and what modifications they need to make to increase their organization's accountability, efficiency, and effectiveness. This is no easy task. As this book will argue, the relentless pressure that the managers of INGO experience means that it often feels like such reflection is a luxury they cannot afford. There is also a real lack of useful literature. While bookshops may brim with the latest and greatest tomes on running a more successful corporation and there are endless courses and seminars to attend, there is little to help leaders of INGOs with the relatively more complex task of managing an INGO. My hope is that this book will contribute to addressing this situation.

I also hope that this book may be useful for students of international relations, international development, and international law. INGOs need to attract the best and brightest to help them address the enormous problems they are seeking to solve. Thankfully, there are an increasing number of relevant courses at university level and a growing interest from many very talented young people in developing a career in INGOs.

Finally, the success of global campaigns such as Make Poverty History have increased the general public's awareness and interest in aid and development issues. I therefore also hope that this book will be useful to those people who donate to INGOs or are otherwise particularly interested in how INGOs function.

Paul Ronalds
January 2010

Acknowledgments

I wrote a significant proportion of this book while on a three-month sabbatical from World Vision Australia. In the aid and development sector, this is an all-too-rare opportunity, so my first thanks go to World Vision Australia and, in particular, its chief executive officer, Tim Costello.

I would also like to thank the large number of people who were willing to meet with me to discuss the issues covered by this book. They included Simon Cowell, David Skinner, and Mark Edington at Save the Children International; Richard Miller at Action Aid; Ian Wishart at Plan International; Judy Mitchell, Adriana Zavos, and Jan Nowell at Oxfam; Robert Glassner at CARE; Nick Roseveare at BOND; Roy Trivedy at DFID; Greg Bourne at WWF; Robert Lloyd and Michael Hammer at One World Trust; Ruwan de Mel at the Global Fund; and, of course, a large number of colleagues at World Vision.

Many colleagues also provided comments on early drafts of this book and pushed my thinking in various ways. Dr. Stephen Slaughter of Deakin University helped shape and mold my original work. Professor Alan Fowler provided some very challenging and insightful comments that significantly advanced my thinking in a number of areas and encouraged me to seek publication. Chris Roche at Oxfam Australia and a number of World Vision colleagues including Janita Nelson, Dr. Brett Parris, Dr David Lansley, Rachel Coghlan, Garth Luke, Jock Noble, Conny Lenneberg, Melanie Gow, Casey Lim, Tracey Darley, Peter McKinnon, Chris Trimble, Joyce Godwin, Joshua Wathanga, and Andrew Newmarch all provided very helpful assistance and insights. I would also like to thank the staff at Kumarian Press, in particular, editor and associate publisher, Jim Lance for his support and helpful suggestions. Nonetheless, the views expressed are my own and should not be attributed to World Vision or any other person.

Finally, I would like to thank my wife, Susannah Tymms, for her unwavering support and encouragement in writing this book.

CHAPTER 1

Introduction:
In the Midst of a Revolution

The French intellectual and journalist Regis Debray claimed, "[W]e see the past superimposed on the present, even when the present is a revolution" (Debray 1967). In many ways, this myopia is at the heart of the challenge facing the largest international nongovernmental organizations (INGOs). They are in the midst of a revolution, but as they have grown and matured as global organizations, their ability to change and adapt has been seriously eroded. In addition, they do not always seem to appreciate the extent to which their strategic context has changed. As a result, they are at risk of being unable to respond to the myriad of challenges they face in the twenty-first century, losing relevance and failing to effectively fulfill their mission.

Although there are many different types of INGOs, this book focuses primarily on those involved in addressing issues of extreme poverty. Over the past ten years, the financial resources of some of the largest of these types of INGOs have grown dramatically. For example, the world's largest aid and development INGO, World Vision, now has an annual budget of around US$2.5 billion, larger than any single United Nations (UN) agency except for the World Food Program (WFP) and larger even than the gross national income (GNI) of some small African and European countries. For any organization, adequately responding to this level of growth would be an enormous management challenge in its own right. However, for large INGOs, this growth has also been accompanied by a dramatic change in the aid and development industry and in global politics.

At the beginning of the twenty-first century, there is unprecedented focus on global poverty. Inspired by global campaigns led by "celanthropists" like U2's Bono and actress Angelina Jolie, solving global poverty has captured the imagination of a larger portion of today's young people than ever before. There has also been an explosion in the number and variety of people and groups now engaged in tackling global poverty. Jane Nelson argues that the emergence of these new players, new models, and new sources of funds for development purposes "represents one of the most fundamental and rapid shifts in the history of international

1

KEY POINTS:

Over the past ten years, large INGOs have encountered fundamental change at three levels.

1. Global politics has become much more multilayered, complex, and fluid.
2. The aid and development industry has changed dramatically. The industry has become much more fragmented, there has been a dramatic rise in nonaid financial flows to developing countries, and we have seen the emergence of some powerful new actors.
3. Large INGOs have enjoyed enormous growth in their financial resources and influence. This has placed considerable strain on their management, people, and processes. It has also dramatically increased stakeholder expectations.

As a result, the greatest challenge facing large INGOs in the twenty-first century is to change and adapt faster than their strategic context.

---

development" (Nelson 2008, 160). This fragmentation of the aid and development industry is reflected in the dramatic decline in the importance of official development assistance (ODA). For example, in the 1970s, ODA funded 70 percent of the United States' resource flow to developing countries. Now, 80 percent of such resource flows come from private citizens, corporations, NGOs, religious groups, and foundations (Nelson 2008, 149). In addition, continued environmental degradation and climate change, ongoing urbanization, a significant rise in food and energy prices, pandemics, and the global "security agenda" have created new challenges and seriously complicated the operating context for aid and development actors. INGOs have also had to respond to significantly increased expectations about their performance and accountability.

The growth in the size of INGOs and increased international focus on global poverty has occurred simultaneously with an enormous change in international relations. The bipolar world of the Cold War and the unipolar world that briefly followed have now given way to a much more multilayered, complex, and fluid international context. The rising power of China, India, and other developing economies have led to a seismic shift in relative power away from European and North American countries, demonstrated by the rise of the G20 as the world's premier economic forum. These changes have been further complicated by the growing power of established non-state actors and the emergence of new players. In addition to INGOs and transnational corporations (TNCs) like McDonald's and Coca-Cola, new megaphilanthropists like Bill and Melinda Gates, and international terrorist networks like al Qaeda are impacting the relative power of states and their decision making. Underpinning this diffusion of power are many features of contemporary globalization. These features include technological innovations such as modern communications that limit states' ability to control information and ideas, international financial flows that limit states' macro-economic choices, and labor mobility, particularly of highly skilled professionals and a cosmopolitan "elite."

The growth in the size and influence of the largest INGOs combined with the dramatic changes that are occurring in both the aid and development industry and in international relations creates significant strategic challenges. If large INGOs are going to continue to effectively fulfill their mission, they will need to respond to these changes by undergoing significant organizational change. However, in the past, achieving such change in large INGOs, with their disperse governance and horizontal power structures, has been difficult and slow. Despite the revolution that has been taking place around them, large INGOs sometimes appear to underestimate the extent to which their strategic context has changed, with profound implications for their future relevance in international relations, their mission, and their organizational sustainability. As a result, whether large INGOs will be able to undertake the necessary organizational change in the time frames now being demanded of them seems, at best, uncertain.

This, then, is the purpose of this book—to examine the "revolution" taking place around INGOs and consider, in particular, whether some of the largest INGOs are equipped to operate in the international context of the twenty-first century, what critical organizational changes are necessary to allow them to effectively respond to the changed international context, and how they may successfully affect such changes.

Definitions

Before moving to more substantive issues, it is important to be clear about the terminology used in this book. Terms such as "civil society," "global civil society," "the third sector," "nongovernmental organization," "nongovernmental development organization," "charity," "voluntary organization," "community service organization," and "nonprofit organization" are all used to varying degrees in the literature and by practitioners in different contexts and countries (Lewis 2007). Sometimes different acronyms are even used for the same term—a testament to the way that the aid and development sector has turned the practice of developing acronyms into an art form. Few of the terms are applied consistently—there are almost no agreed definitions, and some of the terms are highly contested.

The term "civil society" has a long pedigree but, since Antonio Gramsci, has generally been used to denote those parts of society that are neither directly controlled by the state nor form part of a society's commercial activities (the market). A normative element is sometimes also imputed: an expectation that such organizations will promote the public good and only employ nonviolent means. This normative element can probably be traced back to the use of the term in ancient Greece and Rome, where, in a rule of law–based society, citizens actively engaged in shaping institutions and policies, and where rulers were expected to place the public good ahead of private interest (Anheier et al. 2001). Of course, one needs to be cautious about making organizational classifications based on public good. Both the state and the market can be sources of positive social change, and the goals of some parts of civil society can be less than benign. Nonetheless, this normative element is particularly important to INGOs because their moral authority, a key source of their influence in international relations, is based on the widespread belief that they operate to promote the public good. The requirement of nonviolence is also explicitly required for INGOs to be entitled to consultative status with the UN.

As a result, the term "civil society" is incredibly broad and vague. While civil society was traditionally thought of as a concept closely related to the nation state (Anheier et al., 2001, 16), the advent of modern communications and travel has allowed the development of what some term "global civil society," an equally if not more contested term. Anheier et al. (2001, 17) define it as "the sphere of ideas, values, institutions, organizations, networks, and individuals located *between* the family, the state, and the market and operating *beyond* the confines of national societies, polities, and economies." Keane describes it more broadly as a "vast, interconnected, and multilayered social space that comprises many hundreds of thousands of self-directing or nongovernmental institutions and ways of life" (Keane 2001, 23). Some object to this term, preferring to use the term "transnational civil society" on the basis that it is difficult to currently identify an emerging *global* civil society. For example, Keck and Sikkink (1998, 33) argue that the concept of "global civil society" ignores issues of agency and political opportunity that they believe are critical for understanding new international institutions and relationships. There are also debates about the extent to which the concept itself is dominated by Western liberalism, whether it constitutes a mechanism for restraining state power or for increasing the responsiveness of political institutions (see, for example, Anheier et al. 2001, 11). However, these debates can, for our present purposes, be put to one side.

INGOs are the most formal embodiment of this transnational or global civil society, which also includes transnational social movements and transnational advocacy networks.[1] Anheier et al. (2001, 4) define INGOs as "autonomous organizations that are nongovernmental, that is, they are not instrumentalities of government; and nonprofit, that is not distributing revenue as income to owners; and formal, legal entities." Although the term can cover a wide variety of organizations, from

Amnesty International to the World Wildlife Fund (WWF) and the International Confederation of Free Trade Unions, the main focus of this book is on those INGOs involved in providing international aid and development. Some commentators use the term "nongovernment development organization" (NGDO) or even simply NGO to describe these aid and development organizations.[2] For example, Lewis (2007, 44) suggests that an "international" character was historically implicit in the term "NGO" because of its original use in Article 71 of the UN Charter and is now mainly applied to civil society organizations that "work internationally or those which belong to developing country contexts." Nonetheless, I prefer to use the term aid and development "INGO" to describe organizations such as World Vision, Save the Children, or Oxfam for a number of reasons. First and foremost, many of the challenges faced by these organizations arise out of the international nature of their activities and do not apply, or do not apply in the same way, to aid and development organizations with activities in just one state. Hence, their international nature is crucial and worth emphasizing. Secondly, in a number of jurisdictions, Australia for example, the term NGO is used broadly to refer to most formal civil society organizations, not simply those involved in providing aid and development. I will therefore use the term NGO to refer to any formal civil society organization, whether domestic or international; the term INGO to refer to NGOs with operations in more than one country, irrespective of the focus of their activities, and NGDOs to refer to domestic NGOs involved in aid and development. Figure 1.1 illustrates

Figure 1.1 Relationship Between Different Types of Civil Society Organizations

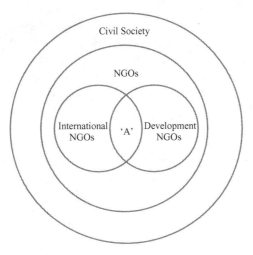

this approach. In this diagram, the organizations that are both international and focused on the aid and development sector—"aid and development INGOs"—occupy the area marked *A* and represent the principal focus of this book.

There are a number of reasons why large aid and development INGOs are the principal focus of this book. One is the financial resources they have at their disposal. Ignoring for the moment quite different global structures and levels of co-operation, the largest six aid and development INGOs by revenue—World Vision, CARE, Save the Children, Médecins Sans Frontières (Doctors Without Borders), Oxfam, and Plan—collectively earned more than US$7 billion in 2008, a threefold increase in the last decade (see Table 1.1).[3] Similarly, the Bangladesh Rural Advancement Committee (BRAC), founded in 1972 and now claiming to be the largest "Southern NGO," had an income of US$316 million in 2007 (BRAC 2007). Even the WWF network, traditionally seen as an environmental INGO but often emphasizing sustainable development rather than species and habitat conservation, raised €447 million in 2008, down from €508 million in the previous year (WWF International 2008).

Other organizations with less structured international partnerships also have quite significant financial resources. For example, there are a number of very large but much looser networks of aid and development organizations united by their denominational affiliation. Caritas Internationalis (known as Catholic Relief Services in the United States) is a "global movement working in solidarity for a fairer world, inspired by the example of Christian faith and Catholic Social Teaching" and one of the largest of these faith-based aid and development networks (see www.caristas.org). It comprises 162 Catholic relief, development, and social service organizations working in over 200 countries and territories. The Association of Protestant Development Agencies in Europe (APRODEV) is another large faith-based aid and development network. APRODEV was founded in 1990 in order to strengthen the cooperation between the European development organizations, which work closely together with the World Council of Churches. There are seventeen members with an annual income in 2008 of some €720 million (see www.aprodev.net). Even larger is ACT Development. Created in 2007, ACT Development is a global alliance of seventy four church based development organizations with a combined staff of more than 39,000 working in 130 countries with a combined annual budget of around US$2.1 billion (see www.actdevelopment.org).

However, it is not just their financial resources that make them important international actors. The large aid and development INGOs also have enormous geographic reach, increasingly global brands, both domestic and international political influence and significant potential to constructively assist states and international organizations more effectively

Table 1.1 Income and Employee Statistics for the Largest Aid and Development INGOs[1]

	1999 TOTAL INCOME(M)	2007 TOTAL INCOME(M)	2008 TOTAL INCOME(M)	TOTAL EMPLOYEES	NO. OF COUNTRY OPERATIONS
World Vision	US$600	US$2,220	US$2,575	40,000	98
CARE	US$525	US$785/€602	US$886/€608	14,500	70
Save the Children	US$368	US$978	US$1,179	14,000	120
Oxfam	US$504	US$941	US$1,043	9,340	100
MSF	US$304	€593	€675	25,973	84
Plan	US$295.2	US$595	€474	7,893	66
	>US$2,500	>US$6,000	>US$7,000	>110,000	

[1]All financial information for 1999 is taken from Lindenberg and Bryant (2001), Table 2.1. World Vision information is based on its annual report for the year ended September 30, 2008. CARE information is from *CARE Facts and Figures 2008* and the CARE International website, www.care-international.org. It is based on the year ended June 30, 2008. Save the Children information is from their 2007 and 2008 annual reports. In 2007, the organization's reported global income of US$1,037 million included US$59 million in transfers between Save the Children offices. In the 2008 calendar year, Save the Children had total income of US$1.276 billion, including transfers of US$97 million between Save the Children affiliates. Oxfam information is based on annual reports and private correspondence. The *Oxfam International Annual Report* discloses total program expenditure of US$704 million for the year ended June 30, 2007 and US$772 million for the year ended June 30, 2008. The 2007 Oxfam employment figure of 8,200 employees is based on an IAWG estimate. As of February 2009, Oxfam employed a total of 9,340 staff, including 5,027 in field offices and 1,385 in retail stores. MSF information is based on MSF's *Activity Report 2008*. Plan's information is based on Plan's *Worldwide 2007 and 2008 Annual Reviews* and *Plan International Worldwide Combined Financial Statement* for the year ended June 30, 2008. In 2008, Plan switched reporting total global income from US dollars to Euros. According to Plan, on a one-to-one basis, worldwide income grew by 6 percent in 2008, excluding the impact of exchange rate movements on non-Euro earnings.

respond to transnational problems like climate change, global poverty, and urbanization. For example, Save the Children operates across 120 countries, BRAC now employs more than 100,000 people, and WWF had a global membership of nearly five million people in 2008. This operational capacity and political clout makes them critical to most humanitarian issues. It is also giving them a more significant role in helping states respond to security threats in a globalized world.

Of course, just because an organization is large does not mean it is effective. One needs to be cautious about assuming influence or effectiveness based on organizational inputs. Many smaller INGOs are not only very influential in specific areas of international relations but also undertake some of the most innovative work. They also tend to be the most responsive to changes in their strategic context. Nonetheless, despite falling technological costs and other advantages of globalization to such smaller actors, economies of scale persist. The largest aid and development INGOs have the resources to invest in broad and sustained engagement with states and multilaterals, operate across the most countries, and because of their broad membership and supporter base, have the potential to influence public opinion in many countries. As a result, they remain among the most powerful members of civil society. It was not surprising then that in July 2008, four of the five most influential INGOs identified by *Foreign Policy Magazine* were large aid and development INGOs: World Vision, MSF, Oxfam, and BRAC. The other one was an organization, the Bill and Melinda Gates Foundation, involved in funding aid and development activities.

Different Types of INGOs

There are a variety of ways to characterize INGOs. One way is by their principal subject of concern, such as human rights, aid and development, or the environment (Lewis 2007). While not meaningless, characterizing INGOs in this way is increasingly difficult. As explained in Chapter 5, aid and development INGOs have been involved in projects designed to improve a community's environment for decades and are increasingly active in supporting both the mitigation of, and adaptation to, climate change. Similarly, some organizations traditionally seen as environmental agencies are engaged in activities that have strong development outcomes. Most aid and development INGOs have also either formally adopted a human rights–based approach to their work or are at least actively involved in promoting human rights through their advocacy and projects (Ronalds 2008a).

Another method of characterizing aid and development INGOs is the "principled," "pragmatist," "solidarist," and "faith-based" typology used by Donini et al. (2008). Those aid and development INGOs with a tradition based on the basic tenets of humanitarianism developed by Henri Dunant (the "Dunantist" tradition) such as the ICRC tend to favor "principle-centered action" and argue for "a narrower definition of humanitarianism limited to life-saving assistance and protection of civilians, based on core principles of neutrality, impartiality, and independence" (Donini et al.

2008, 11). Such INGOs are more wary of accepting government funds and avoid more "ostensibly political endeavors such as advocacy for human rights." Pragmatists, on the other hand, recognize the importance of principles but "place a higher premium on action, even when this means putting core principles in jeopardy." According to Donini et al., many US NGOs fall into this category. Solidarists place greater emphasis on addressing the root causes of poverty, social transformation, and advocacy. Finally, many faith-based agencies seek to express the religious values of compassion and charitable service on which they were founded. While Donini et al.'s approach can be useful to analyze the basis of specific decisions by INGOs or their approach in certain contexts, since most large INGOs adopt some elements of each of the above approaches at different times, its analytical usefulness is limited.

In the past, INGOs have also been divided into those that are predominantly service providers and those that are predominantly activist.[4] The former includes INGOs such as World Vision, CARE, and Save the Children, while the latter includes INGOs such as Amnesty International and Human Rights Watch (HRW). However, this type of categorization of INGOs is also somewhat crude. At Oxfam's birth, it was forced to advocate for access to the blockaded Greece, and, for at least the last few decades, many other aid and development INGOs have sought to promote the empowerment of local community organizations. More recently, many of the largest aid and development INGOs have been developing global advocacy campaigns and increasingly integrating more advocacy with programs. As a result, it is more accurate to envisage this dichotomy as a continuum with various INGOs placed closer to one end or the other. It is also interesting to note that as those INGOs that have been traditionally seen as service providers have grown and matured, and, as there has been increasing demands on them to demonstrate impact, they are being forced to address the underlying cause of poverty, not just its symptoms and have become more involved in advocacy activities.

As a result, the work of the most sophisticated aid and development INGOs can be increasingly portrayed as comprising three inter-related and mutually reinforcing prongs, as illustrated by Figure 1.2.

This outcome is consistent with Korten's (1990) analysis of the way that NGOs evolve over time but the opposite of that suggested by those who argue that these service providers are being co-opted by states (Chandhoke 2002; Kaldor et al., 2003, 8). According to Korten (1990), NGOs naturally evolve through a series of "generations," from the relief agency that meets immediate needs to an organization that seeks to engender a broader social movement to achieve structural change (see also Lewis 2007, 49) Korten's analysis also reinforces that organizational change is an inherent feature of NGOs.

Figure 1.2 The Three Interrelated and Mutually Reinforcing Prongs of the Work of Large Aid and Development INGOs

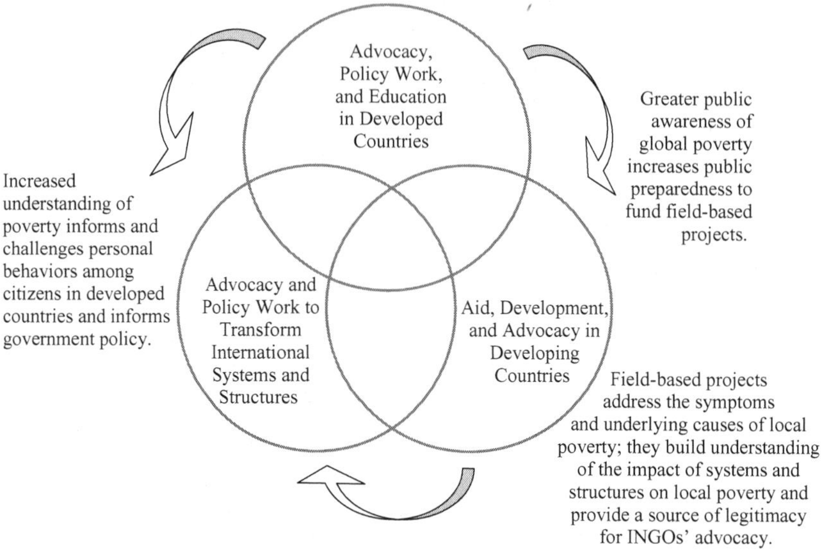

Advocacy, Policy Work, and Education in Developed Countries

Greater public awareness of global poverty increases public preparedness to fund field-based projects.

Increased understanding of poverty informs and challenges personal behaviors among citizens in developed countries and informs government policy.

Advocacy and Policy Work to Transform International Systems and Structures

Aid, Development, and Advocacy in Developing Countries

Field-based projects address the symptoms and underlying causes of local poverty; they build understanding of the impact of systems and structures on local poverty and provide a source of legitimacy for INGOs' advocacy.

Contribution of this Book to the Literature on INGOs

While a growing body of work on civil society and INGOs is emerging, there nonetheless remains a relative lack of data and scholarly debate in the area given the increasing size and significance of INGOs. There are a number of reasons for this. First, both academics and practitioners of international relations largely overlooked the growing importance of INGOs for a long time. During the Cold War, "realism" dominated international relations thinking, and there was little room for such non-state actors. Since realism views the international system as inherently anarchical with power derived primarily from military and economic resources, it is ill suited to making sense of actors like INGOs that "are not powerful in the classic sense of the term" (Keck and Sikkink 1998, x). This meant that most international relations and even many international development theorists largely ignored the role of INGOs. For example, Lewis (2007, 38) claims that a "search of the major development textbooks from the 1960s through to the 1980s for mentions of NGOs or voluntary organizations yields little or no references at all." Similarly, Dichter (1999, 44) argues that during the 1950s and 60s, "most NGOs were not taken very seriously by most government agencies and all but totally ignored by multilateral agencies like the World Bank and the United Nations." Secondly, the study of INGOs crosses a large number of academic disciplines and theoretical boundaries. The penchant for compartmentalization in academic studies has, therefore, undoubtedly undermined our understanding of INGOs. As Ahmed and Potter (2006, 9) argue, many approaches have treated NGOs as issues for domestic or comparative politics rather than international relations; relegated them to specific disciplines such as economics, agriculture, or health; or ignored them, as is largely the case in respect of management theorists, who have focused either on the firm or on public administration.

Thankfully, this began to change during the 1990s as an important body of work emerged examining the role of INGOs in global politics and development. At the University of Manchester, a series of conferences was held, beginning in 1992, which considered the implications of the growing importance and practice of INGOs. Each of these conferences resulted in publications that considered some of the issues raised in this book (Edwards and Hulme 1992; Edwards and Hulme 1995; Edwards and Hulme 1997; Lewis and Wallace 2000; Bebbington et al., 2008). Then, in 1998, Keck and Sikkink published *Activists Beyond Borders*. Taking a constructivist approach, they considered the role of transnational activists in international relations including the role of domestic NGOs and INGOs. However, although Keck and Sikkink has probably done more than any other to raise the profile of INGOs in international relations, even Keck and Sikkink (1998, 217) still conclude by describing their findings as initial and "promising new directions for further research."

In September 1998, a number of the world's largest aid and development INGOs gathered in Bellagio to discuss the ways that globalization was impacting on their organizations. In 1999, the journal, *Nonprofit and Voluntary Quarterly*, devoted an entire edition to some of the papers presented at that conference, and in 2001, two of the contributors at the conference, Marc Lindenberg and Coralie Bryant, published a book that looked specifically at the "implications of globalization for the goals, programs, processes and staff of international aid and development NGOs" (Lindenberg and Bryant 2001, ix). This is the most relevant and substantial piece of work on the issues covered by this book. However, more than a decade after the conference that inspired it, this book warrants updating. Since Lindenberg and Bryant was written, both international relations and the aid and development sector have changed considerably.

In the new millennium, the lack of empirical data on INGOs began to be seriously addressed by the Johns Hopkins Comparative Nonprofit Sector Project, which seeks to document the scope, structure, financing, and role of the nonprofit sector across both developed and developing countries. From 2001, Anheier, Glasius, and Kaldor at the London School of Economics also began to publish Global Civil Society Yearbooks to "analyze and describe, to map both conceptually and empirically" global civil society and to draw relevant conclusions for the various actors who participate within it. While this series of yearbooks was more broadly focused than the work emanating from Manchester University, it has been a critical contribution to our understanding of the place of INGOs within global civil society. In 2003, John Clark published *World Apart*. Clark's book examined the relationship between civil society and globalization. It was followed in 2006 by Ahmed and Potter's *NGOs in International Politics,* which sought to provide a comprehensive and accessible overview of INGOs' involvement in international relations. However, while both Clark (2003) and Ahmed and Potter (2006) address some of the external challenges facing INGOs such as demands for greater accountability, they do not address the organizational implications of these challenges, the focus of much of this book.

During the 1990s, articles on different aspects of NGO management began to appear, and in 2002, many of the best of these were collected and published together (Edwards and Fowler 2002). Over the past 15 years, there have also been a number of books published on management issues associated with NGOs involved in international development. Alan Fowler has published two books (Fowler 1997 and Fowler 2000c) that approach the topic from a more practical perspective while David Lewis's *The Management of Nongovernment Development Organizations* is more academic, written particularly for use by postgraduate students. These works are complemented by the broader, but still highly relevant, studies of the management of third sector or civil society organizations. Good examples of this genre include the 2005 work of Helmut Anheier, *Nonprofit Organizations: Theory, Management, Policy* (Chapter 15 is specifically about INGOs and globalization) and, from the United States, Crutchfield and Grant's (2008), study of *High Impact Not-for-Profits.* This increased attention on the practice of management in NGO is most welcome. Much of the general management literature fails to address the quite unique management challenges faced by managers of NGOs and is generally based on Western ideas and models, a real limitation given the extent to which INGOs work cross culturally. Nonetheless, compared to the business world or public administration, the field of NGO management is still nascent, and what literature exists is often written from an academic's perspective rather than that of a practitioner.

The increasing complexity of the strategic context for aid work has also been a feature of the work of the Feinstein International Centre at Tufts University. Led by Peter Walker, the Feinstein International Centre was commissioned by a number of the largest aid and development INGOs to examine future humanitarian challenges (Feinstein International Famine Centre 2004). This included a survey of the NGO landscape and contains some recommendations for INGOs. A second edition of this publication was released in 2010 called *Humanitarian Horizons: A Practitioner's Guide to the Future.* The

Centre also undertook research into local people's perceptions of the work of humanitarian agencies in twelve contexts during 2006 and 2007. This important "view from below" was used to develop a report, *The State of the Humanitarian Enterprise*, outlining the constraints, challenges, and compromises affecting humanitarian action in conflict and crisis settings (Donini et al. 2008). More recently it has published a review of the humanitarian response function within large aid INGOs (Webster and Walker 2009). The Overseas Development Institute (ODI) in London also investigates these types of issues. Their work on advocacy in fragile states such as Darfur, for example, is very relevant.

Encouraged by the popular appeal of campaigns like Make Poverty History and discussions at international meetings such as the G8, the last few years have seen an increasing number of books written on the efficacy of aid and development. Good examples include Rieff (2003), Sachs (2005), Easterly (2006), Collier (2007), and Riddell (2007). However, most of these have focused primarily on the effectiveness of government-funded aid, and therefore, INGOs have not been a central feature.

A number of recent books also explore the rising number of new actors involved in the fight against global poverty and other transnational challenges. These include Brainard and Chollet's edited *Global Development 2.0: Can Philanthropists, the Public and the Poor Make Poverty History?*, Bishop and Green's book *Philanthrocapitalism: How the Rich Can Save the World*, and David Rothkopf's *Superclass: The Global Power Elite and the World They Are Making*. In particular, Brainard and Chollet's text is a significant contribution to our understanding of how the development world is changing. However, while these texts are important contributions, they do not directly tackle the challenges facing large INGOs.

As this brief overview of some of the key literature on INGOs demonstrates, there is an absence of any text that seeks to connect global trends and changes in international relations with the management challenges faced by leaders of INGOs. While there are many research papers and books that provide information on the various trends affecting INGOs and others that are beginning to map out their increasingly important role in international relations, with the exception of the ten-year-old Lindenburg and Bryant work, none that I am aware of seek to develop a set of specific operational recommendations in response to these changes. On the other hand, while there is literature dealing with specific management challenges facing INGOs, such as becoming a learning organization, addressing human resources challenges or developing new fundraising techniques, neither the broader strategic context nor the interdependencies among the various challenges are addressed.

Therefore the principal aim of this book is to analyze the relevant social, economic, and political trends that are occurring at both a global and industry level and develop an appropriate and coherent range of organizational responses that enable INGOs to be effective in the twenty-first century. As a result, the material this book seeks to cover is necessarily broad. While it is intended to provide practical recommendations for leaders of INGOs, this book nonetheless seeks to engage with some of the key theoretical debates in international relations and development studies that are relevant to their work. In my view, it is important for INGO leaders to be aware of these debates, at least at a high level, because they contribute to a deeper understanding of the thinking behind government policy, the motivations and interests of stakeholders, and of the trends that confront their organizations. This book also seeks to incorporate insights from a diverse range of organizations and contexts. The unique nature of the challenges that INGOs face, the difficulty of their social mission, and the relative lack of tailored management literature means that it has been both necessary and beneficial to seek answers in a great variety of places.

This breadth will no doubt be seen as both a strength and a weakness. Since this book seeks to connect the wisdom of many disciplines, including international relations, development studies, and management, in an accessible way it has been necessary, at times, to limit the discussion to a relatively high level. This may leave some readers wanting more specific advice. However, there is enormous variety among INGOs, even among the largest aid and development INGOs. They are complex organizations, often with as much diversity between affiliates of the same INGO as between different organizations. Therefore, it is not possible, in my view, to provide specific, one-size-fits-all recommendations. Rather, like good development work, INGO leaders need to adapt the analysis and recommendations in this book to their particular circumstances and context.

From the outset, it has also been my intention to provide a balanced assessment of the strengths and achievements of INGOs as well as their weaknesses and failures. This has often been difficult because of the relative lack of reliable data and analysis, the enormous diversity in the sector, and the often high expectations that INGOs create for themselves. It is also, of course, impossible to ever be truly objective. The views and recommendations contained in this book are based on an insider's experience as a senior executive with the largest aid and development NGO—World Vision—and are colored by the biases of my developed-world perspective. This has undoubtedly resulted in my analysis tending to emphasize a top-down view rather than a bottom-up one and, as one reviewer of a draft of this book put it, an optic that is "predominately state rather than civic focused." Accordingly, my selection of the challenges faced by large INGOs, and the suggested organizational responses may be quite different from those compiled by employees of INGOs based in developing countries, from those receiving aid in a humanitarian disaster, or from the leaders of small, community-based organizations that seek to partner with or obtain funding from large INGOs. One's point of view is always a view from a point.

Nonetheless, my hope is that this book will be a useful source of inspiration, ideas, and strategies for those tasked with navigating their organizations through the challenges they face in the twenty-first century. I also hope that it will encourage others, particularly practitioners, to invest far more in analyzing the strategy and operations of individual aid and development INGOs to ensure that they are indeed equipped for the work they must do in the twenty-first century.

Structure of this Book

This book proceeds in three parts. The first part, consisting of Chapters 2 to 4, seeks to outline the strategic context in which large INGOs operate. Chapter 2 examines the impact that globalization is having on INGOs. Adopting a constructivist approach, it argues that globalization has contributed to the increasingly important role that ideas, norms, and culture are having in international relations. It examines states' changing motivations for giving aid and, in particular, the growing awareness of the relationship between extreme poverty and international peace and security in a globalized world. This Chapter also considers the changing role that INGOs are having in the global governance of aid and development. Chapter 3 goes on to chart the growth in the size and influence of INGOs over the recent past. It contains a short history of the role INGOs have played in various campaigns including humanitarian law, human rights, and the more recent Make Poverty History campaign. Chapter 4 contains an analysis of the factors that have driven the growth in the size and influence of INGOs and assesses whether this growth is likely to continue.

The second part of the book—Chapters 5, 6, and 7—outlines the external and organizational challenges created by the changed strategic context. Chapter 5 considers some of the key *external* challenges faced by large aid and development INGOs including new development challenges, the increased politicization of aid and development, growing demands on INGOs to be more accountable and demonstrate their effectiveness, and growing public and government expectations of improved co-ordination and of INGOs' capacity to respond to humanitarian disasters and address development challenges. Chapter 6 focuses on the internal organizational challenges generated by the growing size and influence of INGOs and the changed international context. It outlines six key challenges for the largest aid and development INGOs that mean they must undertake quite radical internal change if they are to be equipped to effectively perform their missions in the changed international context of the twenty-first century. It argues that these external challenges represent a revolution in the strategic context of large INGOs with enormous implications for the nature of activities they undertake, the types of staff they employ, the skills of the leaders they select, the nature of organizations they partner with, how they raise financial resources, and the types of systems and processes they invest in. Chapter 7 explores the difficulties of managing and governing values-driven global organizations. It examines the development of strategy in a rapidly changing context and critically analyzes the different approaches adopted by some of the world's largest INGOs to these issues.

The final part of this book, Chapter 8, provides practical guidance to senior managers of INGOs for achieving the required organizational change. It considers the evidence for the largest aid and development INGOs' ability to change and adapt to the new international context. It investigates why large INGOs appear so resistant to organizational change and suggests six key factors that a number of case studies suggest must be present for transformational organizational change to be achieved.

Chapter 9 concludes by summarizing the key arguments made in the book and outlining an INGO research agenda at three levels: international, industry, and organizational.

Notes

1. Keck and Sikkink (1998, 1) describe transnational advocacy networks as "networks of activists, distinguishable largely by the centrality of principled ideas or values in motivating their formation." The term "transnational moral entrepreneur" is also sometimes used, highlighting the critical role that moral authority plays in advocacy campaigns and the organizations such as INGOs that promote them.

2. Lewis describes NGDOs as "third sector organizations concerned with addressing problems of poverty and social justice, and working primarily in the developing world" (Lewis 2007, 1).

3. The Red Cross is not included because of its status and responsibilities under international conventions, which makes its classification as an INGO problematic.

4. Based on the work of Adil Najam, Lewis (2007, 130) provides a more complex classification system based on the different functions that INGOs can perform: service delivery (acting directly to do what needs to be done), advocacy (prodding governments to do the right thing), innovation (suggesting and showing how things can be done differently), and monitoring (trying to ensure that government and business do what they are supposed to be doing).

CHAPTER 2

Globalization and INGOs

Introduction

Despite the large amount that has been written about it, globalization remains a highly contested concept. While some continue to view it in purely economic terms, globalization is much better understood as "the expanding scale, growing magnitude, speeding up, and deepening impact of transcontinental flows and patterns of social interaction" (Held and McGrew, 2002, 1; Held, 2004, 1). Understanding globalization is also complicated by the way in which it "encompasses two simultaneous, yet contradictory patterns in world politics" (Karns and Mingst 2004, 22). On the one hand, it involves "greater integration and interdependence between people and states, between states and other states, and between states and international bodies." On the other, it engenders significant disintegrative tendencies. One reason for this is that the benefits and costs of globalization are not equally shared. In fact, most of the benefits of globalization have accrued to those 900 million people fortunate enough to be living in the Western world. As Held (2004, 34) explains, they "enjoy 86 percent of world consumption expenditures, 79 percent of world income, 58 percent of world energy consumption, 74 percent of telephone lines . . . By comparison, the poorest 1.2 billion people share only 1.3 percent of world consumption, 4 percent of world energy consumption, [and] 1.5 percent of all telephone lines." Another reason is that by reducing citizens' confidence in the state, globalization has "contributed to the resurgence of ethnic and religious identities, ethnic conflicts, and [the] further weakening if not failure of states" (Karns and Mingst 2004, 23). Paradoxically, both the integrative and disintegrative features of globalization have helped to create an environment more conducive to the proliferation of transnational threats.

The concept is also contested because some view it as a relatively recent Western phenomenon, even a continuation of Western imperialism. However, while it is true that those living in the West have benefited the most from contemporary globalization, it is neither new nor Western. Globalization, defined broadly, is a process that has been

┌───┐
│ (KEY POINTS:)   │

Globalization is having a profound impact on the strategic context for INGOs in a number of ways:

1. The changing nature of power in world politics is increasing the importance of "soft" forms of power that rely on information, persuasion, and legitimacy. It is also changing the relative power of state and non-state actors. INGOs with high levels of credibility that can collect data, synthesize and analyze it, and distribute it widely are likely to benefit from these changes and become increasingly influential.

2. There is a much greater interdependency between the security of the world's rich and poor in a globalized world. This is leading governments to place much more emphasis on the development purposes of foreign aid and to see INGOs as an important part of the overall response apparatus to transnational threats, to generating global public goods, and to improving human security. Broader awareness of the interdependency may also be helping to promote public interest in and build the domestic constituency for foreign aid.

3. The changes in international politics wrought by the intensification of globalization require a radical re-think of the current global governance arrangements associated with aid and development. While some promising reform has occurred, much more needs to be done. Despite the growing role of non-state actors in global governance, too often they remain only on the periphery of decision making. The large INGOs must also become more active themselves in helping to shape the governance architecture of aid in the twenty-first century.

└───┘

occurring since humanity's beginning. Probably the oldest form of globalization is environmental. "[C]limate change has affected the ebb and flow of human populations for millions of years" (Keohane and Nye 2000, 3; Bruhl and Rittberger 2002, 13). From an economic and cultural perspective, the Silk Road is one of the earliest trade routes that had enormous impact on the cultures of China, Central Asia, and Europe and helped to transport new technologies, philosophies, and even diseases such as the bubonic plague. The spread of Islam across the Middle East, Africa, and Asia in the seventh and eighth centuries is another example and Amartya Sen (2006, 126–7) points to the way the spread of science, technology, and mathematics from China, India, and the Middle East around 1000 A.D. changed the nature of Europe at that time.

Nonetheless, despite the long history, contemporary globalization is qualitatively and quantitatively different from these previous forms of inter-connectedness (Held et al. 1999) and is having a profound impact on INGOs' strategic context. While, of course, nation states remain the principal actors, globalization is changing the nature of power in international relations. As global power becomes less hierarchical and more diffuse than in the past, states' influence, and some of their key functions, are declining in relative importance to other actors and issues. This change is benefiting INGOs and creating an environment highly conducive to their growth in both size and influence.

A more connected world allows events to be transmitted globally almost instantaneously and significantly raises awareness of the needs of those living in extreme poverty. In our own living rooms, we can come face to face with the need of our fellow humans living on the other side of the world. This has increased private giving to INGOs as well as strengthened the constituency for increased ODA in many OECD countries. Globalization has also facilitated the geographic spread of INGOs. These issues are discussed further in Chapters 3 and 4. It has contributed to rising stakeholder expectations, new development challenges and increased politicization of INGOs' work. These issues are discussed further in Chapter 5. The effect of globalization on the strategic context of INGOs is therefore a recurring theme in this book.

As a result, it is important that several underlying issues related to globalization are explored at the outset to provide a basis for the more specific issues discussed in later chapters. The first issue to be explored is the increasing importance that globalization gives to the role of ideas, norms, and culture in international relations. It will be argued that this change allows international organizations like INGOs, who have a high level of public trust, legitimacy, and knowledge to become more powerful actors on the international stage. This discussion will set the scene for the exploration of the growing influence of INGOs in Chapter 3. The second issue to be discussed is the much broader conception of national and international security that is emerging in a globalized world. It will be argued that globalization has facilitated the proliferation of transnational threats and there is now a much greater understanding of the relationship between global poverty, a developed state's security, and the well-being of its citizens. It also increases the danger that INGOs will be captured by state's foreign policy goals and the humanitarian imperative lost. The third issue to be considered is the impact of globalization on global governance and the opportunities and challenges that this creates for INGOs. Discussion of these three issues will also deal with some of the more subtle changes occurring at the conceptual level of international relations. While the focus of this book is on the concrete ways that the international context has changed for INGOs, it is nonetheless important that INGO leaders are aware of these conceptual changes because they contribute to a deeper understanding of the thinking behind government policy, the motivations and interests of stakeholders, and of the trends that confront their organizations.

The Power of Ideas and Norms in a Globalized World

While Machiavelli may have argued that it was safer to be feared than to be loved, he did not live in the Information Age. In the Information Age, the main sources of power shift from military and economic resources to informational resources. Organizations with high levels of credibility that can collect data, synthesize and analyze it, and distribute it widely are in a very powerful position. As Keck and Sikkink (1998, x) argue, while information may initially seem "inconsequential in the face of the economic, political, and military might of other global actors," it can help "reframe international and domestic debates, changing their terms, their sites, and the configuration of participants." They use the term "information politics" to describe the strategic use of information in this way by civil society actors such as INGOs. The strategic use of information then becomes one of the most powerful tools that INGOs have at their disposal to influence states. Thus globalization, and the Information Age that it is ushering in, increases INGOs' "structural power," the power to shape frameworks within which states relate to one another and to other actors. As Susan Strange (1988, 30) argues, "[W]hoever is able to develop or acquire and to deny the access of others to a kind of knowledge respected and sought by others; and whoever can control the channels by which it is communicated to those given access to it, will exercise a very special kind of structural power."

However, globalization is also increasing INGOs' "productive power," their ability to harness "socially diffuse production of subjectivity in systems of meaning and signification" and their ability to produce effects on international actors through "constitutive power" (Barnett and Duvall, 2005a). For example, globalization and information technology supports the dissemination and growing awareness of international norms, such as human rights, which allow actors such as INGOs to refer to these norms and demand states' compliance with them (Bruhl & Rittberger 2002, 9). Of course, one would not want to be blind to the equally destructive potential of information technology. The use of radio broadcasts to promote violence during the Rwandan conflict in 1994 is a good example of the misuse of information technology to reinforce prejudice and encourage violence.

Recognizing this shift in power, even the world's most militarily and economically powerful nation, the United States, is replacing the more confrontational style of the Bush presidency with a much greater emphasis on soft power. Keohane and Nye (1998) define "soft power" as

> the ability to get desired outcomes because others want what you want. It is the ability to achieve goals through attraction rather than coercion. It works by convincing others to follow

or getting them to agree to norms and institutions that produce the desired behavior. Soft power can rest on the appeal
of one's ideas or culture or the ability to set the agenda
through standards and institutions that shape the preferences
of others. It depends largely on the persuasiveness of the free
information that an actor seeks to transmit.

Soft power, combined with the United States' military and economic
might is providing the basis for a new approach to foreign policy termed
"smart power," the ability to combine hard and soft power into a winning
strategy (Armitage & Nye 2007). For example, in her Senate confirmation
hearing on January 13, 2009, for the position of Secretary of State, Hillary
Clinton said:

> We must use what has been called smart power—the full range
> of tools at our disposal—diplomatic, economic, military, polit-
> ical, legal, and cultural—picking the right tool, or combina-
> tion of tools, for each situation. With smart power, diplomacy
> will be the vanguard of foreign policy.

However, even in America there is recognition that this requires much
greater reliance on, and interaction with, INGOs. The recent report by a
Committee chaired by Armitage and Nye (2007, 9) recognized that wielding soft power is difficult because many of America's soft power resources
lie outside of government, such as in civil society (emphasizing this point,
the Committee members included the CEO of CARE US and a representative from the Bill and Melinda Gates Foundation). Of course, legitimacy
is central to successfully wielding such soft power, whether you are a super
power or an NGO. As a result, the issue of legitimacy must also become a
central concern of the twenty-first century INGO (see Chapter 6).

In this context, therefore, it not surprising that both practitioners and
theorists of international relations have been placing a much greater
emphasis on "constructivism." Constructivism emphasizes the role of
ideas, norms, and culture in international relations. It sees state interests
"defined in the context of internationally held norms and understandings" and argues that this normative context "influences the behavior of
decision makers and mass publics who may choose and constrain those
decision makers" (Finnemore 1996, 2; see also Keck and Sikkink 1998, 3).
A good example of this influence is the way that international actors rely
on ethically charged claims and counterclaims to justify their behavior or
criticize the behavior of others (Frost 2009, 93). Subjecting powerful
states to ethical criticisms can constrain or change their behavior and
allows relatively weak actors to be significant players on the world stage.

In this regard, the perceived moral authority of INGOs is one of the most important sources of INGO influence and power, an issue discussed further in Chapter 3. Similarly, if nonstate actors such as INGOs can influence and change the normative context in which states operate, they can change state behavior.

Constructivism can be contrasted with "realism," the dominant theory of international relations in the twentieth century. Realist theorists of international relations view the international sphere as a struggle to maximize relative state power and security in an anarchical system. As a result, their approach struggles to accommodate actors like INGOs that "are not powerful in the classic sense of the term" (Keck and Sikkink 1998, x). Realism also has a poor track record in explaining profound changes in international relations. For example, realism is generally considered to have failed to predict or explain the collapse of the Soviet Union. Realism also struggles to account for state behavior that appears to be altruistic or even contrary to national interest, such as Britain's decision to outlaw the slave trade despite the adverse economic consequences it produced (Keck and Sikkink 1998, 213). The result is that realism, at least as a standalone theory of international relations, appears increasingly inappropriate to the current international context.

Rational based theories such as realism are also of limited value in understanding change within complex global organizations like the United Nations, the World Bank, or the largest INGOs. First, such theories say "little about the process of change within international organizations" (Nielson et al. 2006, 107). Second, since such theories rely upon a "logic of consequences," they focus too much on compensation and reward structures within organizations. The motivations of people working in organizations like the UN and INGOs are complex, often including a sense of calling or vocation, which transcends the purely material. That is not to say that traditional theories do not have any insights to offer us. Understanding and changing reward and incentive systems within international organizations like INGOs is critical for achieving organizational change (see Chapter 8), but they are far from sufficient by themselves. In comparison, constructivism is a more useful way of understanding behavior and change in international organizations. For example, recent analysis of change within the World Bank found that employees' strategies and choices become constrained as they internalize "particular logics of appropriateness and come to accept particular causal beliefs about the world that are strongly influenced by their bureaucratic environment" (Nielson et al. 2006, 110). Thus, the rational behavior of staff is both "bounded and socially constructed by the organizational culture" (Nielson et al. 2006, 110). Constructivism also predicts that international organizations "with a deeply rooted bureaucratic culture are difficult to change" (Nielson et al. 2006, 108). Consequently, constructivism is useful both for understanding change in state behavior and within large organizations.

Globalization is also undermining what Mary Kaldor (2003, 4) and others call "methodological nationalism." Methodological nationalism conditions us to ignore the intricacy and nuances of international relations and instead "to believe that nations take stands in international politics en bloc, that governments represent the views of the nation, and that what other people in that country might think is domestic politics and irrelevant at the international level" (Kaldor 2003, 4). It is a "world view that affects everyday language, journalism, and the media as much as it does the social sciences and policy analysis." For INGOs and other transnational activists, the demise of methodological nationalism is a welcome development, since their goals and methods can simply disappear from view in this framework.

However, while the power of ideas and norms in international relations is significant and growing, it would be a mistake to underestimate the ongoing power derived from the military force and economic might of state actors. In addition, many states remain unconstrained by democratic social forces or liberal ideals. The information revolution is also still in its early stages and large parts of the world remain disconnected from it. Using the classification system developed by Held et al. (1999), this position is often described as a "transformationalist" position. Transformationalists believe that the process of globalization has intensified in modern times, become multifaceted, and is changing global governance, with nonstate actors, for example, becoming increasingly important. However, unlike hyperglobalists, transformationalists continue to see states as key actors that will remain important in international relations into the foreseeable future. On the other hand, unlike skeptics, transformationalists nonetheless see the current process of globalization as qualitatively different in form compared to what has occurred in the past. This transformationalist view, sits comfortably with the slow and diffuse process by which ideas, norms and culture spread and the reality that despite the attractiveness of constructivist arguments, material factors do continue to play an important role in international relations. This view also recognizes the way that states and statesmen are able to transfer current beliefs and institutions into new strategic contexts (Keohane and Nye, 1998).

Nonetheless, it is clear that the nature of power in world politics is changing and that this change has the potential to greatly benefit INGOs. The normative context in which states operate is an increasingly important determinant of, and constraint on, state behavior. States must also rely far more on the legitimacy derived from their reputation as good international citizens (a concept originally championed by former Australian

Foreign Minister, Gareth Evans, beginning in the late 1980s). Of course, part of good international citizenship is the provision of financial and other support for peacekeeping, for humanitarian disasters, and for development. This requires states to place more emphasis on their engagement with nonstate actors, such as INGOs undertaking aid and development activities. The growing importance of norms in regulating state behavior also provides INGOs with the opportunity to become more influential actors at both the national and international levels. If they can effectively harness the knowledge they have and combine it with the legitimacy that can be derived from their public support, experience conducting aid and development activities, and their accountability to the people they seek to serve, INGOs can significantly increase their influence, an issue that is analyzed in more depth in Chapter 3.

New Conceptions of International Peace and Security

In the preface to the play *Major Barbara*, George Bernard Shaw states, "[S]ecurity, the chief pretense of civilization, cannot exist where the worst of dangers, the danger of poverty, hangs over everyone's head." One hundred years after the play was first produced at the Royal Court Theatre in London, Kofi Annan echoed this sentiment in his 2005 report to the General Assembly, *In Larger Freedom*. This report and that of the Secretary General's High Level Panel on Threats, Challenges, and Change, *A More Secure World,* argued that "combating poverty will not only save millions of lives but also strengthen states' capacity to combat terrorism, organized crime, and proliferation. Development makes everyone more secure" (Panyarachun 2004). While George Bernard Shaw would have agreed, this much broader view of "security," often associated with the evolving concept of human security, is still considered somewhat contentious among more traditional national security professionals. The 'human security' view, pioneered by the UNDP in its 1994 *Human Development Report* understands the concept of security from the "perspective of people rather than states" and posits that the "best way to achieve security (both at the global, national, and societal levels) is to increase that of people" (Tadjbakhsh 2008). Contrast this with more realist notions of security that focus only on the security of the state. The concept of human security places a much greater emphasis on addressing insecurity caused by direct and indirect sources of violence, such as poverty and climate change, and seeks to tackle these through development and promoting human rights, not just policing and military responses. Human security also blurs the "classical distinctions between foreign and domestic, national and international, internal and external" (Rudd 2008). At its heart, therefore, this concept recognizes that in a globalized world, the security of a developed state and its citizens is closely tied to that of the global poor. As such, it has a number of important implications for the aid and development industry and for large aid and development INGOs in particular. These implications are the subject of this section.

While the UN's founders knew that security, development, and human rights were inextricably linked, ideas about international peace and security have still changed dramatically over the last 20 years, especially since the terrorist attacks on the United States on September 11, 2001. One key turning point was the unanimous decision by the Security Council in 1992 to authorize Operation Restore Hope to use "all necessary means to secure as soon as possible a secure environment for humanitarian relief operations in Somalia" under Chapter VII of the UN Charter (UN Security Council Resolution 794, approved 3 December 1992). Territorial ambition, cold war politics, clan loyalties, and the overthrow of a brutal dictator had, by 1991, left Somalia ravaged by civil war and drought. The poor security situation, particularly in and around the capital Mogadishu, made the delivery of aid to thousands of people desperately short of food very difficult. After "sustained media coverage of the anarchy and starvation in Somalia" (Natsios 1996, 159; Wheeler 2002, 179), it was agreed by the Security Council that the situation in Somalia represented a threat to international peace and security, and a humanitarian intervention was authorized. This was the first time that humanitarian concerns were explicitly used for justifying the use of force and is described by Wheeler as "a groundbreaking decision by the Security Council given its previous reluctance to cross this normative rubicon" (Wheeler 2002, 173).[1] While the intervention in Somalia was ultimately a failure with profound ramifications for later humanitarian crisis in Rwanda and the Balkans, it nevertheless marked a distinct change in the way in which international peace and security was perceived following the end of the Cold War.

However, it was the terrorist attacks on the United States on September 11, 2001, that provide the greatest impetus for a major re-definition of the concept of international peace and security. As Carol Lancaster (2007, 59) argues, the attack was "interpreted by many in the media and among the public as a consequence of the poverty and gross inequalities in the world." While the link may not have actually been strong in this case, it was indubitably clear that failed states could become havens for terrorists. In a globalized world, it was, therefore, in the interests of the international community to prevent and address state failure. Of course, in a globalized world the impact of global poverty on developed world stability and citizen well-being is not limited to merely the threat of terrorism. It also includes the use of failed states as havens for organized crime; the fear of increased refugee flows as a result of war, natural disasters, and climate change;

ongoing human trafficking; and the increased potential for global pandemics arising from poor health systems. The global concern about swine flu, quickly transmitted around the globe via international travel in 2009, is a recent reminder of this relationship. Ashraf Ghani and Clare Lockhart (2008, 4) go so far as to argue that the failed state is "at the heart of a worldwide systemic crisis that constitutes the most serious challenge to global security in the new millennium."

The changing understanding of the concept of international peace and security and the emergence of the notion of human security have had a number of significant policy implications. First, it has led to government policy makers placing a much greater weight on the development purposes of foreign aid. The history of ODA is relatively short. As Carol Lancaster (2007,1) outlines, prior to the Second World War, "foreign aid, as we know it today, did not exist." In addition, historically, the principal purpose of a considerable proportion of foreign aid has not been the alleviation of global poverty. While the World Council of Churches called for governments to dedicate one percent of GNP for the purposes of helping the global poor as early as the 1950s, foreign aid during the Cold War was dominated by a realist understanding of international relations that elevated national interest above all other considerations and saw aid as principally a tool of diplomacy or domestic commercial interests. In fact, Lancaster (2007, 5) goes so far as to argue that, but for the Cold War, the United States may never have "initiated programs of aid or put pressure on other governments to do so." In this environment, little official aid went to the world's poorest countries, any impact that aid had on addressing global poverty was mainly incidental, and INGOs were seen as relatively peripheral to the whole enterprise. As an indication of the low priority that was given to addressing poverty, the percentage of aid given to the least developed countries was only 10 percent in 1970, 25 percent by 1980, and is still only around 30 to 35 percent (Lancaster 2007, 39).[2]

However, while aid continues to be given for a number of reasons, including diplomatic and commercial purposes, one of the important changes in the politics of foreign aid during the 1990s and into the twenty-first century is the much greater emphasis on poverty alleviation. This stronger emphasis is closely related to the broad recognition now by developed states and their citizens of the intimate relationship between global poverty, a developed state's security, and the well-being of its citizens. This change is illustrated by the Australian Prime Minister's first National Security Statement on December 4, 2008. In it, the Prime Minister demonstrated a very broad interpretation of Australia's national security, encompassing helping fragile states in Australia's region to meet the MDGs, responding to humanitarian disasters, and addressing climate change. Not surprisingly, this perspective is also reflected by AusAID,

Australia's bilateral aid agency. It views promoting "an international environment, particularly in the Asia–Pacific region, that is stable, peaceful, and prosperous" as core business and strongly in Australia's national interests (AusAID 2009).

Similarly, there is renewed interest in bilateral agencies like the United Kingdom's Department for International Development (DFID) on how to support so-called failed states. This is good news because fragile states contain 14 percent of the world's population, 35 percent of the world's poor, 44 percent of maternal deaths, 46 percent of children out of school, and 51 percent of children dying before the age of five (DFID 2005). It may also lead to a greater understanding of how the aid complex supports or undermines the task of building effective, functioning states. Ghani and Lockhart (2008, 111) argue that while not intentional, the Cold War had the effect of diverting attention away from state building and therefore contributed to the international aid system undermining the capacity of a state to perform essential social functions.

The second policy implication is the growing debate about the relative importance of military spending compared to foreign aid. For example, commentators like Jeffrey Sachs (2008, 285) are calling on the United States to rethink the amount it spends on its military (US$600 billion in 2008) compared to the amount it spends on development (around US$20 billion in 2008). This debate is even gaining traction within the defense establishment. For example, the latest US national defense strategy acknowledges that force is only a small part of the solution to the United States' security concerns. It recognizes that military efforts "to capture or kill terrorists are likely to be subordinate to measures to promote local participation in government and economic programs to spur development, as well as efforts to understand and address the grievances that often lie at the heart of insurgencies" (US Department of Defense 2008).

Third, the growing awareness of the relationship between global poverty and state security is creating much greater public interest in and possibly even a greater domestic constituency for foreign aid. For example, it has contributed to the growth in private philanthropy for purposes that tackle global poverty. While the spectacular growth in private wealth over recent years has provided the means for individuals to respond, it is events like the September 11 attacks that have provided the impetus to apply this wealth to tackling global poverty. As Matthew Bishop and Michael Green (2008) argue in their book, *Philanthrocapitalism*, in each golden age of philanthropy, "the supply-side expansion in wealth was accompanied by a demand-side surge resulting from growing social need." In the current climate, the newly created wealth of the Gateses, Warren Buffet, Steve Case, George Soros, and Mo Ibrahim is being applied to address the causes of global poverty.

Fourth, the growing awareness of the relationship between global poverty and state security has given civil society, and especially INGOs, a much greater role in national and international security. INGOs are increasingly being recognized by states and IGOs as an important part of the overall response apparatus to transnational threats and critical for generating public goods and improving human security. This growing importance of nonstate actors to security in a globalized world is shown by Kevin Rudd's (2008) concession that "the impact of globalization and advances in technology mean that the partnerships between industry, governments, and the community that have evolved since 2001 are vital and will remain an important part of any future national security policy." INGOs help to breakdown the traditional distinction in international relations between the domestic and international spheres and promote coordinated action by states. They also reinforce the importance of international institutions and participate in the development of multilateral rules and norms. This is critical because modern transnational threats cannot be solved by even the most powerful states acting alone but require "broad, deep, and sustained global cooperation" (Annan 2005). On the other hand, for INGOs, the inter-relationship between national and international security and poverty, infectious disease, and environmental degradation has serious implications for their relationship with bilateral aid agencies. The increased focus on the benefits to state security from aid and development activities increases the danger that INGOs will be captured by states' domestic and foreign policy objectives and that the concept of a 'humanitarian imperative' will be lost. Increased engagement in contexts such as fragile states also raises a number of operational issues. For example, fragile states are the most unsafe and costliest places for INGOs to operate and, as the 2009 ejection of many INGOs from Sudan demonstrates, often highly politicized. Fragile states also raise difficult issues about the proper relationship between INGOs and the military (see Chapter 5).

Of course, the growing recognition of the important relationship between global poverty, a developed state's security, and the well-being of its citizens has, to date, had only a limited effect on some key issues impacting the world's poor and states have continued to adopt policy positions that reflect their narrow rather than enlightened self interest. For example, despite the September 11 terrorist attacks taking place only months before the current Doha Development Round of world trade negotiations began, and notwithstanding the potential economic benefits to developing countries of the Round, the politicians and voters of Europe and North America have not been sufficiently motivated to put aside their protectionist trade policies. More recently, states were unable to achieve even a modest agreement to limit climate change at the

UNFCCC negotiations in Copenhagen, despite climate change's impact on the world's poor and its serious implications for international security. The failure of the Doha Round and the UNFCCC negotiations in Copenhagen reinforce the ongoing challenge that INGOs and others face to convince states to put aside narrow interpretations of national interest in order to effectively address transnational problems. It also reminds us that aid policy is only one of a number of ways in which countries either support or undermine the development of aid–recipient countries. Ensuring that not only the aid system but also international trade and other policies are coherent and support poverty alleviation must be a high priority for statesmen, the UN, and civil society. Despite the progress that has been made, peace in the twenty-first century will require a much more express policy, governance and operational relationship between not only national and human security but also trade and other policies than currently exists. It will also require significant global governance reform. Although the UN gave birth to the notion of human security, it is currently poorly equipped to provide it (Panyarachun 2004, 13). The issue of global governance reform is the focus of the next section.

Globalization, Global Governance, and INGOs

At a press conference following the G20 conference in London in April 2009, Barack Obama was asked by a Chinese journalist what he would do to ensure that US domestic politics did not prevent him from acting for the greater good (Davies 2009). His response was to argue that he was the President of the United States, not of China or some other country, and that his responsibility was to improve the lives of his constituents in the United States. However, he also went on to acknowledge that in "an era of integration and interdependence," statesmanship was much more complex (Davies 2009). The journalist's question, and Obama's response, neatly encapsulates the challenge faced by modern leaders in fashioning a response to such divergent challenges as the current global economic crisis, climate change, or threats to international security from fragile states and extreme poverty. No longer can unilateral action by even the most powerful states effectively address the challenges they face. At the same time, electoral realities limit their political responsibility to domestic constituents. A corresponding dilemma exists at the international level, giving rise to one of the key challenges for global governance in the twenty-first century: How do our current international institutions, created and controlled by sovereign states, overcome the national interests of their members to respond decisively to the transnational threats that we face in a globalized world?

This same challenge extends to the global governance of international aid and development. Since states began to provide ODA following World War II (see previous section), they have not only established national bilateral agencies to distribute their aid but also cooperated with one another to create a broad array of IGOs, institutions and regimes at the international level. However, the intensification of globalization, the economic growth enjoyed by newly industrialized countries, the increasing acknowledgment of the relationship between security and poverty, the international attention from global campaigns such as Make Poverty History, and the proliferation of international actors involved in aid and development activities demand a re-think of the current global governance arrangements associated with aid and development.

Despite the magnitude and urgency of the transnational problems facing the world, existing international organizations have struggled to overcome the national interests of states and respond decisively. This creates an institutional deficit at the global level well illustrated by the glacial speed at which the UN has undertaken institutional reform. In fact, there has been little innovation in organization forms of any type since the industrial revolution, something Dee Hock (1995, 2) describes as a "global epidemic of institutional failure." There are also a number of systemic issues that undermine international aid effectiveness. These include problems associated with the allocation of aid, the volatility of aid, the number of donors that each recipient must interact with, and the ongoing, lopsided nature of aid relationships (Riddell 2007, 386–7). This section therefore will outline how the governance architecture that has developed over the past sixty years to support international cooperation on aid and development must change to better adapt to a globalized world, improve aid coordination, and accommodate the very significant role that nonstate actors such as INGOs now play in addressing extreme poverty. The impact that these global governance reforms may have on the operations and capabilities of INGOs is addressed at length in Chapters 5 and 6.

Arguably, states and IGOs are required by international law to cooperate on aid and development issues and, in particular, to support the fulfillment of the MDGs. This requirement to cooperate is an explicit part of Goal Eight of the MDGs, which some commentators contend have become customary norms of international law (Alston 2005; Lancaster 2007). Certainly, the frequency with which states have affirmed, reiterated, and restated the MDGs in so many international forums provides a strong basis for such a view. However, there are also other sources of such an international obligation to cooperate. These include the general undertaking given in Article 62 of the UN Charter; Article 28 of the Universal Declaration of Human Rights;[3] and the reference in Article 2(1) of the International Covenant on Economic, Social, and Cultural Rights to states' obligation "to take steps, individually and through international assistance and co-operation" (Alston, 2005, 776).

To further this collective responsibility, states have responded in a number of ways. Firstly, they have established a broad array of IGOs, institutions, and regimes. These include large, formal multilateral organizations such as the World Bank, the UNDP, and the WFP. There are also a number of high-level coordination mechanisms. These include the United Nations Conference on Trade and Development (UNCTAD), the Office for the coordination of Humanitarian Affairs (OCHA), the Triennial Comprehensive Policy Review (TCPR), and the newly created Development Cooperation Forum (DCF). Outside of the UN system, the international governance of aid and development also includes the DAC, "the principal body through which the OECD deals with issues related to co-operation with developing countries" (see www.OECD.org). All DAC members are signatories to the Paris Declaration, an international agreement created in March 2005 "to increase efforts in harmonization, alignment, and managing aid for results with a set of monitorable actions and indicators" (see www.OECD.org).[4] The Paris Declaration has been signed by the ministers, heads of agencies, and other senior officials of over one hundred countries and is intended to create a strong global mechanism for accountability in relation to aid and development. The G7, G8, and most recently, the G20 have also all become much more engaged in the global governance associated with aid and development issues. Starting with the G8's meeting at Gleneagles in 2005, aid and development issues have been constantly on the Group's agenda, and it has continually committed itself to increases in aid.[5]

Finally, a range of specific measures have been established to provide global governance of the MDGs. In 2004, UN Secretary General Kofi Annan argued that the MDGs had already "transformed the face of global development cooperation" and "generated unprecedented, coordinated action" on the part of the United Nations, the World Bank, the International Monetary Fund, the major donors of international development assistance, and the developing countries at which the Goals are targeted.[6] While the judgment of other commentators has been more circumspect, it remains clear that the MDGs have the potential to be one of the frameworks for holding "key actors accountable for their commitment to eradicating global poverty in the twenty-first century" (Fukuda-Parr 2004, 400). As a result, all of the key development focused IGOs have aligned activities with the MDGs. In addition, the Millennium Project was established in 2002 to provide the UN Secretary General with a detailed plan for achieving the MDGs. In 2007, the UN Millennium Project secretariat was integrated into the UNDP. Another interesting accountability mechanism established by the UN is the Millennium Campaign, an initiative that seeks to mobilize civil society to hold states accountable for achieving the MDGs (see www.endpoverty2015.org). Between October 17 and 19, 2008, the Millennium Campaign mobilized over 100 million people under the slogan "Stand Up—Take Action" at events in more than 100 countries around the globe. In relation to Goal 8, there is also a MDG Gap Task Force, comprising more than 20 UN agencies. Finally, there is a regime for monitoring progress on the MDGs at both the international and country levels. At the global level, the UN Secretary-General reports annually to the General Assembly on the implementation of the Millennium Declaration. Country reports are released every five years or so. These reports help engage political leaders and mobilize civil society and communities in support of the MDGs at the country level.

With such a plethora of organizations, institutions, and regimes, it is not surprising that the effectiveness of the global governance of aid and development remains an issue subject to intense scrutiny. For example, the Dutch Minister for Development Cooperation, Agnes van Ardenne, said in a speech in February 2006, "It makes no sense to carve up development problems and divide them among no fewer than 38 UN organizations. The result is too little efficiency and too much overlap, too little action and too much talk" (Freiesleben 2008a, 42; see also Burall et al. 2006, 3). Given that there has not been a single example of closure or merger of a major international institution in over 60 years (Bezanson 2005, 6), this fragmentation is not surprising. However, perhaps an even more significant issue is that the governance of international aid and development activities remains too state-centric and a vast array of nonstate aid and development actors remain largely at the periphery of this system of state-based governance. Transnational corporations, new megaphilanthropists, "celanthropists" like U2's Bono and actress Angelina Jolie, and faith groups have joined more traditional nonstate actors like World Vision and Oxfam in the fight against global poverty. The result of this proliferation is that answering questions about who and how aid priorities are set and how aid programs are organized and funds channeled has seldom been more urgent.

As Jane Nelson (2008, 160) argues, the emergence of new players, new models, and new sources of funds for development purposes "represents one of the most fundamental and rapid shifts in the history of international development." Successful economic development has led to the creation of more than twenty new bilateral agencies, not only by emerging powers such as India and China but also newly industrialized countries such as Taiwan. Globally, there are now, approximately "225 bilateral and 242 multilateral agencies funding over 35,000 activities each year" (see www.OECD.org). Donor proliferation is particularly "pronounced in the health sector, where more than 100 major organizations are involved"

(IDA 2007). At the same time, there has been a significant growth in the use of partnership-based global and regional programs for the channeling of ODA. Nearly a third of ODA now flows through such institutions (Lele et al. 2006). Lele et al. (2006, 2) argue that the emergence of these global funds is a direct response to the "recognition of the need to promote global public goods . . . Since the world lacks a system of global governance with the authority to tax and mobilize resources to provide global public goods, global collective action is needed to produce them."

However, the fragmentation of the aid and development industry is also reflected in the dramatic decline in the importance of ODA, despite its quantitative growth. In the 1970s, ODA funded 70 percent of the United States' resource flow to developing countries. Now, 80 percent of such resource flows come from private citizens, corporations, NGOs, religious groups, and foundations (Nelson 2008, 149).[7] New private actors have also emerged such as the Bill and Melinda Gates Foundation, and many large companies are donating significant funds to aid and development. The result is that traditional aid and development actors have now been joined by "billionaires, foundations, multinational companies, social entrepreneurs, NGOs, actors, rock stars, eccentrics, [and] preachers," and this "remarkable variety of voices and ideas" must be taken into account as part of the humanitarian cacophony (Bishop 2008, 43).

The more traditional multilateral actors and the associated state-based governance institutions have been slow to respond to this change. Although the UN Charter allowed ECOSOC to "make suitable arrangements for consultation with nongovernmental organizations which are concerned with matters within its competence" (Article 71), until recently their role was limited. It is only since the 1990s that NGOs have participated in UN organizations and international institutions to any significant degree (see Chapter 3). Similarly, during the 1980s and 1990s, the World Bank attracted considerable criticism for their lack of engagement with civil society and associated concerns about accountability. At the DAC's most recent High-Level Forum on Aid Effectiveness at Accra, there was recognition that non-DAC donors, civil society, and other funders of aid and development needed to be involved. More than 300 civil society groups were consulted in the lead-up to the meeting. However, despite this change, governance of global aid and development remains state-centric, with nonstate actors having relatively little influence over the reform process and remaining largely relegated to the periphery of official decision-making bodies.

There are a number of reasons for this resistance to a more significant role for nonstate actors. First, governments of some developing countries have reacted cautiously to an increased role for INGOs, concerned that it may negatively impact their own agenda for increased representation and participation in international forums (see Chapter 3). Second, the UN and DAC have both struggled to navigate competing agendas and state anxiety over reforms of aid and development governance without the complications that incorporating a whole range of nonstate actors would bring. For example, at the urging of the General Assembly, during the World Summit the UN Secretary-General established a high-level panel to examine ways to improve coordination among UN agencies in the areas of development, humanitarian assistance, and the environment.[8] However, when the Panel's Report, *Delivering as One*, was delivered in November 2006, the recommendations were hotly debated. On the one hand, large, OECD based donors were generally supportive of the report's recommendations. These donors emphasized the need for efficiency and accountability and prioritized security, human rights, and gender issues (Freiesleben 2008a, 50). On the other hand, the G77 and nonaligned movement "largely resisted imposing stronger conditions and stricter accountability standards on UN entities" (Freiesleben 2008a, 50). They were concerned that the push for greater aid coherence would adversely impact their sovereignty and were resistant to any conditionality based on gender or human rights. These disagreements continue to stifle the reform process.[9] Similar divisions have emerged in the DAC-initiated aid effectiveness process. The Paris Declaration is seen by many critics as donor driven, lacking ambition, and doing little to hold donors accountable. The process has also been criticized for progressing too slowly.

The challenge of balancing national interest with improved global governance of aid and development has also created a real credibility gap for traditional multilateral actors. As McNeill and St Clair (2009, 3) argue, on the one hand, "multilateral organizations derive moral authority from being seen to promote the well-being of people of the world," while on the other they remain controlled by sovereign states. For example, the World Bank has been criticized for blocking reforms at the Accra conference, allegedly due to pressure from its largest shareholder, the United States. Similarly, while the UNDP gains considerable credibility from its close working relationship with many developing country governments, this same relationship can undermine its moral authority where the states it works with do not appear to share its poverty alleviation goals. For this reason, McNeill and St Clair (2009, 10–11) argue that such organizations have a responsibility to "'rise above the states that created them." As laudable as this goal may be, it is not clear how they are expected to do this in practice under the current global governance arrangements.

The reform of aid and development governance is therefore caught in a conundrum. The current proposals are seen as insufficiently ambitious by many state and nonstate actors and out of step with the reality on the ground. On the other hand, a more ambitious agenda is likely to be even more controversial and slow down the current change process further. Similarly, multilateral institutions established for the purpose of assisting states with their collective responsibility to address global poverty remain captured by the national interests of those very same states. At the same time, growing ODA budgets are leading to much greater scrutiny from commentators and the public. If aid and development actors are unable to demonstrate more effective governance of aid, it is likely that the recent public support for the increases in ODA will evaporate, particularly if economic conditions remain difficult. As a result, a way through the impasse must be found. Thankfully, although much more reform is required, there are some positive steps being taken at both the global level and at the grassroots level that show significant promise.

The first positive change is a growing role for the G20 in global affairs, including the global governance of aid and development. The preparedness of the G20 to adopt a broader agenda is a positive change for a number of reasons. Compared to alternatives such as the G7, G8+5, or the mooted League of Democracies, the value of the G20 as a forum for resolving issues between states on global poverty is that it partially transcends developed and developing country interests and represents close to two-thirds of the world's population. It also remains small enough for issues to be resolved in a timely manner. On the other hand, the G20 remains an informal, voluntary structure, which still excludes a large number of developing countries. It also remains structurally disconnected to other aid and development global governance arrangements.

The second positive change is the growing role of ECOSOC in coordinating aid and development issues. Over many years, a number of reforms have sought to give ECOSOC a greater role in coordinating the UN's development activities. These reforms include establishing Annual Ministerial Reviews (AMRs) to assess progress on the goals and targets set at major UN Conferences, especially the MDGs, and the creation of the DCF. ECOSOC is now also able to respond to humanitarian emergencies by convening ad hoc sessions. There is therefore significant potential for the DCF to become the principal mechanism to achieve a much greater degree of coordination and policy coherence among UN actors, the Bretton Woods Institutions, and DAC members. However, this will not occur without a determined effort on behalf of all parties and a real willingness by developed countries to cede some authority and control in return for an overall improvement in the governance system. At present, this still seems some way off. The report of the inaugural DCF, held from June 30 to July 1, 2008, identified significant ongoing issues with the governance of aid and development. These included poorly allocated aid, a failure to mainstream the MDGs, and concern from developing countries about the Paris Declaration and conditionality (see www.un-ngls.org). On the one hand, major donors such as the European Union and United States see a more limited role for the DCF and remain concerned about any watering down of standards or sustainability requirements. On the other hand, many developing countries desire a more ambitious agenda for the DCF, preferring a UN-based body that gives them greater influence compared to "the proceedings of the Development Assistance Committee where industrialized countries call the shots" (Manning 2006; Fues 2007, 26). As a result, all sides need to be prepared to make concessions and engage the legitimate concerns of others if real progress is going to be made.

Of course, reform of ECOSOC could go much further. The Institute of Global Policy (2009), for example, has called for the "full activation" of UN Charter Article 57 by placing the Bretton Woods Institutions and even the G20 formally within the remit of ECOSOC. Alternatively, the High-Level Panel on System-Wide Coherence recommended the establishment of a Global Leader's Forum (L27), comprising the heads of state of half of ECOSOC's members, rotating on the basis of equitable geographic representation (A/61/583, Para. 54). ECOSOC, or a subcommittee of it, could also take on the substance of the work currently managed through the DAC's Paris Declaration, allowing this narrow and somewhat anachronistic coordination mechanism to wither away. The advantages of using ECOSOC as the basis for greater coordination are that it utilizes an existing organization that is already recognized as the main economic and social organ of the UN, there is already some momentum for reform from recent changes to ECOSOC's remit, it is part of the UN system and members are appointed out of the General Assembly making it more representative, and it already has a track record of engaging nonstate actors. The disadvantages are political. It will be difficult to convince the DAC, the Bretton Woods Institutions, or the G20 to surrender some of their authority to ECOSOC.

The third important change is the emergence of a number of new hybrid international organizations. These new organizations are a complex combination of old actors that challenge traditional distinctions in the "purposes and modus operandi of commercial, private nonprofit, and public institutions" (Zadek 2008, 189). Since they incorporate a much broader range of aid and development actors than just states, they better reflect the more dispersed nature of the sector. They also have the ability to reshape markets and instill new behavioral norms on traditional international actors consistent with a constructivist interpretation of international relations. Their diffuse governance structures ameliorate against capture by the national interest of states. These so-called hybrid organizations also help to address the fragmentation of the aid and development industry, since they have an inherent collaboration and harmonization agenda.

The largest example of such a hybrid organization is the Global Fund to Fight AIDS, Tuberculosis, and Malaria (GFATM).[10] Jeffrey Sachs (2008, 298) was one of the key proponents for the creation of GFATM, motivated by the perceived inability of donor governments, international financial institutions and the business sector "to organize an effective response . . . within the existing institutions." While governments around the world have supplied a significant proportion of GFATM's funds, so too have private foundations like the Bill and Melinda Gates Foundation and private enterprises. Civil society and multinational corporations also have significant roles in GFATM (see Case Study 2.1). For example, GFATM's board includes representatives of donor and recipient governments, NGOs, the private sector, and affected communities. GFATM has also set new standards in IGO transparency. "Its web site posts virtually everything that is done or discussed and does this almost on a 'real time' basis. This includes detailed financial information on disbursements, contributions, administrative costs, and shortfalls" (Bezanson 2005, 10).

While supporters like Sachs (2008, 301–2) are so pleased with the outcomes that he has recently called for the creation of six more global funds to meet the majority of development challenges, not all commentators are as effusive. Lele et al. (2006, 9) argue that GAFTM programs often compete with "vital ongoing national and local programs for scarce aid resources as well as for national and local budgetary resources, staff, and institutional capacity" and do not necessarily streamline procurement and disbursement procedures or reduce the number of different drug regimes. There have also been questions raised about the sustainability of the GFATM's business model (Benzanson 2005). Further, some critics argue that vertical funds such as GAFTM can lead to large imbalances in aid allocation at the country level. For example, in Rwanda US$48 million was available for HIV/AIDS that affected 3 percent of the population while only US$1 million was available for maternal and child health (Kharas, 2008, 67). Finally, the governance and accountability of such organizations becomes a critical issue because they "profoundly reconfigure the basis on which public goods and private gains are related in their creation and exploitation" (Zadek 2008, 189). As a result, while these hybrid approaches contain significant promise and are likely to be part of the solution to the global governance challenge, they are unlikely to be a panacea for all of its problems.

These global governance challenges create a number of opportunities and challenges for INGOs. Bruhl and Rittberger (2002) identify four "governance gaps" faced by states as a result of globalization—a jurisdictional gap, an operational gap, an incentive gap, and a participatory gap—and suggest that INGOs can make a positive contribution in addressing each of them. First, they argue, INGOs can help to address the predominantly national nature of most policy development underlying

---

Case Study 2.1: Global Fund to Fight AIDS, Tuberculosis, and Malaria (GFATM)

GFATM is a good example of a new type of international collaborative organization, describing itself as a "partnership between governments, civil society, the private sector, and affected communities."

Founded in 2002, following an article published in the *Lancet* by academics Amir Attaran and Jeffrey Sachs, the GFATM has become the main source of finance for programs to fight AIDS, tuberculosis, and malaria. By the end of 2007, funding of US$10.1 billion has been provided to more than 550 programs in 136 countries. It provides a quarter of all international financing for AIDS globally, two-thirds for tuberculosis, and three quarters for malaria.

Government agencies have channeled large amounts of funds through the GFATM, and international organizations like WHO, UNDP, and the World Bank are also involved. However, the GFATM has also mobilized corporate partners who, through programs like (PRODUCT) RED, channel a percentage of their profits to the GFATM. Current private sector partners include Starbucks, American Express, Apple, and Gap. In August 2006, the Gates Foundation contributed $500 million to the GFATM, calling it "one of the most important health initiatives in the world."

Civil society and aid and development NGOs in particular have significant roles in the GFATM. These roles include supporting advocacy and resource mobilization, holding two positions on the GFATM Board, and implementing programs.

In the field, the GFATM does not implement programs directly, relying instead on a broad network of partnerships with other development organizations utilizing Country Coordinating Mechanisms (CCMs). CCMs include "representatives from both the public and private sectors, including governments, multilateral or bilateral agencies, nongovernmental organizations, academic institutions, private businesses, and people living with the diseases."

---

the jurisdictional gap by developing and promoting global policies to combat the transnational threats that we face. Second, INGOs' broad community engagement—in both developing and developed countries—allows them to assist states in addressing the operational gap by providing policy makers and public institutions with relevant and timely information and policy analysis. Third, they can address the incentive gap by undertaking activities that encourage states to adhere to the international agreements that they enter into. Finally, INGOs can help to address the participatory gap in a number of ways: by participating themselves in international decision-making bodies; by providing ways for domestic groups to circumvent domestic political constraints to access international organizations; and by building the capacity of civil society to advocate in the international arena.[11]

In contrast to INGOs, Bruhl and Rittberger, (2002, 23) argue that because international institutions like the UN are state-centric and because of the "distance between decision makers and the people affected by these decisions . . . the input legitimacy of public policy making within these institutions is rather low." Thus, INGOs can have a significant ameliorating effect on the governance deficits created by the ongoing process of globalization.

However, to perform these new global governance roles will require significant change on the part of INGOs. First, they will need to invest more in developing policy on the global governance of aid and development. This includes not merely views about global aid reform but also deeper questions about the underlying political architecture of aid giving. Currently, evidence of policy positions or advocacy on the global governance of aid and development by NGOs, even the large aid and development INGOs, is hard to find.[12] They will also need to engage IGOs in a more sophisticated way. In fact, Puchala (2007, 189) argues that NGOs are "not yet legitimate and effective political players at the international level . . . because there are very few legitimate or institutionalized linkages among international civil society, world politics, and global governance." Second, they will need to acquire or develop a range of new technical skills and capabilities and transition from what Clark (2003, 103) calls problem focused advocacy to solution-focused advocacy (see Chapter 6). Third, it will require INGOs to consider how they will respond to demands for better coordination and harmonization of their own aid and development activities (see Chapter 5).

In a special preparatory report to the Millennium Summit, Secretary-General Kofi Annan (2000, 30) stated that the time had come for the UN to shift from multilateralism to globalization because "while the postwar multilateral system made it possible for the new globalization to emerge and flourish, globalization, in turn, has progressively rendered its designs antiquated." Almost a decade later, the global governance of aid and development remains one of the areas still to make this transition from multilateralism to globalization. Despite recent reforms and despite eight almost universally accepted goals around which a more coordinated international response could be built, the UN agencies involved in aid and development issues still lack sufficient coherence. The Bretton Woods Institutions and DAC initiatives such as the Paris Declaration are even more disconnected. Further, multilateral agencies remain captured by narrow state interests, which can undermine their poverty alleviation mission. Finally, the current global governance arrangements fail to include the plethora of important new actors now involved in delivering aid and development on the ground. As a result, it is clear that the current international architecture is not well placed to discharge states' collective responsibility to alleviate extreme poverty.

Further reform is desperately needed. These reforms need to create an international architecture for aid and development that is more coherent, that better represents the interests of both donor and recipient countries, and that includes emerging state donors and nonstate actors. In particular, there is a need for further reform of ECOSOC so that it becomes the central point, not just for the coordination of aid and development activities in the UN system but so that it can also drive better policy coherence with the Bretton Woods Institutions and the DAC. In addition, existing multilateral institutions should take the role of nonstate actors much more seriously or be replaced by the emerging hybrid forms of international organizations such as GFATM, which have a more effective, inbuilt harmonization and coordination capability.[13] Of course, while these emerging organizational models hold great promise, they still require refinement if they are to realize their potential and remain accountable to both donors and the poor they seek to serve.

Achieving such reform will not be easy. There are many competing agendas and priorities in the aid and development sector. Donor countries remain concerned about demonstrating to their citizens that the increased funds being invested in ODA are being used wisely. Developing countries worry about competing donor demands, high transaction costs, potential loss of sovereignty, and influence. Nonstate actors are skeptical that their views will be taken seriously by state actors and uneasy about the costs of bureaucratic engagement and the loss of their independence and responsiveness. While these concerns are all legitimate, in such an interconnected world, the threat to our common good from extreme poverty demands that we work to overcome them and reach a workable accord between all international actors. While commentators such as Roger Riddell (2007, 390) argue that fundamental problems with the aid system can only be addressed by "prizing official aid away from the overarching political influence of the main donor governments who provide and control it," it may be far more practicable and ultimately effective to reconstitute political incentives around aid by emphasizing the interdependencies with national interest in a globalized world. If such a position can be achieved, the benefits will be considerable. Donor countries and their citizens should enjoy a more stable and secure global environment. For developing countries, aid and development governance reform may result in more funds, far greater coherence in both aid policy and implementation, and ultimately, more impact on the ground. It may also enhance their political sovereignty: as US President John F Kennedy said in a 1961 speech to the General Assembly, "Political sovereignty is but a mockery without the means of meeting poverty and illiteracy and disease" (Jolly et al. 2005, 18). However, the most important prize may be a significant improvement in the human dignity, equality, and equity of the billion or more people living in extreme poverty.

Conclusion

Multilateralism was the twentieth-century response to the challenges of globalization. In the twenty-first century, the pace and depth of globalization, the importance of nonstate actors and the scale of transnational problems mean we must go beyond multilateralism to a new underpinning concept for global governance. The nature of today's transnational threats combined with the power and influence of nonstate actors such as NGOs and TNCs means that global governance cannot be based on states alone. As the Commission on Global Governance (1995) encouraged, "the world needs a new vision that can galvanize people everywhere to achieve higher levels of co-operation in areas of common concern and shared destiny." Almost 15 years later, the unsuccessful UNFCCC negotiations in Copenhagen in 2009 demonstrate that our approach to global problem solving is still stuck in the last century. Instead, in the same way as states responded to the horrors of World War II by establishing a new form of global governance for the twentieth century, we need to respond to the massive challenges of the twenty-first century—climate change, terrorism, income inequality, and poverty—by establishing a new global governance framework. In this new framework, INGOs can play a critical role in a number of ways.

INGOs can use their unique access to information and knowledge to help reframe international and domestic debates. They can reinforce the importance of international institutions and participate in the development of multilateral rules and norms. They can encourage the dissemination of international norms and provide information about states' compliance with them. They can also undertake activities that encourage states to adhere to the international agreements that they enter into. INGOs' broad community engagement allows them to provide policy makers and public institutions with relevant and timely information for policy analysis. They can develop and promote global policies to combat the transnational threats that we face, thereby challenging the predominantly national nature of most policy development and helping to promote coordinated action by states. INGOs' activities in developing countries are also an increasingly important part of the overall response apparatus to transnational threats and critical for generating public goods and improving human security. INGOs help to breakdown the traditional distinction in international relations between the domestic and international spheres. INGOs' cosmopolitan-based approach to policy issues helps combat nationalism. INGOs can improve the accountability of global governance by participating themselves in international decision-making bodies. They can increase participation in global governance by providing ways for domestic groups to circumvent domestic political constraints, facilitating access to international organizations, and by building the capacity of civil society to advocate in international arenas. However, to perform these new global governance roles and achieve a more just form of globalization will require some significant change on the part of INGOs. These changes and how to achieve them are the focus for the remainder of this book.

Notes

1. A similar resolution had been passed by the Security Council in relation to Bosnia a few months earlier, but China, India, and Zimbabwe had all abstained. See Security Council Resolution 770 approved on August 13, 1992.

2. US ODA remains highly skewed toward middle-income countries. Only 5 percent of US ODA goes to the poorest 10 countries, and only about 25 percent of all US ODA to those countries the OECD classifies as least developed (Singer 2009, 115). In total, only about one-quarter of the DAC aid currently goes to the world's least developed countries (Singer 2009, 116). Ten percent of aid, or US$11 billion, goes to countries too rich to qualify as recipients of ODA (Riddell 2007, 358).

3. Article 28 states: "[e]veryone is entitled to a social and international order in which the rights and freedoms set forth in this Declaration can be fully realized."

4. The Paris Declaration followed earlier statements in favor of greater aid harmonization such as Para. 43 of the Monterrey Consensus in 2002 and the Rome Declaration on Harmonization in 2003.

5. For example, at their 2009 Summit in L'Aquila, they said: "We renew all our commitments towards the poor, especially in Africa. We are determined to undertake measures to mitigate the impact of the [financial] crisis on developing countries, and to continue to support their efforts to achieve the Millennium Development Goals" (Final Declaration, Para.6).

6. Implementation of the United Nations Millennium Declaration: Report of the Secretary-General, U.N. GAOR, 59th Sess., Agenda Item 56, Para. 39, U.N. Doc. A/59/282 (2004).

7. Natsios (2006) puts the figure at 86 percent.

8. Concerns about the coordination of UN actors led the General Assembly to identify, in the World Summit Outcome Document, four general areas to improve the overall coherence and effectiveness of the

UN's development-related activities. See Paragraphs 168 and 169, A/RES/60/1.

9. The High Level Panel recommended a new coordination mechanism, the Sustainable Development Board, and a UN headquarters-level UN Development Coordinator, neither of which have been approved by the General Assembly. On the other hand, increased coordination at the country level has been piloted in a number of countries with early indications suggesting some improvements, although the formal evaluations of the pilots will not be available until late 2009 (Freiesleben 2008b).

10. Other examples include the Global Alliance for Vaccinations and Immunization, the Equator Principles governing project finance, the Global Reporting Initiative, the Extractive Industries Transparency Initiative, and the Forest Stewardship Council. For a list demonstrating the diversity and breadth of these actors, see Zadek 2008, 196.

11. Development tools such as Community Based Performance Monitoring, used by CARE, the World Bank, and World Vision, can also enable and empower communities to influence the quality, efficiency, and accountability of service delivery, particularly education and health services. In Uganda, World Vision staff found that the tool was used by the local community to increase World Vision's own accountability. When a World Vision "contractor attempted to deliver a cracked water tank to a primary school, the community rightfully refused to accept it, demanding instead to be provided with the quality tanks to which they were entitled" (WVA 2007: 73).

12. Exceptions include: Action Aid International (2005), *Real Aid: An Agenda for Making Aid Really Work*, Action Aid International, Johannesburg, and Action Aid International and Oxfam International (2005), *Millstone or Milestone: What Rich Countries Must Do in Paris to Make Aid Work for Poor People*, Action Aid International, London.

13. Puchala (2007) suggests that the most promising reform of international institutions is constitutional change that would allow "legitimate and responsible elements of transnational society into formal roles in global governance" (198).

CHAPTER 3

A New Era in International Relations?

Introduction

Less than 10 years ago, Allen and Thomas (2003, 213), in a leading introductory text to global poverty, argued that "in spite of the enormous amount of hype that is generated by some development NGOs and their supporters about 'making a difference' and 'empowering' the poor and the fact that NGOs can obviously achieve a great deal in certain situations, they are never going to change the world." Their argument, adopting a realist perspective, was based on the relatively small financial resources at the disposal of INGOs.[1] Since then, the financial resources of the largest aid and development INGOs have grown dramatically (see Table 1.1). Perhaps more importantly, these large INGOs have increased their involvement in policy development, advocacy, and international relations, recognizing that the power of their ideas may be much greater than the impact of their activities on the ground. As a result, the extent to which INGOs influence global politics and contribute to changing the world now appears more open to debate.

This Chapter will begin by examining the growth in the number and financial resources of INGOs. It will then explore the growing influence of INGOs, arguing that, contrary to Thomas and Allen's view, INGOs are increasingly influential in international relations. However, assessing the extent of this influence is complicated by the influence states also have on the attitudes and activities of INGOs and the growing number of critics seeking to limit or undermine INGO influence in both the domestic and international arenas.

Before proceeding, it is worthwhile placing the relatively more structured and sophisticated modern form of the INGO within its historical context by providing a brief overview of the history of INGOs. According to Florini and Simmons (2000, 8), the first modern transnational policy campaign was the nineteenth-century campaign to end slavery. It did not rely on military power—although it later co-opted the British Navy—nor economic power—in fact, it sought to ban an economically profitable activity. Instead, it was successful because the abolitionists were able to convince large groups of people to reconsider what was acceptable behavior, to reconsider the 'norms' of civilized society. Similarly, the purpose of

┌─── KEY POINTS: ──┐

The enormous increase in the size of INGOs over recent years and the significantly increased interconnections between them means that they present much more complex management challenges than in the past.

INGOs are also increasingly influential in international politics. This influence takes at least four forms:

1. INGOs are involved in formal norm creation and standard-setting through their involvement as official members of government delegations and at the UN and other international meetings;
2. They influence the broader process by which new norms emerge and become part of the international agenda;
3. They influence many IGOs through their involvement in the governance of IGOs, formal and informal consultation mechanisms, and as operational partners of IGOs; and
4. The size and scale of INGO activities in developing countries gives INGOs significant influence on developing country governments.

However, this influence should not be overstated. INGOs remain only one of a number of influential actors in international relations, and the relationship between governments and INGOs is complex, with the constitutive effects working both ways.

While INGOs must remain vigilant to ensure that governments do not capture them, cooperation and constructive engagement is as critical to INGOs' success as is challenging existing power structures. INGO leaders must therefore constantly strive to achieve a delicate balance between constructive engagement with governments and other powerful institutions on the one hand and challenging the status quo and dominant paradigms on the other.

└───┘

the International Committee of the Red Cross (ICRC), founded by Henri Dunant in 1864 after his experiences at the Battle of Solferino, was intended to reconstitute the norms of war.[2] Since the ICRC has certain status and responsibilities under international conventions, it is not technically classified as an INGO. Nonetheless, its founding and growth forms part of the same tradition as the large aid and development INGOs that are the principal focus of this book. In the twentieth century, peace groups, such as the League to Enforce Peace and the League of Nations Society of London supported the development of the League of Nations, and labor unions were active in the formation of the ILO (Karns and Mingst 2004, 225). While the influence of NGOs in international relations diminished during the 1930s as governments became preoccupied with rising security and economic concerns, they became important sources of ideas as planning for the post–World War II order proceeded, shaping, for example, the UN Charter (Karns and Mingst 2004, 225).

All of the six largest aid and development INGOs were founded in response to war, demonstrating the complex inter-relationship that exists between them and international affairs. The oldest, Save the Children, was founded in 1919 in response to the First World War; Foster Parents Plan (now Plan International) began in 1937 in response to the Spanish Civil War; Oxfam began in 1942, campaigning for food supplies to be sent through an allied naval blockade to starving women and children in enemy-occupied Greece during the Second World War; CARE started by sending food parcels from the United States to Europe in 1946; and World Vision was founded in 1953 to help orphans of the Korean War. The youngest, Médecins Sans Frontières (MSF), was born in response to Nigeria's civil war in 1971.[3]

Growth in Size and Complexity of INGOs

Since the 1970s there has been an explosion in the number of INGOs. While quantitative information on INGOs is poor, according to Anheier et al. (2001), in 1874, there were 32 registered INGOs. This number had increased to 1,083 by 1914, continued to grow after World War II, and then accelerated in the 1990s so that "around one quarter of the 13,000 INGOs in existence today were created after 1990" (Anheier et al. 2001, 4). The Union of International Associations, which adopts a broader definition of INGO, estimates that in 2004 there were more than 50,000 INGOs (See www.uia.be/en/stats; Glasius et al. 2005, 3). Interestingly, this number is comparable with United Nations Conference on Trade and Development (UNCTAD) estimates of the number of TNCs: over 60,000 in 2001 (Kaldor et al. 2003, 10). In fact, Simeant (2005) suggests similarities between some of the factors that are driving the growth of INGOs and TNCs, including the desire to better facilitate the acquisition of human and financial resources. As Glasius et al. (2005, 3) argue, this growth represents the "institutionaliza-tion of a social movement industry." Not surprisingly, this growth in numbers has been accompanied by a similar or even greater growth in membership, staff, and share of national income.[4] World Vision now employs around 40,000 people globally with a number of individual World Vision offices employing more than 1,000 staff. The largest development agency by employees, the Bangladesh Rural Advancement Committee (BRAC), has more than 100,000 staff. In some of the poorest countries, aid and develop-ment INGOs are also delivering key services that the "failed" state is no longer capable of delivering. For example, Cohen et al. (2008) claim that 80 percent of basic services in Afghanistan are delivered by local or interna-tional NGOs. As a result, these organizations are now much larger and face far more complex management challenges than in the past.

The complexity is compounded by the increased inter-connections between INGOs. The data suggest that global civil society is becoming "thicker" (Anheier et al. 2001, 4; Kaldor et al. 2003, 14; Anheier 2005, 337). The greater density of INGO networks is demonstrated by factors such as the increased information exchange, project collaboration, participation in joint meetings, and membership of advocacy coalitions. However, INGO density is still considerably less than the density, for example, of international trade and TNCs (Katz and Anheier, 2005). INGOs are also less a Western-based phenomenon than in the past as the geographical spread of INGOs has increased (Kaldor et al. 2003, 12–14).

Analysis of the sources of aid and development INGO funding demonstrates how both public and private giving has grown to support this proliferation and growth in INGOs. ODA remained stagnant in nominal terms from the 1980s to the 1990s (although declined as a percentage of gross national income) but then rose sharply in the first decade of the new millennium (see Figure 3.1). Based on 2005 prices and exchange rates, total DAC ODA in 1985/6 was US$64 billion, in 1995/6 US$63 billion, but by 2005/6 it had risen to US$105 billion, admittedly inflated by debt relief (OECD DAC, 2006, Table 9). In 2006/7, total DAC ODA fell by 8.4 percent in real terms to US$103.7 billion, but in 2007/8 it rose by 10.2 percent to total US$119.8 billion (in 2008 dollars, see OECD 2009). For the first time, non-debt relief ODA was over US$100 billion. ODA increased in 20 of the

Figure 3.1 Total DAC ODA and Average Country Effort, 1990–2008.

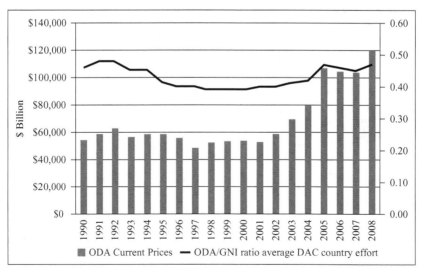

Source: DAC Online Database

22 DAC countries in 2008. Global aid increases have averaged 5.9 percent in real terms each year since the 2005 G8 meeting in Gleneagles. This compares with an average increase of 8.4 percent required to reach the Gleneagles commitments.

In addition, the percentage of ODA received by INGOs increased over this period. According to Kaldor et al. (2003, 11), since the 1970s, "the INGO share has doubled, with most of the gain in the 1990s, a period which coincides with the significant expansion of INGO operations more generally."[5] The proportion going to INGOs is even higher in relation to humanitarian crisis. In 2006, the DAC donors spent 23 percent of their combined official humanitarian assistance through NGOs and a further 8 percent through the Red Cross and Red Crescent Movement. In comparison 43 percent was channeled through UN agencies and other international organizations (Development Initiatives 2008).

Private giving to INGOs has also grown. In 1990 dollars, private donations more than doubled from US$4.5 billion in 1988 to US$10.7 billion in 1999 (Kaldor et al. 2003, 12). This figure includes individual, foundation, and corporate contributions. Growth has continued into this decade with private giving to INGOs in the DAC countries now more than US$14 billion (2006 DAC data, Table 13). In fact, NGO private funding often outstrips humanitarian financing from DAC donors. For example, in 2006, MSF France spent US$81 million of French private citizens' money on humanitarian crises, compared to just $48 million spent by the French government (Development Initiatives 2008). Such private giving provides INGOs with the capacity to respond more quickly to humanitarian disasters. For example, World Vision uses a US$6 million Emergency Preparedness Response Fund to finance the initial response to a humanitarian crisis until government grants can be obtained or specific fundraising appeals launched. This allows World Vision to respond within hours or days rather than wait for governments, which in 2006 took an average of six weeks to disburse funding for emergencies (Development Initiatives 2008).

As a result, the six largest INGOs have increased their total annual revenue (in nominal terms) from around US$2.5 billion in 1999 to more than US$7 billion in 2008 (see Table 3.1). This sustained level of double-digit growth has resulted in the resources of large INGO being comparable to the ODA provided by some members of the OECD. For example, in 2005 the annual income of World Vision exceeded the ODA of Italy or Australia in the same year (see Koch 2008).[6]

In addition, to these traditional sources of funding, the emergence of significant new donors has provided additional sources of funds for INGOs. The most significant is the Bill and Melinda Gates Foundation, formed in 2000, with a US$35.9 billion endowment (since supplemented with additional funds from Warren Buffet). In 2009, the Bill and Melinda

Gates Foundation disbursed approximately US$3.5 billion. The GFATM was formed in 2001 to fight AIDS, tuberculosis, and malaria and has already raised over US$11 billion (see Case Study 2.1). In addition, many large companies are donating significant funds to aid and development, some of which is spent through INGOs. For example, BHP Billiton is now one of the largest Australian funders of international development projects—it contributed US$103 million to community projects around the world in 2007 (BHP Billiton, 2008).

Growth in Political Influence of INGOs

Not only are INGOs now much larger, with more staff in more countries contributing often very significantly to local economies, they now have considerable domestic and international political influence. As Hurrell (2005, 42–3) argues, this influence takes at least four forms. First, they are involved in formal norm creation and standard setting through their involvement as official members of government delegations and at UN and other international meetings such as the World Economic Forum (WEF). Representatives of Oxfam, Save the Children, and World Vision have all attended the WEF in the past, and approximately 30 INGO leaders attended the 2010 meeting (see www.weforum.org). Second, they are involved in the broader process by which new norms emerge and become part of the international agenda. For example, their role as a key source of information and comment for the media and their extensive public communication activities help to shape and influence public opinion. Third, they are involved in the functioning of many international government organizations (IGOs), including representation at board level and through mandated requirements for IGOs to consult with INGOs. Fourth, they have influence through their direct involvement in many government activities, such as humanitarian relief, promoting good governance, and political development. However, as this section will show, it is a complex relationship, the constitutive effects work both ways, and there are real limitations to INGOs' influence in both domestic and international politics.

While INGOs' greater role in international policy formulation and treaty formation is not entirely new, it is now much more commonplace and successful. While the nineteenth century crusade to end slavery was probably the first transnational campaign with a specifically moral goal that played a significant role in world politics, it was closely followed by INGO involvement in the development of humanitarian law. Based on the groundwork of the ICRC, at the Hague Peace Conference in 1899 "non-governmental groups organized a parallel salon for diplomats to meet with concerned citizens, various petitions with numerous signatures were submitted to the official conference, and an independent activist produced a daily conference newspaper" (Anheier et al. 2001, 5). More recently, NGOs have played a critical role in the development of our international human rights framework. As Ishay (2004, 224) argues, NGOs "were responsible for the incorporation of human rights clauses into the UN Charter, for a significant part of the language used in the Universal Declaration, and for the adoption and domestic ratification of major human rights treaties." NGOs were also instrumental in convincing the UN to establish the office of the UN High Commission on Human Rights in 1994 (Korey 2001). The role of NGOs in this area continues with NGOs often pivotal in convincing the deeply divided Human Rights Council and its predecessor to act. While formal consultative status gives NGOs the right to speak at human rights meetings, it is often the information provided informally by NGOs and the potential threat of media attention that is critical. States are also more likely to "frame their proposals in terms of appropriateness and justice in the presence of civil society actors" (Glasius 2005, 130). However, involvement in human rights promotion and monitoring presents significant challenges on the ground for aid and development INGOs. These challenges are discussed further in Chapter 5.

INGOs have also contributed to the emergence of an international norm that the governments of rich countries should provide resources for the economic and social development of poor countries. Carol Lancaster argues that this norm, which certainly did not exist in the 1950s, has emerged, in part, due to the "rise of development-orientated NGOs which created a domestic constituency for aid's development purpose" (Lancaster 2007, 5). Further, in those countries where INGOs have been weak, such as Japan, the purpose of aid has been dominated by non-development purposes, such as commerce and diplomacy. Even in the United States, where INGOs and the aid lobby have been relatively weak in the context of the US political system and there has been a constant struggle between those who have supported aid and those who have argued that it is inappropriate (see Case Study 6.1), INGOs have played a critical role in supporting a development-oriented aid norm (Lancaster 2007, 100–105). The success of campaigns like Make Poverty History has strengthened this emerging development-orientated aid norm. However, one consequence of the success of such campaigns in convincing rich countries to provide more aid to address global poverty is that if such aid is shown to be ineffective, it will undermine the domestic political support that it has helped to garner. According to Lancaster, this is "one of the most serious threats to the future of foreign aid" (Lancaster 2007, 8). As a result, it reinforces the importance to INGOs of demonstrating aid effectiveness, discussed further in Chapter 5.

INGOs have supported a large number of high-profile campaigns with significant implications for international relations, even in the litmus test area of international security. Domestic and international NGOs were critical to the development of the Convention on the Rights of the Child (CRC) through the 1980s. While it took some time for NGOs to operate with the required professionalism, sometimes making spontaneous, ill-prepared proposals and even "disagreeing with each other in the presence of the Chair and delegates," once they established an Ad Hoc Group they helped to drive the process and were taken seriously as key participants (Cantwell 2008, 23–24).

One of the reasons for the World Bank's and IMF's changes of policy toward highly indebted poor countries was civil society criticism led by the Jubilee Campaign. The Jubilee Campaign was an international campaign seeking to pressure the G7 leaders to "cancel the unpayable debts of the poorest countries by the year 2000, under a fair and transparent process." By the end of the campaign, 24 million signatures had been gathered for the Jubilee 2000 petition, the first-ever global petition. There were Jubilee 2000 campaigns in more than 60 countries around the world (see www.jubilee2000uk.org). The Jubilee Campaign and others, such as the 50 Years is Enough Campaign (see www.50years.org), prompted significant changes in the way one of the most powerful international organizations operates. Under President James D. Wolfensohn's leadership, the World Bank sought to build bridges to NGOs to the point where seventy

---

Case Study 3.1: Reform of the World Bank

Despite vested political and economic interests and the ever-present difficulty of implementing change in multilateral organizations, the World Bank achieved significant reform of its structure and policies at the beginning of this decade. These include improving accountability and transparency through the establishment of the Development Economics Center, the Operations Evaluation Department, and the Inspection Panel. The World Bank also became much more attuned to environmental issues and instituted a much more sustained engagement with civil society.

There were a number of drivers for this organizational change. First, the criticism from increasingly influential NGOs and others contributed to creating an environment in which the World Bank was more open to change. In particular, the mobilization of public opinion through the Jubilee Campaign and the socialization of the reform agenda through increasing meetings between NGO advocates and Bank bank staff were critical. Second, internal advocates were skillful in presenting reforms in ways that did not clash with the Bank's bank's existing norms, values, and beliefs. Third, the leadership of Wolfensohn, politically supported by Bill Clinton, was key.

NGO specialists worked in the World Bank's field offices, and more than half of World Bank projects had NGOs as partners (Mallaby 2004, 262), although subsequent structural changes at the World Bank may have undermined some of these reforms and the influence of INGOs. The World Bank has itself acknowledged the impact of NGOs on its policy on the environment and in relation to the debt of some of the world's poorest countries (Riddell 2007, 297).

More recently, the Make Poverty History campaign has been instrumental in placing aid volumes on the domestic agenda of governments and in international meetings of the G8, the WTO, and the UN. The International Campaign to Ban Landmines (ICBL), which started in 1991 and within six years resulted in the adoption of the Ottawa Convention, is particularly noteworthy, not so much because it won a Noble Peace Prize in 1997,[7] but because it achieved a significant policy change in the area of security despite the objections of major states.[8] It was also used as a model for the campaign to increase the powers of the International Criminal Court (ICC) and campaigns to ban cluster weapons, reduce the use of light weapons, and eliminate the use of child soldiers (Ahmed and Potter 2006, 162).[9]

Finally, INGOs also now play a much more significant role in the governance and operations of IGOs.[10] Karns and Mingst (2004, 230) identify five types of NGO activities in IGOs: "(1) consultation in regime creation and implementation, (2) lobbying, (3) surveillance of governmental activities, (4) involvement in international program implementation, and (5) participation in decision making." This broad engagement with IGOs is well illustrated by the much greater role that INGOs play in most UN meetings. When the UN was established, Article 71 of the UN Charter allowed the Economic and Social Council (ECOSOC) to "make suitable arrangements for consultation with nongovernmental organizations which are concerned with matters within its competence." NGOs with consultative status have access to the areas used by diplomats at the UN, useful for informal discussion with delegates. They are also able to attend meetings and proceedings. However, despite this status, even into the 1970s and 1980s, the involvement of NGOs in international meetings of states was an exceptional event. This began to change with the Rio Conference on Environment and Development in 1992, and since then every major UN conference has involved large scale NGO participation in parallel conferences and meetings (Falk 2005, 156). The 2009 UNFCCC negotiations in Copenhagen are a good example of this trend. As Figure 3.2 illustrates, out of a total of 32,506 first-day registrations at the Conference, 20,506 were from NGOs, including business oriented NGOs. While in 1948, only 41 NGOs had been formally accredited to ECOSOC (Karns and Mingst 2004, 231),

Figure 3.2 Registrations at Day 1 of the 2009 UNFCCC Negotiations in Copenhagen

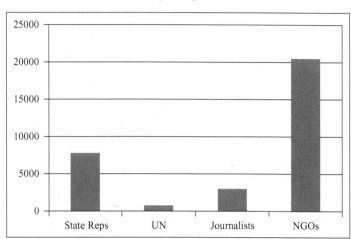

as of September 1, 2009 this number had increased to 3,287 NGOs across 3 categories (United Nations, E/2009/INF/4).

Unlike ECOSOC, neither the General Assembly nor the Security Council has any formal or legal framework for NGO participation. However, recognizing their unique role in international relations, the ICRC and the IFRC now both hold observer status at the General Assembly (Karns and Mingst 2004, 231). The General Assembly has also opened up to "NGOs in recent years, for example with the '+5 Special Sessions' and the informal Civil Society Hearings in the run-up to the 2005 World Summit" (Martens 2006). In the Security Council, a contentious protocol (the so-called Arria Formula) has enabled individual consultations with NGOs to take place, although these happen outside Security Council premises and do not appear on the official Council agenda (Paul 2003; Martens 2006). In 1995, Amnesty International, the Global Policy Forum, Earth Action, the World Council of Churches, and others organized an NGO Working Group that now regularly meets with the Council President (Karns and Mingst 2004, 233). Representatives of INGOs have also briefed Security Council members on a number of occasions. For example, in 1997 representatives of CARE, MSF, and Oxfam appeared before the Security Council to brief members on the situation in the Great Lakes (McDonald 2004; Karns and Mingst 2004, 233).

By 1997, this significantly increased involvement in the UN led then–Secretary General, Kofi Annan, to say, "Nongovernmental organizations are now seen as essential partners of the United Nations, not only in mobilizing public opinion but also in the process of deliberation and policy formulation and—even more important—in the execution of policies in work on the ground" (Opening Address to the DPI/NGO Fiftieth Annual Conference, Sept. 10, 1997). In recognition of this new role, Kofi Annan commissioned a high-level panel in 2003 to provide advice on the UN's relationship with civil society. The Panel's report, *We the Peoples: the UN, Civil Society, and Global Governance* (called the Cardoso Report after the name of the Panel's chair, former Brazilian President, Fernando Cardoso, see www.un-ngls.org), was delivered in 2004 and contained proposals on simplifying the accreditation process, on financial support for participation of NGOs from developing countries, and on strengthening the Security Council's engagement with NGOs (Martens, 2006). While these recommendations are not, in one sense dramatic, they do indicate that international politics has changed and global civil society, including INGOs, is now a core part of it.

However, IGOs outside of the UN system are also now much more engaged with INGOs. For example, the World Bank now has a much more sustained engagement with civil society. McGann and Johnston (2005) argue that "over half of World Bank projects are currently executed in partnership with NGOs" and that this move has created a situation in which "NGOs are at the center of World Bank policy, and moreover often determine it." Similarly, the GFATM has two NGO representatives on its board. These representatives actively promote civil society's interests at the governance level of an organization that will distribute more than US$3 billion in funding as part of its Round Eight grants. NGO board representatives were also instrumental in ensuring that civil society has a larger role to play in the administration of grants. Under the newly introduced dual track financing, a civil society organization will normally be a principal recipient of GFATM grants alongside government. Since Global Fund (2008) analysis suggests that the performance of NGOs is, on average, better than that of governments, the proportion of GFATM grants awarded to NGOs may well be expected to increase further, making them even more operationally important to the GFATM.

Limitations to and Critiques of the Growing Influence of INGOs

Of course, not everyone welcomes an increased role for INGOs in international or domestic politics. Many see them as less representative than even international organizations such as the World Bank. Others argue that often narrowly focused single-issue advocacy groups can create significant policy distortions. For example, after Wolfensohn increased the

World Bank's engagement with NGOs, a group of the Bank's executive directors, mostly from developing countries, "started to complain that management had gone too far, had opened the doors so wide to NGOs that the Bank's integrity had been compromised" (Clark 2003, 170). Larry Summers, Director of President Obama's National Economic Council and former US Treasury Secretary under Bill Clinton, told a World Bank management committee that he was "deeply troubled by the distance the Bank has gone in democratic countries toward engagement with groups other than governments in designing projects" (Clark 2003, 171). More colorfully, Sebastian Mallaby (2004, 6) warns that the World Bank is in danger of becoming captured by what he describes as "Lilliputians."

Many states have also resisted an increased role for NGOs at the UN for a number of reasons. Governments of some developing countries have resisted an increased role for INGOs based on concerns that it would negatively impact their own agenda for increased representation and participation in international forums, as well as based on opposition from domestic business and political interests (Kahler 2004, 153–4). States have resisted an increased role for INGOs in the global governance of aid and development for similar reasons (see Chapter 2). This concern may be one of the reasons behind the reluctance of many governments to endorse the recommendations of the Cardoso Report. Despite support from Secretary General Kofi Annan, at the Millennium+5 Summit preparatory processes, the recommendations of the Cardoso Report were not only *not* implemented but "governments largely excluded NGOs both from preparations for the Summit and from the Summit itself" (Martens 2006). Others fear that reform of the UN system is already difficult and slow enough without further complications from adding a large number of non-state actors.

For some, it is a distraction from INGO's "core" work. According to Anderson and Rieff, INGOs should "devote fewer of their resources to advocacy and more time and care to the actual needs of their actual constituencies" (Anderson and Rieff 2005, 36). Others argue that the goals of some NGOs are not always consistent with cosmopolitan values, human rights, or even the public good. For example, "pro-family" INGOs have lobbied conservative religious governments, including majority Catholic and Muslim nations such as Nicaragua, Pakistan, Iran, Sudan, Libya, Algeria, and Egypt with considerable success. They have also worked through the Vatican, which has observer state status at the UN and participates fully in UN conferences. In addition, such groups are behind the United States' refusal to ratify the CRC. INGOs also do not always act honestly and sometimes lack accountability.[11]

We should also be cautious to ensure we do not exaggerate INGOs' influence. As Keck and Sikkink (1998, 23) outline, a key tactic used by civil society actors and networks involves recruiting powerful state allies to their cause as one step in achieving policy change (a tactic they describe as "leverage politics"). For example, nearly all successful campaigns to change international law involve a collaborative effort with state actors. In the development of the CRC, Poland was critical; in the development of the Ottawa Convention, Canada was the essential state actor. The campaign for the birth of the ICC was, in diplomatic terms, a similar hybrid, neither traditionally state-ist in character nor an example of non-state transnationalism (Falk 2005, 151). There are also many examples where global civil society and INGOs in particular failed to achieve their policy objectives. For example, despite the mobilization of 11 million people in approximately 800 cities on February 15, 2003, to protest the possibility of war with Iraq—a protest that prompted the *New York Times* to describe global civil society as the "second superpower" (Kaldor et al. 2003, 3)— within weeks the United States, Britain, and Australia had nonetheless gone to war.[12] Through the 1980s and much of the 1990s, INGOs also failed to have much impact on changing the neoliberal orthodoxy that dominated development economics, despite their criticisms. Similarly, notwithstanding the number of NGO representatives at the unsuccessful UNFCCC negotiations in Copenhagen (see Figure 3.2), one commentator claimed that the negotiations proceeded "as if democratization and the flowering of civil society, advocacy, and self-determination had never happened" (Monbiot 2009). While there are often many reasons for such failures, one common limitation for INGOs is that the sources of their power are diffuse, often decentralized, and can sometimes take considerable time before having impact on state actors. Achieving normative change is also inherently difficult, because it requires actors to question established practices and replace them with new ones (Keck and Sikkink 1998, 35). In the past, they have also lacked the policy depth to provide viable policy alternatives.

Furthermore, we need to acknowledge the influence that states and IGOs have over INGOs. Successful development work also requires a complex relationship between INGOs and local and national governments. While registration requirements vary considerably, an INGO must always obtain approval to operate within a particular jurisdiction. In some countries, registration can be used either directly or implicitly as a way of controlling the statements or activities of INGOs. For example, in June 2008 Sudan expelled the head of MSF from the South Darfur region for refusing to cooperate with an investigation into alleged misconduct by the agency arising out of a 2005 report by MSF documenting widespread rape cases in Darfur.[13] This followed the expulsion in November 2004 of the country directors of both Oxfam and Save the Children. Sudan claimed they had breached the law by making political statements about the crisis in Darfur.

Usually, however, governments are more subtle. In many developing countries, regular registration renewal often hangs over the head of local directors of INGO offices as an implicit threat. In developed countries, INGO funding rather than registration is used as a way of influencing the agenda of INGOs. Most government grants are made with specific sectoral and geographical targets and can be accompanied by requirements around the methodology to be adopted or even what public statements an agency must make. A recent example of US government influence over the programming choices of aid and development INGOs is the requirement imposed on those agencies that accept HIV funding to "emphasize abstinence as the primary strategy for prevention and to pledge to condemn prostitution despite the additional stigma and hence outreach problems such an approach involves" (Ellis 2010). In 2003, Save the Children and Mercy Corps objected to USAID contractual restrictions on their freedom to speak to the media on programming issues in Iraq (Read 2003). Similarly, under the Howard Government in Australia, AusAID contracts routinely included a "gag" clause requiring Ministerial approval for any public comments by a contractor (including INGOs) on an AusAID funded program (this clause was removed by the Rudd Government).

The use of competitive tenders and short term, renewable contracts by governments may also generate incentives that produce dysfunctional outcomes. As Cooley and Ron (2002, 6) argue, these contracts are "often performance based, renewable, and short term, creating counterproductive incentives and acute principal-agent problems." For those INGOs for whom government funding is a significant proportion of their overall income, the prospect of staff redundancies and program cut backs can be a powerful way to curb INGOs independence. As many commentators note, this a particular problem for US-based INGOs (Ahmed and Potter 2006, 112–119; Clarke 2003, 196–7). Clarke (2003, 196) argues that US-based INGOs do not criticize their own government because they are reluctant to "[be] labeled political or unpatriotic" or in the case of development NGOs, because "their sector receives so much USAID funding." On the other hand, governments are critical to the long-term success of INGO development work. To be effective, local government needs to be an intimate part of any development activity to promote sustainability and the long-term transformation of society. Aid and development INGOs, therefore, want to promote strong local and national governments that can provide key public services such as health and education, promote the rule of law, and develop strong, fair, and free markets for economic exchange and the creation of wealth (Slim 2007a). As a result, INGOs need to guard against their size or influence undermining government or leading to official resentment that might reduce the effectiveness of development work.

The extent to which INGOs offer alternative approaches to dominant economic, social, and political models is also open to question. In Alan Fowler's (2000b) opinion, development NGOs "have not really succeeded in co-opting the official aid system; more the other way around." A number of other commentators agree (Ellis 2010; Ahmed and Potter 2006, 119). Sassen (1999) goes even further and argues that INGOs are part of the "West's hegemonic project" and that they merely create a more conducive environment for western-style capitalism "by instituting standards and . . . strengthening Western-style liberal democracy." Similarly, Lipschutz (2005, 247) argues that global civil society is based on a liberal worldview that avoids foundational questions of politics and power, so-called constitutional issues, but rather focuses on power distribution: "such a focus accepts the deployment of power as a given and begs for dispensations from the powerful." Anderson and Rieff (2005) continuing this theme, argue that INGOs can be viewed as a "contemporary secular, postreligious missionary movement." These commentators then see global civil society and particularly large aid and development INGOs, as deeply enmeshed in existing power structures. This means that they are more likely to be in "collaboration with those who exercise dominion and institutional power" and therefore unlikely to challenge or seek to change the dominant discourse (Lipschutz 2005, 248). For Bebbington et al. (2008, 3), such collaboration is contrary to the underlying purpose of NGOs. They argue that such organizations can only be NGOs "in any politically meaningful sense if they are offering alternatives to dominant models, practices, and ideas about development." In my opinion, the views of these commentators are too pessimistic and fly in the face of the very real examples of success outlined here. In the same way as the ICRC and other INGOs changed states' views about the appropriate conduct of war in the nineteenth century, so too have INGOs driven the growth in the discourse of human rights—described by some commentators as the most striking change in both the theory and practice of international relations in the last 50 years (Brown 2002, 116). While INGOs must remain vigilant and ensure that they are not captured by dominant interests and thereby compromise their missions, cooperation and constructive engagement is as critical to their success as is challenging existing power structures. INGO leaders must, therefore, constantly strive to achieve a delicate balance between constructive engagement with governments and other powerful institutions on the one hand and challenging the status quo and dominant paradigms on the other.

While the precise extent may still be debated, it is clear that INGOs wield considerable influence in contemporary international relations. The source of this influence is the power they now wield in a globalized world (see Chapter 2). By working toward a common good and championing values beyond state interests, civil society actors can, even without formal status, constrain state behavior and change the terms of the debate. Aside from their active involvement in the formation of treaties and promoting state compliance through monitoring activities, the activities of INGOs' can create normative pressure on states to comply with international obligations that they have not formally consented to. For example, although the United States has not signed the Ottawa Convention, they have ceased to produce landmines (Ahmed and Potter 2006, 163). However, this increased power and influence is extremely fragile, hanging as it does on INGO's ability to effectively navigate an increasingly complex external environment and to maintain their legitimacy despite the inherent contradictions in their strategy and operations, discussed further in Chapters 5 and 6.

Conclusion: The Impact of INGOs on State Sovereignty

A key underlying theme of this chapter is the extent to which ideas, norms, and culture matter in international relations. The position one takes on this issue will influence the extent to which one accepts that global civil society (and INGOs in particular) is transforming the international system. Realists continue to point to the use of force by the US government in response to 9/11, the 2008 invasion of Georgia by a resurgent Russia, and the growing economic and military power of China to argue that the world remains dominated by material structures rather than normative ones. However, in my view this is not the case. While military force and economic power continue to be very important in international relations, the failure of the world's pre-eminent military to use force to successfully respond to 9/11 has, in fact, led to a greater acknowledgement, at least by Western states, of the importance of soft power. For example, the unilateral rhetoric of US Defense Secretary Robert Gates' predecessor, Donald Rumsfeld, has now been replaced by a view that acknowledges that force is only a small part of the solution. The most recent US defense strategy suggests that military efforts "to capture or kill terrorists are likely to be subordinate to measures to promote local participation in government and economic programs to spur development, as well as efforts to understand and address the grievances that often lie at the heart of insurgencies" (US Department of Defense 2008, 8).

Instead, world politics is socially constructed, and states and other international actors—including INGOs—are shaped by shared inter-subjective understandings and social practices such as discourse, culture, norms, and ideas. As Martha Finnemore (1996, 2) argues, "states are embedded in dense networks of transnational and international social relations that shape their perceptions of the world and their role in that world." While I am cautious to avoid overstating the influence of INGOs, if one accepts that state interests are determined through social interactions, more frequent engagement with states by INGOs in more effective ways will have a greater impact on how a state will define its interests.

For this reason I believe that INGOs, as the most powerful and organized form of global civil society, are having a significant transforming affect on international relations and state sovereignty in particular. They achieve this transformation in a number of ways. They blur the distinction between the domestic and international by straddling the divide and by providing a mechanism and resources for domestic groups to raise issues at the international level. Since they are private but operate in the public realm, they also blur the traditional distinction between public and private spheres in international law. As Mills and Joyce (2006) argue, INGOs operate at the geographic and conceptual fault lines on international relations and, as such, are having a significant impact on its development. INGOs also encourage states to become involved in the treatment of inhabitants or the environment of other states. By championing values beyond state interests, they constrain state behavior. For example, the humanitarian values of large INGOs are "premised on a worldview not easily accommodated within the principles and rights associated with state sovereignty" and by "asserting that human beings have rights and value simply by virtue of their humanity, humanitarians create a set of normative claims that compete with the claims made by states" (Finnemore 1996, 71). While as recently as the 1970s, "the idea that the human rights of citizens of any country are legitimately the concern of people and governments elsewhere was considered radical" (Keck and Sikkink 1998, 79), this is no longer the case. I also disagree with more skeptical interpretations that view the impact of global civil society as merely a phase, which in a post–September 11 environment has run its course (Anderson and Rieff 2005, 26–7). No longer can political communities be seen as "self enclosed political spaces," instead, they are now "enmeshed in complex structures of over lapping forces, relations, and networks," thanks, in part, to the work of INGOs (Held and McGrew 2002, 123).

However, INGOs' past successes in norm creation and influence at the international level have given them a much more prominent role in international relations and significantly increased expectations of their capacity to contribute to policy development and in other ways. These expectations fall particularly heavily on the largest INGOs. Whether or not the largest INGOs will be able to meet these new expectations and continue to be an important influence on international politics into the twenty-first century will be largely dependent on how they respond to the plethora of challenges that now confront them. These challenges are the subject of Chapters 5, 6, and 7. However, before considering these challenges in detail, it is worthwhile examining more fully the underlying drivers of INGO growth and considering whether they are likely to continue to support the growth in size and influence of INGOs. This examination is the task of Chapter 4.

Notes

1. At the time, they estimated that the INGO sector had total resources of around US$10–15 billion.

2. For a comprehensive history of the Red Cross, see Moorehead (1999). Martha Finnemore (1996) also provides a very useful constructivist account of the way in with the ICRC socialized states to accept new political goals and new values that have had a lasting impact on the conduct of war.

3. Lindenberg and Bryant (2001, 13–17) provides a brief overview of the history of each of the largest six aid and development INGOs. See also Clark (2003, 133–6); Gnaerig and MacCormack (1999, 140–146); Henry (1999, 109–120) and Offenheiser (1999, 121–139).

4. Anheier (2005, 330) sets out a range of employment data for INGOs across twenty-eight countries. He suggests that in these countries, INGOs amount to 1 to 2 percent of total nonprofit sector employment. However, this data relates only to developed countries rather than developing countries where one would expect INGO employment to be much higher. It was also collected in 1995 meaning it is now quite out of date.

5. There seems to be some discrepancy in the numbers. Ahmed and Potter (2006, 117) use a number of sources to show that the average NGO share of ODA of selected OECD countries has increased from 6.5 percent in 1983 to 1986 to 10.9 percent in 2000, while Table 18 of the OECD DAC Development Cooperation Report 2006 suggested an average at that time of 8.8 percent. Nonetheless, the trend of an increasing proportion of ODA being spent through NGOs is clear.

6. This appears to be broadly consistent with the growth in the overall INGO sector, which I estimate to have approximately US$25 billion of annual income in 2006. This figure is calculated using the 2006 DAC

data which estimates private giving of US$14.6 billion, bilateral funds to NGOs of 8.2 percent of total bilateral aid of approximately US$100 billion and funds from multilateral organizations of around US$2.4 billion. For a more detailed analysis of private giving and a much higher estimate of the total amount given privately for international purposes, see Kharas (2008, 62–64).

7. NGOs, including MSF, and their founders have won 13 Nobel Peace Prizes, see Ahmed and Potter (2006, 154) for a list.

8. The six founding NGOs of the ICBL were not from the traditional disarmament community but rather were mostly aid and development NGOs working directly with affected communities: Mekata (2000, 146). This background may have increased their perceived legitimacy and made it harder for their advocacy to be dismissed.

9. For a detailed account of NGO involvement in the ICC (mostly by large INGOs), see Glasius (2005).

10. Full a complete list of INGO involvement with UN agencies, see Reinmann (2006, 56–7).

11. For a survey of NGO wrongdoing, see Gibelman and Gelman (2004).

12. Of course, George Bush became one of the most unpopular presidents in American history, the decision to go to war certainly contributed to Tony Blair stepping down as prime minister of Britain, and John Howard lost both the prime ministership and his own seat at the Australian election in November 2007.

13. In 2005, the Darfur head and country director of MSF were arrested on charges of crimes against the state, publishing false reports and spying in relation to the report. The government of Sudan had denied that rape was common in its remote West.

CHAPTER 4

Factors Driving the Increased Size and Influence of INGOs

Introduction

There are many forces behind the increased size and influence of aid and development INGOs discussed in Chapter 3. Certainly, the increased financial resources that the sector now has at its disposal are one factor. However, it would be simplistic to see this as the underlying cause. More fundamentally, it is such things as changing views about the nature of development which have favored a growing role for INGOs; new forms of communications and transport that have dramatically lowered the costs for these transnational actors; increasing political freedoms for civil society; the apparent inability of states to act in a collective way to address global problems such as poverty, climate change, ethnic and religious tension, and ongoing population growth; and the gradual emergence of a more cosmopolitan mind-set in some countries. However, whether or not these factors will continue to drive the growth of INGOs' size and influence is uncertain. Some will certainly continue to support this trend; other factors, however, appear to be waning. Furthermore, the impact of a dramatic slowing in global economic growth on these issues needs to be considered, at least in the short run. This Chapter will therefore identify and examine the main drivers for the historical growth in the size and influence of INGOs and consider the extent to which this growth is likely to continue.

Changing Understanding of Development and Policy Priorities

In the immediate postcolonial period following World War II, there was a strong emphasis on nation building, and "development" was defined almost exclusively in material terms and measured by growth in per capita gross domestic product. This approach can be contrasted with the more recent and much broader understanding of development that emphasizes people's capabilities and freedoms, not simply their material poverty. Drawing on the

---

KEY POINTS:

A large number of factors have been driving the increasing size and influence of INGOs. They include

- changing views about what development is and how it occurs
- increased political openness to civil society in many parts of the world
- increased awareness and concern about transnational problems like global poverty and climate change
- a growing confidence gap between citizens and governments. High-profile scandals, financial collapses, and other problems have also led to a loss of public trust in corporations
- a rise in cosmopolitan values, a preference for democratic forms of governance, an appreciation for cultural diversity, and increased interest in global issues in developed countries
- increased outsourcing and privatization by many governments
- improvements in and the reduced costs of information, communication, and transport technologies

It is less clear that global economic growth is a long-term determinant of the size and influence of INGOs. While the current global economic slowdown may dampen INGO growth rates in the short term, it is probably unlikely to be a significant long-term impediment.

Overall, most of the external factors that have driven INGO growth over the last decade appear to remain largely positive. As a result, if INGOs can address the external and organizational challenges they face, the underlying environment for their ongoing growth in size and influence remains strong.

---

work of Amartya Sen, the UNDP has championed this broader view of development in its annual *Human Development Reports* and its Human Development Index. According to the UNDP their approach is "guided by the belief that development is ultimately a process of enlarging people's choices, not just raising national incomes" (see www.UNDP.org). Similarly, Kingsbury (2007, 16) describes this broader approach to development as one that focuses on creating an environment in which people can develop their full potential and lead productive, creative lives in accord with their needs and interests. As such, it has been characterized as a people-centered approach rather than a growth-centered one. Since participation and empowerment are central to this approach, it is seen to be more aligned with the work undertaken by NGOs that favor participative development at the local level and seek to redistribute power and transform institutions.

Related to this change in our understanding of development, there has also been a growing policy emphasis on good governance and promoting political development. This includes programs that strengthen civil society, improve the legal and institutional underpinnings of the rule of law, strengthen the role of the media and other sources of independent information, increase human rights education, promote grass-roots demand for good governance, and fight corruption (see Chapter 5). Once again, these changing policy priorities have played to the perceived strengths of NGOs, although whether NGO activities actually promote increased political participation varies depending on the extent to which a social mobilization paradigm is adopted as opposed to a service delivery one (see Rahman 2006). More recently, the growing role of INGOs in global governance and the growing awareness of the relationship between poverty and international peace and security in a globalized world, discussed in Chapter 2, have both continued to support the growth in size and influence of INGOs.

Views about how best to facilitate development have also shifted. Development is no longer understood as a linear process to which top-down planning can be applied. Instead, the development process is seen as nonlinear and far more complex and multifaceted. These policy changes and new approaches have all been supported by the perceived ineffectiveness of bilateral aid and encouraged by INGOs themselves. Using their increasing public profile and influence, INGOs have successfully lobbied bilateral agencies for a greater role in the development process and a greater share of ODA.

NGOs also came to be seen as one of the primary sources of development alternatives in terms of both ideas and practices. While Lewis (2007, 40) suggests that this may still be the case, the emergence of new aid and development actors, such as the Bill and Melinda Gates Foundation, are certainly challenging this view now. Like the Rockefeller Foundation before it, the Gates Foundation has stimulated new thinking in the development sector, and it is having an impact on practice well beyond its considerable size. The Gates Foundation has also set aside nearly $500 million for the Grand Challenges in Global Health Initiative, which supports a range of innovative research projects. There is also a plethora of other aid and development actors that bring a "remarkable variety of voices and ideas, combined with a mixture of expertise [and] naiveté" (Bishop 2008, 43). As a result, while aid and development NGOs will undoubtedly remain important sources of new thinking, whether they will continue to be the principal source of development alternatives is, at best, uncertain. As Chapters 5 and 6 will detail, particularly in relation to the largest aid and development INGOs, they do not have a good track record of capturing and disseminating good practice and continue to lag other actors in terms of investment in policy expertise.

Increased Political Openness

Another factor that has driven INGO growth is increased political openness. Since 1945, the globalization of political structures, international institutions, and the spread of Western liberal democratic values have created an environment "highly conducive to NGO growth" (Reinmann 2006, 46). Reinmann argues that in some instances, this political openness has extended to tacit encouragement by states and IGOs of a "new pro-NGO international norm" that has placed pressure on other states to "support and include NGOs in both international and national politics." The result has been that the increase in the number of democratic governments during the 1970s and 1980s was accompanied by expanded civil rights, which allowed Northern-based INGOs to enter countries where they previously could not work.[1]

This trend continued throughout the 1990s, with the fall of the Berlin Wall and the dissolution of the USSR, the redemocratization of Latin America, and greater government tolerance in Japan, South Korea, and South Africa, all significantly increasing opportunities for INGOs (Kaldor et al. 2003, 19). Of course, there were also examples of reducing political openness in places like the Balkans, the Middle East, and in Central Asia, but in general "the world was on a course for greater political openness that welcomed citizen participation and involvement to an extent unknown in the past" (Kaldor et al. 2003, 19). This trend, however, now appears to have come to an end, at least for the foreseeable future. Freedom House's 2009 survey suggests that from 2006 to 2008, global political rights and civil liberties declined (Puddington 2009). In just 2007, one-fifth of the world's countries experienced a decline (Puddington 2008). This includes countries where previous significant progress had been achieved, such as Bangladesh, Sri Lanka, Philippines, Lebanon, Palestine, Nigeria, and Kenya. In 2008, although the pace of erosion seemed less severe than in previous years, "most regions experienced stagnation, with sub-Saharan Africa and the non-Baltic former Soviet Union experiencing the most acute deterioration" (Puddington 2009, 1). There has also been a marked increased in the politicization of aid (see Chapter 5), growing religious fundamentalism in some countries and added bureaucratic burden and restrictions imposed as a result of new global security and counter terrorist measures (Fowler 2008). It is therefore unlikely that political liberalization will continue to significantly support growth of aid and development INGOs, at least in the short term.

Increased Awareness and Concern about Transnational Problems

The second factor that has driven INGO growth is increased awareness and concern about transnational problems. There have been, for example, a plethora of UN reports on transnational threats, including the 2006 report, *Meeting Global Challenges: International Cooperation in the National Interest,* by the Task Force on Global Public Goods; the February 2004 report by the World Commission on the Social Dimensions of Globalization, *A Fair Globalization*; the 2004 report by the Secretary General's High-Level Panel on Threats, Challenges, and Change, *A More Secure World*; and Kofi Annan's own report, *In Larger Freedom: Towards Development, Security and Human Rights for All*. All of these reports identified similar problems including poverty, infectious disease, and environmental degradation; nuclear, radiological, chemical, and biological weapons; terrorism; and transnational organized crime. There has also been a range of popular books that have highlighted the issue. In 2002, Jean-Francois Richard wrote a book titled *High Noon: 20 Global Problems and 20 Years to Solve Them* in which he identified three types of issues requiring a globally coordinated response: issues involving the global commons, like global warming and water deficits; issues whose size and urgency requires a global commitment, like the fight against poverty or conflict prevention; and issues needing a global regulatory approach, such as global financial flows or rules for e-commerce. More recently, both the economist Jeffrey Sachs (2008) and *New York Times* columnist, Thomas Friedman (2008), have written popular books highlighting the need for a coordinated response to global transnational problems. In fact, according to Sachs (2008, 3) the "defining challenge of the twenty-first century will be to face the reality that humanity shares a common fate on a crowded planet." This common fate will require new forms of global cooperation yet, despite the magnitude and nature of the threats, states appear increasingly unable to act in a collective way to address them. Furthermore, with intergovernmental organizations subject to the national interests of states making decisive and responsive action difficult, there remains a significant institutional deficit at the global level. As a result, there is increased demand for non-state, transnational, public good orientated actors. Aid and development INGOs are one such type of actor.

Interestingly, Ulrich Beck suggests that even more fundamental changes in international relations are occurring. He argues that the nation-state was established to protect and insure citizens against risk such as natural calamities, poor health, unemployment, and those posed by foreign enemies (Glasius et al. 2005, 1).[2] However, since many key risks impacting people's lives have been largely de-bounded from the nation-state in spatial, temporal and social terms, the underlying value of the nation-state as an institution is being questioned. Not only is the point of origin of a risk often unrelated to its place of impact, there is often unequal power between those exposed to the risk and those creating the risk, not only between countries but also within them (Beck 1999, 143). In fact, Karns and Mingst (2004, 23) argue that the "disjuncture between states' persistence as central structures of the international system and an eroding loyalty and confidence of individuals in the institutions of the state has contributed to the resurgence of ethnic and religious identities, ethnic conflicts, and further weakening, if not failure of some states."

There are a number of potential responses to Beck's unbounded risk. One response is for nation-states to seek to reassert control through increased immigration controls and through trade or physical barriers such as the Israeli separation wall. While this can be a popular response, most analysis would appear to question its long-term effectiveness. Another is to seek to establish global markets for transnational goods and externalities. For example, Ruggie (2004, 499) sees transnational actors such as INGOs as part of a system of states that is becoming "embedded in a broader, albeit still thin and partial, institutionalized arena concerned with the production of global public goods." A third route is to establish global regulation (e.g., WTO or Kyoto Protocol). The inability of states to cooperate despite the obvious transnational nature of the problems is one of the reasons for increased support for INGOs.

Even in the United States, where donors have traditionally taken a somewhat skeptical view of foreign aid, in the latter half of the 1990s the proportion of total private giving for international purposes doubled from 1 to 2 percent (Lindeburg and Bryant 2001, 11). Since the forces of globalization will continue to amplify the unbounded nature of key risks but their unequal burden makes reaching agreement on international agreements politically difficult domestically—as evidenced by the failure of the Doha trade round and the difficulty in negotiating a successor to the Kyoto Protocol—we can expect that this factor will support continued growth of INGOs.

Growing Confidence Gap Between Citizens and Governments

The failure of states—and, in some cases, their inability—to deal with transnational problems combined with examples of corruption, concern about self-interest, and questions of competence has led to the third factor that has driven INGO growth: an increasing confidence gap between citizens and governments (Glasius et al., 2005, 3). Clark (2003, 70) points to worldwide "falling voter turnout, declining membership of political parties, reduced confidence in politicians and governments, increasing citizens' actions against corporations, widespread hostility toward IGOs, and the rapid growth of the global protest movement" as evidence of the waning of public confidence in democratic processes. In the United Kingdom, research by the London School of Economics suggests "people are more cynical about politics than anything else" and this cynicism is growing (Davies 2008). Paul Skidmore (2008) argues that the British public's trust in government has almost halved since the 1970s, and this has no doubt been made worse by the MPs' expenses scandal that led to the resignation of the Speaker of the House of Commons in May 2009. However, Skidmore argues that this trend is not restricted to Britain but can be identified across a broad number of different societies and political systems. Research by the University of Southampton shows that the public's cynicism extends to the international development arena—the public tends to doubt that the government is genuinely interested in addressing global poverty or that it will deliver effective results (Atkinson and Eastwood 2007). The state of cynicism in the United States can perhaps best be measured by the fact that a US comedian, Jon Stewart, is now ranked alongside the *New York Times* as a key opinion former.[3] Barak Obama's 2008 Presidential campaign certainly harnessed perceptions that politics used to be a nobler and more ambitious enterprise than it is today to encourage American voters to support a call for political change.

Public trust in corporations is also declining. High-profile scandals, financial collapses, environmental vandalism, labor and supply-chain issues, and human rights abuse have all led to a loss of public trust in corporations. For example, Gibelman and Gelman (2004, 358), argue that "the downfall of Enron, ImClone, WorldCom, Tyco, and other large conglomerates created a general state of suspiciousness and mistrust toward corporate America." This has been further exacerbated by the recent economic crisis that has been blamed by some analysts on corporate greed, particularly in the financial industry. Increased transparency brought on by new communication methods such as the Internet has arguably also had the effect of decreasing rather than increasing public trust in regulators and industry (Glasius et al. 2005, 2). Any dissonance between a company's marketing messages in one country and its actual practice in another are now quickly revealed.

INGOs are benefiting from this confidence gap between citizens, governments, and corporations. "[T]he new social movements, and the NGOs they spawned, provide the institutional connection between the drop in confidence in conventional, nation-state institutions and the growth of global civil society" (Glasius et al. 2005, 3). The same University of Southampton research referred to previously, found that, in contrast to the UK government, the public engagement activities of credible NGOs was seen to build public support for aid. A 2003 Gallup Poll found that NGOs ranked second out of 17 institutions as the most trusted social and political institutions, well ahead of both government and business (Ahmed and Potter 2006, 244). However, as will be argued in Chapter 5, the same factors that are leading to a loss in confidence in government and business could impact on INGOs without significant attention to their own accountability and effectiveness.

Value Shift in OECD Countries

The fifth, and perhaps most-contested, factor behind the rise of INGOs is the purported value shift in OECD countries that is claimed to have given rise to cosmopolitan values, a preference for democratic forms of governance, an appreciation for cultural diversity, and increased interest in the types of global issues that many INGOs are involved in, such as global poverty. Kaldor et al. (2003, 16) cite the work of a large number of social scientists to support this hypothesis. Further evidence for such a values shift can arguably be seen in the global response to the Asian tsunami in December 2004 and the rise of third-way politics in places like Britain under Tony Blair and in Germany under Chancellor Schröder. According to Anthony Giddens (1998, 78), "the fostering of an active civil society is a basic part of the politics of the third way." While many factors influenced the outcome, the election of Barak Obama can also be seen as a rejection of the unilateralism of George Bush. Obama's multicultural background certainly suggests a growing willingness on the part of the American voting public to embrace diversity. In Australia, the election of Kevin Rudd may be interpreted as a reaction against some of the regressive globalization of the Howard government, such as its treatment of asylum seekers, and a return to the values that allowed Australia to welcome large numbers of Vietnamese boat people in the 1970s and to undertake significant proglobalization economic reform in the 1980s.[4] Certainly, Rudd's support for increased foreign aid played a part in some marginal seats in the 2007 election.[5]

The support for increased foreign aid can be seen in many developed countries and is reflected in the agenda of a number of recent international meetings. For example, in 2005 there were three events that all sought to highlight the issue: the G8 Summit in Gleneagles in July,[6] the UN Millennium +5 Summit in September in New York, and the World Trade Organization (WTO) meeting in December in Hong Kong. It is notable that a coalition of INGOs and other civil society groups campaigned under the Make Poverty History banner around all of them. Kaldor et al. (2003, 28) has also argued that the broad based support for anti war demonstrations held in February 2003 support the potential of a "new cosmopolitan approach, which integrated immigrant and developing-country communities into the global political process for the first time."

A number of reasons have been promulgated for this shift. One reason is that growing material affluence from economic growth has created a middle class whose values increasingly moved from an emphasis on economic well-being to "concerns about democracy, participation, and meaning, and involved, among other things, a formation toward cosmopolitan values such as tolerance and respect for human rights, social equity, and quality of life" (Kaldor et al. 2003, 29; see also Abramson and Inglehart 1995). If this is a major factor, it will be interesting to see whether countries become more domestically focused or inward looking as a result of the 2008 global economic crisis.

Another reason for this values shift is that communication technology and more frequent international travel mean that the public in OECD countries has much greater knowledge of and empathy with people living in developing countries (undoubtedly a factor in the public response to the Asian tsunami). Certainly, Keck and Sikkink (1998, 43) believe that "technological and institutional change can alter the 'moral' universe in which action takes place by changing how people think about responsibility and guilt." Increased education also plays a part. For example, in countries that incorporate global education into their curricula, such as Scandinavia, support for significant levels of ODA remains high. INGOs themselves have played a role here. By undertaking and supporting global education activities aimed at supporters, schools, and religious groups and through advocating for global education to be formally incorporated into school curriculums, INGOs have contributed to increased awareness and understanding in many countries.

Nonetheless, the extent—and perhaps even the existence—of such a values shift remains highly contested. For example, German political scientist Ernst Hillibrand (2008) argues that Europe is seeing the end of a political-ideological cycle and that the third way in Britain and *neue mitte* in Germany have reached their political expiry date. He argues that one of the reasons for this is that "globalization and Europeanization have affected European workers' relative economic situation for the worse. The wage share . . . has fallen in the European Union during the past 25 years, from 72.1 percent to 68.4 percent. The Gini Index of income inequality has risen in most Western European countries since the 1980s." Nationalism's ongoing strength is evidenced by the numerous demands of peoples around the world for secession or for greater autonomy within states or in protests about migration or free trade. Some commentators are also arguing that there is a "marked trend toward greater tribalization with groups who feel that globalization is destroying their identity and who long for more traditional, less-inclusive notions and beliefs in an effort to find a sense of personal belonging" (Schwab 2007, 344). One reaction has been the "regressive globalization" described here. This phenomenon is evident in the success of populist right movements in Europe that have taken a hard line against continued immigration and is difficult to reconcile with the globalization friendly and pro-European discourse of the center-left establishment that until recently dominated European politics.[7] It is also evident in the way that the term "cosmopolitan" was used by Republicans in the 2008 US presidential election as a means of slurring Barak Obama (Cohen 2008).[8] As a result, it is very difficult to determine whether or not this value shift is real and whether it will continue or recede.

Outsourcing and Privatization

The sixth factor that has driven INGO growth, particularly financial growth from the 1980s onward, is the neoliberal outsourcing and privatization agenda and the new roles it gave INGOs (Bebbington et. al. 2008, 13). Large INGOs "benefited enormously from the increasing tendency of government and intergovernment organizations to channel aid and development funds through INGOs rather than to national or local governments" (Florini and Simmons 2000, 8). As concerns about the efficiency and effectiveness of bilateral aid grew, INGOs were increasingly turned to as an alternative model for deploying ODA (Lewis 2007, 39). Thus INGOs also benefited from the broader perceptions that NGOs were "more efficient, more flexible, and more innovative than state agencies" (Anheier 2005, 340) and the preference, especially among conservative politicians and proponents of third-way politics, to transfer traditional state social welfare functions to civil society (Sassen, 1999). This phenomenon was not limited to Western Europe, North America, Japan, and Australia but extended to former communist countries of Eastern Europe and to some least developed countries as well (Mathews 1997; Ahmed and Potter 2006, 24).

Increased government "outsourcing" to INGOs raises significant issues for INGOs themselves. For example, there are concerns that it can lead to INGOs becoming captured by state actors, and there is certainly clear evidence that a high proportion of INGO funding from government sources can *potentially* "distort accountability upwards and overemphasize linear approaches to performance measurement with damaging effects on the ability of INGOs to be effective catalysts of social change" (Edwards and Hulme 1995b, 219). Recognizing the potential downsides of significant government funding, many INGOs have policies in place governing the proportion of government funding they are prepared to accept. This is an issue that MSF is particularly cognizant of and one of the reasons that in 2008, 89.9 percent of their total global income was from nongovernment sources.

However, it is likely that the past zeal for privatization and outsourcing is abating somewhat. As the *Spence Report* (World Bank 2008) demonstrates, and as reinforced by government reaction to the 2008 global financial crisis, there has been a significant shift in economic thinking away from the policy prescriptions of the Washington consensus. Instead, there is increasing recognition for policy to be sensitive to contextual differences between countries and for policy experimentation. Economic orthodoxy is much more likely now to recognize a legitimate role for government, thereby reducing government privatization and deregulation. While still favoring free trade, the *Spence Report* even recognizes that there are risks and dislocations from opening up an economy too quickly.

On the other hand, if official aid budgets continue to rise in line with commitments in many developed countries (despite the global financial crisis), the ongoing reluctance to expand the staff employed by bilateral agencies means that such agencies will continue to seek mechanisms that allow them to expend large sums in a way that meets public sector goals around accountability. This trend is therefore likely to continue to provide opportunities for large aid and development INGOs to grow, although they will need to compete with multilateral institutions and the new collaborative organizations, discussed in Chapter 2, for a share of these funds. That in turn will require them to address the issues explored further in Chapters 5 and 6.

Technology

The seventh factor that has driven INGO growth has been improvements in and the reduced costs of information, communication, and transport technologies. Since television advertising allowed the largest aid and development INGOs to become household names in the early 1980s, modern communication technologies have facilitated increased fundraising and allowed INGOs to mobilize supporters in greater and greater numbers. In addition, new technology has facilitated the geographic spread of INGOs by lowering internal communication costs. In fact, in 1986, Greenpeace was one of the first organizations of any type to use a computer network to link its thirty offices together (Clark 2003, 98). New communication technologies have also allowed for much more cost-effective networking between organizations. For example, the International Campaign to Ban Landmines (ICBL) used modern communications forms to allow members to share information, political strategies, and to jointly plan activities without a secretariat (Williams and Goose 1998, 22; Bruhl and Rittberger 2002, 8). Bruhl and Rittberger (9) conclude that "without the technological revolution, these INGOs could never have worked so closely together." Modern communication technology had a similar impact in the campaign for the ICC and the anti-MAI campaign.

The increased speed of communications via the Internet and other technology has helped INGOs partially address one of the limitations of their influence: the slow pace at which they are able to reflect public support for their views to politicians and international statesmen. E-mail based campaigns are fast, cheap, and require less effort from supporters than letter writing, increasing response rates. Mobile phones can be even more powerful. They allow for large numbers of people to be mobilized quickly for campaigning purposes, and they are far more ubiquitous than the Internet. Mobile phones are now regularly used by activists to create instant street protests, can be used to disseminate information, including pictures, to counter government propaganda, and increasingly as a fundraising tool. For example, mobile phones were used by activists to organize street protests in the 2001overthrow of Joseph Estrada in the Philippines. Of course, they have a dark side too. Mobile phones were used as detonators in the Madrid train bombings in 2004 and can just as easily spread disinformation and rumors.

Opportunities for civil society to harness new technologies continue to emerge. For example, the use of Twitter during the 2009 presidential election in Iran—a technology that did not even exist at the time of the last Iranian election—facilitated information sharing between activists around the world and may have tempered the government's response to street protests. This election was the first time that Twitter had been used to support a large-scale social movement. Twitter's attractiveness to these types of situations is not surprising. As Lev Grossman (2009) argues, Twitter is "ideal for a mass protest movement, both very easy for the average citizen to use and very hard for any central authority to control . . . It's free, highly mobile, very personal, and very quick. It's also built to spread, and fast." It is "promiscuous by nature: tweets go out over two networks, the Internet and SMS, the network that cell phones use for text messages, and they can be received and read on practically anything with a screen and a network connection" (Grossman 2009). Of course, it also has real limitations. As the more traditional *Economist* (2009b) argued, the site gave a very one-sided view of events and, like YouTube, was hobbled as a news source by its clumsy search engine. Still, even President Obama was using technology like YouTube to bypass conventional media and speak directly to large numbers of people on critical issues of foreign policy. In March 2009, the Obama administration developed a YouTube video that was intended to influence young Iranians.[9] In addition to Twitter and YouTube, a range of web 2.0 applications, new high-definition video, such as CISCO's TelePresence or Hewlett-Packard's Halo, and other technologies are likely to continue to make the job of managing a large, geographically dispersed global organization easier and more cost effective (see Chapter 7).

New technologies have the potential to enhance the effectiveness of aid and development programs. For example, Sachs (2008, 307) describes mobile phones as "perhaps the greatest development tool of our age."

While the introduction of mobile phones in developed countries was an incremental change, complementing existing fixed-line telephony, in much of the developing world the change is revolutionary. Mobile phones help to make markets more efficient, reduce transaction costs, provide direct and indirect business opportunities, and improve productivity. It is therefore not surprising that a number of studies have shown that an extra 10 mobile phones per 100 people can add 0.6 to 0.8 percent to a developing country's GDP (for example, see Waverman, Meschi, and Fuss 2005). As such mobile devices continue to increase in computing power—the Apple iPhone already has more processing power than the entire North American Defense Command did in 1965—and as networks in developing countries are upgraded from second generation to third generation technology, the ways in which they can be used to facilitate economic and social development will continue to increase.

New Technologies can also help INGOs respond to stakeholder demands for increased transparency and provide donors with a more realistic understanding of the complexities of aid and development work. A good example of this potential in relation to donors is a joint venture between the African Medical Research Foundation (AMREF) and the *Guardian* newspaper. *Guardian* readers have been jointly funding a three-year integrated development project in Katine, Uganda, with most information (budgets, plans, and progress reports) available online. The Katine web site contains video, allowing comments and questions to be posted for the country director. A Ugandan reporter also visits the project area two weeks each month (see www.guardian.co.uk/katine). Perhaps even more significant is the potential for community members to use new technologies to keep INGOs more accountable or to even communicate directly with donors. For example, World Vision–sponsored children sometimes use Facebook to find and communicate directly with their sponsors. As Internet access in poor communities expands, such interactions are likely to significantly increase.

While activists, small NGOs, and civil society more broadly have remained relatively good at adapting new technologies to their purposes, the large INGOs have not shown the same level of innovation. Their websites are generally basic and they have not innovated in the way that, for example, Get Up (see www.getup.org.au) has in campaigning or the Obama presidential campaign did in fundraising. While exceptions exist, their forays into social networking sites such as Facebook or MySpace are nascent at best, and they have largely failed to date to use sites like YouTube, despite their enormous potential for viral marketing. The view that large INGOs have become very poor at utilizing new technology is reinforced by a survey of press relations conducted by Steven Ross (2008), which found that "the potential of Internet technologies has barely begun to be exploited" by INGOs. One of the reasons for this is that, overall, INGOs invest too little in technology. While their financial systems have been improved to meet donor requirements, they have failed to employ information management technologies despite them being seen as critical to improved effectiveness. Large INGOs also appear generally unaware of the way new technologies could disrupt, either positively or adversely, their field activities (Geldof 2005).

These technology failures will need to be addressed if the large INGOs wish to remain relevant in the twenty-first century as the information revolution continues to gather pace. While phone calls over copper wire could carry one page of information per second in the 1980s, it is claimed that the Nippon Telegraph and Telephone company of Japan is now testing a fiber optic cable that pushes 14 trillion bits per second down a single strand of fiber, equivalent to 2,660 CDs or 210 million phone calls every second. In Africa, for example, the mobile phone market is increasing by close to 50 percent per annum, one of the fastest growth rates in the world (Garreau 2008). This growth in mobile phone penetration is likely to be replicated in Africa by Internet penetration, currently only around 5 percent, as undersea fiber-optic cable is laid in the Indian Ocean, linking East Africa to the inland broadband networks of Asia. This may cut bandwidth costs for some African countries by up to 90 percent and massively expand penetration. Globally, Internet penetration is still only around 23 percent, suggesting that we are only at the beginning of the revolution that it will bring (see www.Internetworldstats.com). If the large INGOs fail to identify the opportunities for their organizations and for their customers from the increased availability of these types of technology, other organizations will emerge who are better able to use technology to achieve their mission. As a result, while it is clear that new technologies have been crucial to the past growth in size and influence of the largest INGOs and that new technologies have enormous potential to support the work of INGOs, there is some doubt over the ability of the large INGOs to grasp these opportunities and continue to grow and prosper in the twenty-first century.

Global Economic Conditions

The final factor to be considered is the impact of global economic growth on the size and influence of INGOs. Global economic growth can impact INGOs in a number of interrelated ways. Slowing or negative economic growth may reduce the ability of INGOs to raise financial resources. Since private philanthropic giving is highly discretionary, it becomes one of the first items to be reduced as economic conditions become less certain and household budgets constrained. Hence, philanthropic giving is highly sensitive to, and a lead indicator of, unemployment. In 2009, for example, UK-based INGOs experienced reductions in private giving of up to 10 percent as a result of deteriorating economic conditions in that country. Such falls in private giving can be exacerbated by other factors. For example, constrained economic conditions can combine with donor fatigue, public concerns about INGO effectiveness, and competing domestic issues to lead to significantly reduced support for INGOs. Since slowing economic growth will also reduce corporate earnings, it is likely to reduce distributions by trusts and foundations, leading to further falls in INGO incomes. For example, around 6 percent of disbursements by US-based foundations went to international development and related activities, either through US- or overseas-based NGOs (Anheier 2005, 340).

One may also expect reduced economic growth to lower government tax receipts and increase competing demands on a government's budget, leading to a decrease in ODA. In addition, since OECD governments are likely to come under increasing pressure in the next few years to reduce the debt they incurred to stimulate their economies in 2009 and 2010, there will be increasing pressure to find budgetary savings by deferring increases or reducing ODA. This is the view of the ODI that believes that ODA could fall by up to a fifth (Economist, 2009a). The ODI's view is supported by the experience of the global economic recession in the early 1990s where large fiscal deficits led to deep cuts in ODA.

On the other hand, total global ODA did not fall during the economic downturn after 2000, demonstrating that the relationship between GDP and ODA is not straightforward. Despite the deteriorating economic conditions in many developed countries and significant increases in government borrowings, many OECD countries have so far retained their commitments to increasing ODA. For example, Australia's foreign minister reiterated the Australian government's commitment to increasing Australia's ODA to 0.5 percent by 2015 in the 2009 Budget (see www.foreignminister.gov.au), both sides of politics in the United Kingdom remain committed to increasing the United Kingdom's ODA to 0.7 percent of GDP by 2013, and the Obama administration in the United States appears committed to its pledge of doubling US aid to Africa by the end of his first term.[10] The DAC believes that based on current commitments, ODA will continue to rise from US$120 billion in 2007/8 to US$145 billion in 2010, an increase of 21 percent (in 2008 dollars, see OECD 2009, Table Four). While this increase is at least US$10 billion short of the promises made by the G8 at its 2005 Gleneagles meeting, it does suggest that they will achieve their US$50 billion target for Africa—at Gleneagles, the G8 committed to lift total aid from US$80 billion to US$130 billion by 2010 and to increase aid to Africa to US$50 billion *in 2004 dollars.* In any event, should the DAC projections be met, it will provide the basis for solid government revenue growth for the largest INGOs, despite the economic downturn.

Slowing or declining economic growth will also increase poverty in developing countries. The global economic crisis caused capital inflows to poor nations to fall by around 85 percent. Remittances are also likely to have fallen in 2009, despite their greater resilience relative to many other categories of resource flows to developing countries.[11] According to Martin Ravallion, Director of the Development Research Group at the World Bank, 65 million people will fall below the $2-a-day poverty line in 2009 due to the impact of the global financial crisis. Some 53 million will fall below the level of absolute poverty, which is $1.25 a day (World Bank 2009). To put this into perspective, this equates to between 200,000 and 400,000 more children, mostly female, dying every year between 2009 and 2015 than would have perished without the crisis (World Bank 2009). Not only do these statistics suggest that there will be increased demand for INGO services, these statistics will also be a powerful advocacy tool for ensuring that OECD governments honor their ODA commitments.

Overall, then, it is difficult to predict the effect that economic growth has on the size and influence of INGOs. However, even if the current global economic slowdown does dampen INGO growth rates in the short term, it is unlikely to have a significant long-term impact.

Conclusion

A large number of factors have been driving the increasing size and influence of INGOs. They include changing views about what development is and how it occurs; increased political openness to civil society in many parts of the world; increased awareness and concern about transnational problems like global poverty and climate change; a growing confidence gap between citizens and governments; a rise in cosmopolitan values, a preference for democratic forms of governance, an appreciation for cultural diversity and increased interest in global issues in developed countries; increased outsourcing and privatization by many governments; and improvements in and the reduced costs of information, communication, and transport technologies. It is less clear that global economic growth is a long-term determinant of the size and influence of INGOs.

However, whether the growth rates enjoyed by INGOs over the past decade will continue into the next one appears uncertain. Factors such as political openness, the privatization and outsourcing push, and the value shift in OECD countries all appear to be unlikely to drive ongoing growth.

On the other hand, ongoing concern over transnational problems, which citizens do not believe governments have the capacity to effectively address, and especially ongoing technological development appear to remain supportive of ongoing growth. Although potentially more fragile than in the past, policy changes that reinforce the role of INGOs in the development process and even in global governance also appear likely to sustain ongoing growth in both size and influence. Finally, while the current global economic slowdown will probably dampen INGO growth rates in the short term, it is unlikely to be a significant long-term factor. On balance, then, the overall environment appears largely supportive of the continued growth in size and influence. However, whether or not individual INGOs are able to take advantage of this environment will depend on how they respond to the myriad of challenges that face them. These challenges and the organizational changes needed to adequately respond to them are the subject of the next three chapters.

Notes

1. Between 1973 and 1989, the number of governments classified as democratic in the developing world increased from 17 to 38 (Lindeburg and Bryant 2001).

2. Bruhl and Rittberger (2002, 6) have identified three, slightly different, key functions of the state. They are: "to ensure a population's physical security; to sustainably manage the environment; and to [promote] the production and distribution of goods and services necessary to a population's livelihood." Other functions that people may look to governance to provide include promoting the rule of law, mechanisms for people to participate on issues that affect them, and addressing market failure, including, at least, severe income inequality.

3. Demonstrating its power, Jon Stewart's program, *The Daily Show*, was used by Barak Obama as his last TV appearance before the critical Pennsylvania primary. The show is "perfectly attuned to an era in which cogitative dissonance has become a national epidemic", Smith, D (2008), "How a Satirist Became America's Most Influential TV Personality" *The Observer*, Sept. 14, p. 32.

4. Kaldor et al. (2003) define regressive globalization as those "individuals, groups, firms, or even governments that favor globalization when it is in their particular interest and irrespective of any negative consequences for others. Regressive globalizers see the world as a zero-sum game, in which they seek to maximize the benefit of the few, which they represent, at the expense of the welfare of the many, about which they are indifferent at best."

5. Based on information about internal party polling obtained by WVA and public comments by Australia's Parliamentary Secretary for International Development Assistance, Mr. Bob McMullan.

6. Make Poverty History attracted more than 225,000 people to the Edinburgh demonstration on July 2, four days before the G8 meeting. See Glasius et al. (2005, 10).

7. In Austria's 2008 election, far right parties won 29 percent of the vote. The far right Swiss People's Party is the largest in Switzerland; Denmark's government relies on the support of the anti-immigration People's Party; and the explicitly xenophobic Northern League in Italy is part of the ruling right-wing coalition. "The European Far Right: Dark Tales from the Vienna Woods," *The Economist*, October 4, 2008.

8. Ironic since Stalin also used the term *kosmopolity* (cosmopolitans) to undermine opponents.

9. See "Obama's Norouz Message to Iran," developed by Voice of America and distributed via www.youtube.com.

10. Recent research by World Vision Australia found that, notwithstanding the economic crisis, support for ODA had increased from 83 percent in 2007 to 86 percent in June 2009. Most importantly, the share that strongly supported government aid increased from 31 percent to 43 percent of total respondents. World Vision Australia (2009).

11. According to Ratha et al. (2008) remittances are normally a stable or even countercyclical source of funds during an economic downturn in the recipient economy, and resilient in the face of a slowdown in the source country.

CHAPTER 5

External Challenges: Responding to a Rapidly Changing Context

Introduction

While the enormous growth in the size and influence of the largest aid and development INGOs outlined in Chapter 3 presents a significant challenge in itself, it has been accompanied by a rapidly changing international context. Climate change, reduced food security, peak oil, urbanization, and a more politicized operating environment present significant new development challenges for INGOs and make responding to humanitarian emergencies more difficult. In addition, there is now a much greater focus on INGO accountability, effectiveness, policy engagement, and coordination. This Chapter explores these challenges and suggests that large INGOs will need to make some significant operating changes if they are to effectively respond to the changed international context. In particular, this Chapter will argue that INGOs not only need to acquire new skills in order to meet the challenges of the changed international context, they require a much more sophisticated and politically sensitive approach to their work. Given their new role in international relations and the influence they now have, good intentions are certainly no longer good enough. If INGOs are to remain relevant in the international arena of the twenty-first century, they will need to better understand the expectations that the public, governments, and international organizations now have of them and respond accordingly.

Meeting New Development Challenges

Overall, our understanding of development has matured significantly over the last twenty years with profound implications for the work of aid and development INGOs. As discussed in Chapter 4, the emphasis on nation building and economic development that characterized the postcolonial period has been replaced by broad acceptance within the development community of the relationship between economic development and human capital, institution building, and political development. While this

```
┌─( KEY POINTS: )────────────────────────────────────────┐
```

The rapidly changing external environment creates enormous challenges that further complicate the already difficult task of managing aid and development INGOs in the twenty-first century. These challenges include

1. Expectations that aid and development INGOs will become more involved in programmatic areas that encourage grassroots demand for good governance, fight corruption, and even promote political development. Combined with the increased activism of the ICC, the emerging concept of the responsibility to protect, and the War on Terror, these expectations are leading to the increased politicization of aid and development work and a more dangerous operating environment for INGOs.
2. Responding to the impact of human-induced climate change on poor communities including coping with large increases in the size and frequency of natural disasters, increased migration, and potentially increased conflict and social tension over resources.
3. Helping poor communities deal with ongoing population growth and food shortages while growing sustainably. On the one hand, population and economic growth are both increasing demand for food, yet the impact of climate change, under-investment in agriculture, and peak oil are all undermining the world's capacity to adequately respond.
4. Creating and advancing effective development approaches in urban areas where an increasing proportion of the world's poor will live.

In addition, there is now a much greater focus on INGO accountability, effectiveness, policy engagement, and coordination. While the increasing importance of INGOs in international relations has led to a greater focus on their activities, responding to the disparate demands of donors, governments, IGOs, and communities requires careful reflection.

While there are examples of issues where specific INGOs have good technical depth, the largest aid and development INGOs generally need to acquire much greater technical skills and policy depth in order to meet the challenges of the changed international context. They also need to approach their work in a much more sophisticated and politically sensitive way.

change has contributed to the growing size and influence of aid and development INGOs, it has also had two other important effects. The first is that it has played a role in the growing politicization of aid and development activities, discussed in the next section. The second effect is that aid and development INGOs are increasingly involved in activities that seek to strengthen civil society, improve the legal and institutional underpinnings of the rule of law, strengthen the role of the media and other sources of independent information, increase human rights education, promote grass roots demand for good governance, fight corruption, and even promote political development. This has been matched by donors' interest; according to Uvin (2004, 83), positive programmatic support for human rights has been one of the fastest growing areas in international development assistance, now comprising more than 10 percent of aid budgets. However, not only do these new programmatic activities require a range of new technical skills, they are also a much more contentious area for INGOs than traditional programming. For example, David Rieff (2003) argues that the involvement of aid and development INGOs in these activities erodes the humanitarian principles of impartiality and neutrality and results in development agencies losing their moral bearings. Many more conservative media commentators also object to aid and development INGOs' involvement in such a political area.

The second, and perhaps even more profound, change is the growing impact of anthropogenic climate change on the work of aid and development INGOs. Setting aside the fact that Gro Harlem Brundtland's report, *Our Common Future,* put the concept of sustainable development on the map as long ago as 1987, for most of the next two decades, the poverty and climate change agendas proceeded independently (La Fleur et al. 2008, 3). While aid and development INGOs did undertake projects that better positioned poor communities to adapt to climate change and reverse local environmental degradation, this was generally seen as marginal to their principal development activities. Similarly, most climate experts focused "primarily on mitigating greenhouse gas emissions in developed countries rather than on bolstering climate resilience or encouraging sustainable development" (La Fleur et al. 2008, 4). An exception was WWF, which often sought to emphasize sustainable development in some of the less-developed places that it worked rather than species and habitat conservation (Clark 2003, 132). Demonstrating just how recent and deep the separation of the development and environment agendas has been, neither the MDGs nor the official indicators of progress toward these goals even mention climate change.

However, while some media commentators continue to identify climate change as an environmental problem, most aid and development INGOs now see it as at least as much of a development challenge. Human induced climate change is already having an enormous impact on the world's poor, and it has the potential to undo much of the progress made by developing countries in recent decades. For example, in the last decade, the number of people affected by disasters was three times higher than in the 1970s (www.emdat.be/natural-disasters-trends, World Vision International 2006, 19). This has contributed to aid and development INGOs spending a growing proportion of their budget on aid rather than development. For example, in 1998, World Vision spent 15 percent of its income on aid, but by 2008 this had grown to 35 percent.

Without concerted international action, the ongoing effects of climate change will continue to fall most heavily on the poor. The World Bank's *World Development Report 2010* estimates that poor nations will bear between 75 and 80 percent of the cost of floods, increased desertification, and other disasters caused by global warming. Nations in Africa and South Asia may lose as much as 5 percent of their GDP if temperatures rise by just two degrees Celsius above pre-industrial levels. Within these poor countries, it will be those on the lowest incomes that will suffer the most. The poorest people tend to live in the most vulnerable areas, such as low-lying land prone to flooding or on marginal agricultural land prone to drought (Parris 2007).

The poor are also least able to protect themselves and recover from the effects of an increasing number of climate-induced disasters. Since the 1970s, the number of reported natural disasters has increased from an average annual total of 90 to a figure close to 450 per year in this present decade (Webster et al. 2009, 5). According to Webster et al., the total economic cost of natural disasters in 2008 was US$181 billion. However, the number of natural disasters is expected to continue to increase in both number and severity so that the number affected each year will increase from around 250 million people per annum in 2009 to around 375 million a year by 2015 (Oxfam 2009). This will require an increase in humanitarian aid spending from 2006 levels of US$14.2 billion to at least $25 billion a year by 2015 (Oxfam 2009). Webster et al. (2009) estimate an even larger increase in funding needs. Their findings suggest that climate change could lead to increases in humanitarian costs of between 32 percent and 1600 percent depending on what criteria are used (Webster et al., 2009). Their report also highlights that "extreme weather events do not occur in isolation and that the increasing interconnectedness of world economic and political systems has made disasters more complex and destructive" (Webster et al. 2009).

The poor are also the most susceptible to the spread of tropical diseases, and they are the "most vulnerable to the effects of the conflicts likely to arise from international tensions over water, energy, and displaced people" (Parris 2007). Burke et al. (2009) estimate that armed conflict could increase by more than 50% if Africa by 2030 and lead to another 393,000 battle deaths if climate model projections of future temperature trends are correct. For example, the ten lowest-ranked countries in terms of development are all water stressed. In the Horn of Africa, the water situation is so dire that conflict is pervasive in countries such as Sudan, Chad, Northern Uganda, Ethiopia, and Somalia (Sachs 2008, 121, 129-130). This is expected to become much worse as between 75 million and 250 million people are exposed to increased water stress due to climate change in Africa alone (Wallace 2009). The strong correlation between poverty, water stress, and conflict and its relationship to the security of developed states is contributing to governments changing motivations for giving aid (see Chapter 2). For example, a 2009 report by the Australian Defence Force (ADF) titled *Climate Change, The Environment, Resources and Conflict* recognizes the potential impact that environmental stress will have on Australia's security and the demands on the ADF (Pearlman and Cubby 2009). The security threat posed by climate change is also explicitly recognized in Australia's first National Security Statement (Rudd 2008) and is increasingly prominent in national security strategies and military policies in Europe (Wallace 2009; see also German Advisory Council on Global Change 2007; Council of the European Union 2008).

Massive increases in migration are also likely to result from climate change. Even in 2008, a report by OCHA and the Internal Displacement Monitoring Centre estimates that approximately 18.9 million people were driven from their homes by rapid-onset climate-related disasters (OCHA 2009). This figure is likely to significantly increase if greenhouse gas emissions lead to the expected sea-level rises of between one and two meters by 2100. As a recent World Bank study of 84 developing countries showed, even a one-meter rise in sea levels would affect more than 56 million people (Dasgupta et al. 2007, 2). All told, the IASC (2008) estimates that the number of people who will be obliged to move as a result of climate change and environmental degradation by the year 2050 range from 25 million to one billion. The world's political and humanitarian systems are unlikely to cope with mass movements of people on such a scale.

Climate change therefore creates a number of specific operational challenges for aid and development INGOs. It requires aid and development INGOs to be at the forefront of developing programmatic interventions that seek to both mitigate and adapt to climate change. They must also join with environmental INGOs to ensure that the post-Kyoto framework for addressing climate change recognizes both the size of the threat posed as well as the special vulnerability of the poor. For those aid and development INGOs that have traditionally been more service orientated than activist, they will also need to engage their supporters to ensure that they understand the relationship between climate change and poverty. Without establishing such a link, such INGOs will be vulnerable to a loss of public support, particularly in contexts like the United States, Canada, and Australia, where human induced climate change has been a highly politicized issue.

However, it is not just climate change that is placing increasing stress on the environment. Notwithstanding the 2008 global financial crisis, Jeffrey Sachs (2008, 23) predicts that in 2050 the world's economy will have grown by around six times its current size. Given the enormous strain the world's ecosystems are already experiencing, without significant changes in the way we currently live *and* technological improvements, this economic growth will undoubtedly lead to a further deterioration in our environment. In addition, since our natural systems are often characterized by thresholds and positive feedback loops, INGOs need to prepare for abrupt changes when the system crosses a threshold and positive feedback loops are established.[1] This will require aid and development INGOs to become much more adept at responding to larger natural disasters and more unpredictable events. It will also require them to think much more explicitly about the relative merits of investing more in rapid response capacity relative to investing in advocacy and long-term programmatic responses, particularly those that enhance a community's own ability to adapt. For example, to date, World Vision has prioritized increasing its investment in response capacity rather than developing greater policy and programmatic expertise in climate-change mitigation and adaptation. While this will help to ensure that World Vision can continue to meet donor expectations about its capacity to respond to humanitarian disasters across the world, it is not at all clear this strategic choice is in the long-term interests of the world's poor.

In addition to the effect that their consumption is having on the planet's climate, fossil fuels are creating development challenges in another way. Rising oil prices directly feed into the price of food, particularly affecting urban consumers. They increase the costs of inputs like fertilizers and pesticides for poor farmers and contribute to more general price inflation, which erodes the purchasing power of the poor. As a result, when oil prices hit record highs, above US$147 a barrel in July 2008, so did food prices. Combined with other factors such as the increased consumption of an emerging middle class in China and India, prolonged drought in Australia, increased biofuel production, speculation, and export restrictions, the price of oilseeds and grains, such as wheat and maize, doubled between January 2006 and June 2008 (Brown and Pomeroy 2008). According to the World Bank, this led to an additional 100 million people becoming food insecure (UN News Service 2008). While the price of oil declined as the global economic crisis reduced demand, most oil analysts expect the long-term price of crude oil to rise significantly. For example, the International Energy Agency is predicting that the price of a barrel of oil will average more than US$100 from 2008 to 2015 and more than US$200 by 2030 (Macalister 2008). While more investment is going into exploration, it is unlikely to be sufficient to keep up with burgeoning demand, especially in China, India, and the Middle East. As Shell's energy scenario team predicts, global consumption of all forms of energy will at least double between now and 2050 because of a growing global population and increased per capita consumption (see www.shell.com).

While world food prices have, like oil, retreated from their price peaks, this is likely to be only temporary since the underlying drivers of this challenge are long term social, environmental and economic trends. In this context, it is quite possible that food insecurity will become the greatest development challenge of the twenty-first century. While population and economic growth are both increasing demand for food, the impact of climate change, underinvestment in agriculture, and increasing oil scarcity are all undermining the world's capacity to adequately respond. According to a recent report from Deutsche Bank (2009), agricultural productivity must increase by at least 50 percent between now and 2050 if we are to provide food for an expected nine billion people[2] the world. This will require a dramatic transformation in agricultural production. Unfortunately, we are ill prepared to undertake such a transformation.

The world has allowed investment in agricultural research to fall dramatically since the success of the Green Revolution in the 1960s and 1970s. The result has been massive underinvestment in agricultural for many years. For example, the share of total ODA that was spent on agriculture declined from its 1979 level of 18 percent down to just 3.5 percent by 2004 (Bertini and Glickman 2009, 37). This fall in the proportion of ODA spent on agriculture was mirrored by similar falls in public spending by many agriculturally based developing countries: from roughly 7 percent in 1980 to only 4 percent by 2004 (Bertini and Glickman 2009, 37). These statistics have led the FAO (2008) to lament that, despite the underlying growing demand for food, "land and water constraints remain for the most part unaddressed, investments in rural infrastructure and agricultural research are still low, agricultural inputs remain expensive relative to farm-gate prices, and the need to adapt to climate change is more urgent than ever before."

The situation is even worse in sub-Saharan Africa, where one out of every three people is currently malnourished. Investment in agriculture in Africa has declined enormously. For example, US ODA to agriculture in Africa "declined approximately 85 percent from the mid-1980s to 2006" (Bertini and Glickman 2009, 16). In agriculturally based African countries like Uganda, total public spending on agriculture fell from around 10 percent in 1980 to just 3 percent and in some years less than 2 percent (Bertini and Glickman 2009, 37). Yet most African countries continue to experience high levels of population growth, and climate change is likely to lead to Africa experiencing the most pronounced reductions in agricultural production. This will be devastating for many African countries since agriculture accounts for such a large share of their economies and so many of their citizens live at subsistence levels. Increasing oil prices and climate change will also exacerbate the impact of an extended economic downturn on poor countries as they simultaneously seek to contend with reduced demands for their exports, adverse exchange rate movements, and a reduction in capital inflows. On the other hand, since yields are so low in Africa (about 20 to 30 percent of the yield in many developed countries), there is a terrific opportunity to substantially lift food production by small-plot African farmers, an area where aid and development INGOs could play a significant role.

The size of the problem and long-term nature of the underlying trends makes it, therefore, surprising that so many large aid and development INGOs appear to have been taken aback by the food crisis in 2008, slow to understand the impact on poor communities and slow to develop appropriate programmatic and advocacy responses. Arguably, this is because the issue highlights a number of systemic weaknesses of the large aid and development INGOs: their lack of economic analysis capacity; the disconnect between their field work and global policy positions; their relatively small investment in identifying programmatic best practice; and their poor track record in scaling up nonfood aid interventions. These are all weakness that the largest INGOs will need to urgently address if they are to meet the challenge posed by rapidly growing demand for food. For those aid and development INGOs that are able to meet the necessary changes, there will be growing funding and influence opportunities. Thankfully, many large donors are beginning to increase their investment in agriculture, and there is growing recognition of the need to develop long-term solutions to food insecurity and malnutrition.

Global migratory patterns are also dramatically shifting the face of poverty from a predominantly rural to an urban phenomenon. It is estimated that in 2008, for the first time in history, half of the world's population (around 3.3 billion) lived in urban areas (IRIN 2007). A recent UN Habitat (2008) report predicts that urbanization will reach 70 percent of the world's population by 2050. At the end of 2007, nearly one billion of the world's poor were expected to be living in urban slums and according to research by CARE (2006), this number increases by about 100,000 every day (see also Sachs 2008, 27; Kupp 2007; and Beall and Fox 2006). This movement of people from rural areas to towns and cities is a long-term trend, likely to also be exacerbated by climate change as more people seek better lives in cities. The CARE (2006) report says that by 2030, the total number of city dwellers will be nearly five billion. Since nearly all of the world's population increase is expected to happen not just in the developing world but in developing world cities, such growth is bound to outstrip the capacity of poorly resourced governments and feeble urban economies to absorb new residents and provide them with adequate jobs, shelter, services, and protection. At a time of rising food prices, it also leaves them much more exposed to food insecurity. As a result, there is an urgent need for aid and development INGOs to become much more adept at responding in urban settings.

However, despite the long-term nature of this trend as well, once again the largest aid and development INGOs have been slow to respond. While most large aid and development INGOs have well-established models of rural development, their urban interventions tend to be far more nascent. According to Kupp's (2007) research, "northern-dominated international NGOs have generally been slower than other organizations to adapt to and engage with urban poverty. Their involvement in urban settings has been limited—few are seen as major players in eradicating urban poverty." They have generally had significant difficulty in developing new sources of funding, reallocating resources, and adopting development approaches more suitable to urban areas.[3]

Finally, these development challenges are all occurring in the midst of the worst slowdown in global economic growth in decades. Capital inflows to poor nations shrunk by 85 percent in 2009 and remittances are also likely to fall. According to the IMF (2009), Africa is being hit by three main shocks simultaneously: reduced demand for Africa's exports and reduced remittances from workers overseas; the sharp fall in commodity prices; and still-tight credit in world financial markets, which is squeezing both long and short term investment inflows. As a result, growth rates for sub-Saharan Africa have been significantly reduced in the medium term. According to the World Bank (2009), this slowing of economic growth will lead to an additional 65 million people falling below the US$2-a-day poverty line in 2009, and some 53 million will fall below the US$1.25 level of absolute poverty. This could further exacerbate rising inequality, leading to increased social tensions, unrest, and insecurity. According to a recent UN Habitat (2008) report, income inequalities in cities in South Africa, Brazil, Colombia, Argentina, Chile, Ecuador, Guatemala, and Mexico are "not only increasing but are becoming more entrenched." While it is still too early to fully appreciate the impact of the global financial crisis on the world's poor, the impact of the Asian financial crisis on, for example, Indonesia's poor was dramatic. Unemployment leaped, poverty levels increased by a third, malnutrition returned, and children of poor parents were withdrawn from school (see Stiglitz 2002; World Bank 2006). It will also be critical that aid and development INGOs assist communities to re-establish economic growth in a sustainable way. As LaFleur et al. (2008) argue, how they grow, "that is, whether they pursue the same unsustainable, carbon-intensive path that led to the industrial world's prosperity or adopt new, clean technologies that fuel nonpolluting growth" is as important as "*whether* they grow . . . for as difficult as the [climate] challenge is, its burden will be magnified if developing countries are too poor to invest in protecting their own people."

Any one of the new development challenges outlined above would be significant in its own right; collectively they represent a massive challenge for aid and development INGOs. Combined with rising inequality, increased immigration, and the prospect of reduced global economic growth for at least the next few years, it is not surprising that aid and development INGOs are therefore struggling to adequately respond. However, to some extent this challenge has been exacerbated by their reluctance to re-allocate resources in the face of quite apparent, long-term trends and the difficulty that some agencies are having in developing new fundraising methods. It also highlights their need to acquire new skills, increase technical analysis, find new partners, and develop new approaches to their field work, challenges that they must invest more in overcoming if they are to better respond to the changing international context.

Managing the Politicization of Aid and Development Work

While there were Cold War struggles over civil and political rights versus economic, social, and cultural rights, in the past, aid and development work was often viewed (and even represented) as largely technical exercises. However, over recent years, the political nature of aid and development work has become increasingly evident for a number of reasons.

First, our changing understanding of development has led to an explicit recognition of the relationship between development issues and human rights. As a result, all UN agencies and many INGOs have adopted rights-based approaches to their development activities. A rights-based approach can be described as a way to integrate "the norms, standards, and principles of the international human rights system into the plans, policies, and processes of development" (see www.unhchr.ch/development). A rights-based approach encourages a much greater focus on the broader social, political, and economic issues that create the context for development work when compared to welfare, charity, or philanthropy-based approaches. This increases INGOs involvement in activities that question or even challenge existing power structures of a society. Thus, to some extent, INGOs themselves have directly contributed to their work having a more explicitly political flavor.

Second, the humanitarian context for INGOs is also becoming more politicized. In addition to the continued growth of the human rights discourse, the increasing activism of the ICC and the gradual (and grudging) emergence of a "responsibility to protect" (R2P), both further complicate INGOs' relationships with host governments in emergency contexts. This political complexity leads to a less stable operating environment for INGOs. For example, despite dire humanitarian conditions, in the lead up to the 2008 Zimbabwean elections the government suspended operations of all aid and development NGOs. As was widely reported, it is reasonably clear that this action was taken to minimize witnesses to the acts of intimidation and violence that the government used to influence the outcome of the election. The response to Cyclone Nagris that devastated Myanmar in 2008 was also complicated by the French foreign minister's suggestion that the R2P concept could be invoked to ensure aid got through to the people of the Irrawaddy Delta. A similar call was made in 2008 by the Kenyan prime minister in relation to Zimbabwe. The indictment of Sudanese President Omar Hassan al-Bashir by the ICC has also certainly made the operational context in Sudan more difficult for INGOs (see Case Study 5.1).

INGOs also legitimize the claims of local opposition groups and may provide some form of protection for their activities. When combined with their human rights advocacy, this contributes to a transnational structure that pressures regimes simultaneously from above and below (Risse 2000, 203–4). The result is that even where INGOs have worked in a country for decades, they cannot necessarily expect to be permitted to continue to

---

Case Study 5.1: The Impact of the Indictment of Sudanese President Omar Hassan al-Bashir

Within hours of the formal indictment of Sudanese President Omar Hassan al-Bashir, thirteen INGOs received notice to leave Sudan. These included Oxfam, Save the Children, CARE, and MSF. Demonstrating the relationship between the expulsion and the ICC's indictment, MSF's summons to government offices occurred "within minutes after the announcement of the ICC," according to MSF's operational director in Darfur. Sudan accused the agencies of spying for the ICC.

In one of the world's poorest countries, the impact of the expulsion of these INGOs was dramatic. Oxfam indicated that the revocation of its license would affect more than 600,000 Sudanese people. CARE said its expulsion would affect 1.5 million beneficiaries. Save the Children said the decision by Sudanese authorities to suspend its operations would affect 50,000 Sudanese children. The UN estimated that, in total, the expulsions would impact 6,500 aid workers in Darfur, where 4.7 million people rely on foreign assistance for food, shelter, and protection from fighting.

While UN agencies such as WFP, WHO, and UNICEF were not among those ordered out, the expulsion of the INGOs had an enormous impact on the UN system, illustrating the extent to which INGOs are now a key part of the UN delivery mechanism. The UN indicated that the expulsion of INGOs would paralyze up to half of its programs.

By June 2009, some of the INGOs had been able to re-establish operations by adopting new names and applying for new registrations.

Sources: IRIN (2009), MacInnes (2009)

operate effectively when the country's international political relations become more strained (Ronalds 2008a).

Third, international action to assist and protect the most vulnerable has become linked to the security and political agenda of the United States and its allies (Donini et al. 2008). The relationship between poverty and fragile states and the violence that inequality often breeds has been recognized by states and overseas aid has taken its place alongside diplomacy, trade, and defense as key instruments in the "war on terror" (Fowler 2008; Atwood et al. 2008; Sachs 2008). In contexts like Iraq, Afghanistan, and Pakistan, the war on terror is a battle for hearts and minds resulting in aid activities becoming a so-called force multiplier and a key battlefield tactic on all sides. Many groups seek to manipulate aid to further their own goals, and it is not by accident that on some calculations nearly a quarter of the US government's aid is distributed by the Department of Defense.[4] Military personnel are also directly involved in delivering humanitarian aid, blurring the distinction between them and aid workers. According to a study Donini et al. (2008, 10) undertook in Iraq, it was virtually impossible for Iraqis "to distinguish between the roles and activities of local and international actors, including military forces, political actors and other authorities, for-profit contractors, international NGOs, local NGOs, and UN agencies." This confusion led to MSF deciding to cease operations in Afghanistan in 2004 after several MSF aid workers were killed there. Similarly, in Pakistan five employees of the WFP were killed in October 2009 by a suicide bomber. Neither the organization's "bomb proof" offices nor the fact that it was providing relief to more than eight million Pakistanis prevented the agency from becoming a Taliban target. Concern over the blurring of political, military, and aid objectives in the UN system has also led to MSF declining to participate in many of the recent UN reforms to increase humanitarian coordination and harmonization. Conversely, World Vision has continued to remain engaged but developed the HISS-CAM process, a tool to assist staff in considering operational and policy decisions around civil–military engagement (Thompson 2008; World Vision International 2008).

This renewed emphasis on the relationship between aid, a state's security and stability, and the changed operating environment means that the lack of integration and coherence that sometimes exist between different government agencies must be addressed (see Case Study 5.2). It also means that aid issues have a much greater prominence among senior government decision makers.

The organizational implications of this more political operating environment is that aid and development actors need to spend much more time engaged in analysis of the costs and benefits of INGO actions, not just to the organization itself but to the broader humanitarian context. Their

Case Study 5.2: Reforming Bilateral Agencies

Other development actors also face a change dilemma.

In a recent article in *Foreign Affairs*, three former heads of USAID, the US foreign aid agency, called for significant reform not only of USAID but also of the US government's coordination of foreign aid (Atwood et al. 2008). The article argued that the organizational structures governing the US aid program had become "chaotic and incoherent" and that "major institutional reforms" were required. In particular, the head of USAID lacked influence not only over government decisions affecting the overseas development agenda but also over a significant portion of development activities.

These criticisms also apply to other bilateral agencies. In Australia's case, AusAID is merely a subdepartment of the Department of Foreign Affairs and Trade (DFAT), the head of AusAID is equivalent to a deputy secretary of DFAT, and political responsibility rests with a parliamentary secretary rather than a minister.

In light of the intimate relationship between poverty, security, the environment, trade, and investment, the heads of bilateral agencies must be in a position to effectively influence policy in these areas. The Department of International Development in the United Kingdom has achieved this through cabinet-level representation, and this has certainly contributed to it becoming one of the world's most influential bilateral aid agencies.

However, achieving organizational reform of bilateral agencies will be at least as difficult as achieving change in large INGOs. Increasing the prominence of any government department is always perceived by rivals as a zero-sum game, resulting in significant political resistance. The siege mentality that developed as some bilateral agencies suffered significant staff cutbacks will need to be overcome. Bilateral agencies must also reinvigorate their appetite for risk and improve their capacity for innovation and partnership development.

failure to sufficiently understand the complex politics surrounding a humanitarian emergency has been criticized in the past, most prominently in connection with the genocide in Rwanda in 2004. However, aid agencies remain ill prepared to avoid a repeat of this situation. For example, in 2008 World Vision acquired, through its US office, a large food aid grant for North Korea that may have been perceived as associated with the denuclearization process agreed to by North Korea with the United States, China, Japan, Russia, and South Korea. It appears that no detailed political analysis was undertaken by World Vision before the decision to accept the grant was made, despite the highly politicized context, the risk of being associated with US foreign policy objectives and North Korea's history of manipulating foreign aid. For example, in 2003, the MSF's Fiona Terry alleged that refugees who had fled North Korea to China claimed that food aid meant for famine victims was diverted to citizens deemed to be loyal to Kim Jong-il's regime (see also *The Economist* 2008). A failure to insist on an independent needs assessment leaves agencies open to the accusation that they are collaborating with the regime.

Instead, all INGOs must be much more alert to the political impact of their humanitarian and development activities. This means that INGOs must be more prepared to confront "that age-old humanitarian dilemma" of choosing between alleviating suffering in the here and now or addressing root causes through political change in the hope of potentially alleviating a lot more suffering in the long run (Walker 2008a). This in turn requires staff with well-developed political-science skills, not an area of expertise that many large aid and development INGOs have much depth in, and requires development actors to engage with a much broader range of actors if their work is to be effective. They need to partner more and use collective advocacy to maintain operations while continuing to address some of the underlying issues. Finally, these are often life-and-death decisions for severely disempowered people so INGOs need to remain deeply pragmatic and accountable to the poor whom they seek to serve.

Another organizational implication of this more political operating environment is that INGOs must invest more in ensuring the safety of staff and their activities. As aid and development INGOs have grown, so has the number of their staff in conflict settings. The value of goods that INGOs control has also grown dramatically, making them a more attractive target. Not surprisingly then, 2008 was the deadliest year ever for aid workers with 122 deaths, more than that suffered by peacekeepers. For example, in February 2008, Plan suffered the first direct attack on its staff and premises in its history. The armed attack, in Mansehra, North Western Frontier Province, Pakistan, claimed the lives of three staff members. According to the ODI, in total, 260 humanitarian workers were attacked in 155 serious incidents in 2008, up from 32 incidents a decade ago (Stoddard et al. 2009). The ODI argues that "attacks against aid workers have increased sharply since 2006, with a particular upswing in kidnapping" and that "NGO international (expatriate) staff and UN local contractors" are specific targets (Stoddard et al. 2009). They also believe that attacks on aid workers in the most insecure contexts—Sudan, Afghanistan, and Somalia—were increasingly politically motivated, reflecting a broad targeting of the aid enterprise as a whole (Stoddard et al. 2009).

Aid and development INGOs need to respond carefully to this upswing in violence against staff and balance their desire to provide humanitarian assistance in such contexts with the protection of their staff and others. If not implemented carefully, security measures can exacerbate conflict or have a detrimental impact on an agency's relationship with local communities or have longer-term security implications. Not only is the relationship with the local community key to the success of the agency's program, as Mary Anderson (1999, 64–65) argues, local communities can also be the key to ensuring the security of staff and activities. The increased security costs also reduce the amount of funds available for programmatic purposes and increasing overheads, exacerbating the fundraising challenge discussed further in Chapter 6.

Improving Stakeholder Accountability

According to Litovsky and MacGillivray (2007, 17), accountability is about "civilizing power." It describes a "relationship between power holders and those affected by their actions." Looked at in this way, it is, therefore, not surprising that as the power of INGOs has grown, so too have demands for greater accountability.[5] Hugo Slim provides a more formal definition. He defines NGO accountability as "the process by which an NGO holds itself openly responsible for what it believes, what it does, and what it does not do in a way [that] shows it involving all concerned parties and actively responding to what it learns" (Slim 2002). However, it remains a deeply contested issue in the aid and development sector.

For some, accountability is seen as "the key to effective development in the twenty-first century" that unlocks "progress that is stalling in the face of dramatic new challenges, a range of new actors, fast-growing financial flows, and complex collaborative arrangements" (Litovsky and MacGillivray 2007). Yet many practitioners claim that, in practice, accountability focuses too much on control functions, logical frameworks, and short-term quantitative targets and encourages hierarchical management structures. INGO accountability mechanisms are also criticized for Westernizing aid and development "through the implementation of organizational standards and codes across borders and through imposition on people who may have a very different experience or perspective on an event or notion of politics" (Sassen 1999). Certainly, the research supports the view that the development of standards, procedures, and techniques by the sector has come at the cost of flexibility, spontaneity, proportionality, and mutuality (Donini et al. 2008, 28). Recent research in Afghanistan also "shows that poor accountability and bad technique and behavior are the greatest causes of mistrust and discontent between aid agencies and assisted communities" (Walker 2008). Compared to other transnational actors, the large international aid and development INGOs must balance the needs of their different stakeholders: beneficiaries, partners, host governments, staff, donors, and other supporters. Where tax deductibility is provided for donations to INGOs or ODA is channeled through INGOs, the taxpayers of a country should also be considered a stakeholder. The requirements of accountability will also be different for their different activities—what is appropriate for humanitarian activities will be different from what is appropriate for long-term development work or advocacy activities.

The divergence of views and the inherent complexity of the concept of accountability underpins the difficult task facing aid and development INGOs. Nonetheless, it is critical that they come to grips with it. International funders like the GFATM are placing higher expectations on both themselves and on their partners (Bezanson 2005, 10). Poor accountability also undermines INGOs' legitimacy, weakening their influence and effectiveness.

Many of the largest aid and development INGOs have responded, both as individual agencies and collectively as a sector. Individual efforts include Action Aid's Accountability, Learning, and Planning System (ALPS), introduced in 2000 (See David and Manchini 2004), and World Vision's Learning Through Evaluation, Accountability, and Planning (LEAP).[6] In addition, there has been a range of sector-wide responses. There are a number of codes of conduct: the Red Cross Code of Conduct,[7] Sphere,[8] and domestic codes such as the Australian Council for International Development's Code of Conduct managed by the sector's peak body. In 2006, the INGO Accountability Charter was launched by a consortium of large INGOs, including Oxfam and Save the Children and supported by CIVICUS (See www.ingoaccountabilitycharter.org). There is also ALNAP,[9] the Humanitarian Accountability Project (HAP),[10] People in Aid, and others.[11] INGOs also face accountability mechanisms in various domestic jurisdictions. For example, in the UK, all NGOs are monitored by the Charities Commission.[12] More broadly, the One World Trust's Global Accountability Project has sought to compare accountability across transnational actors (www.oneworldtrust.org). In addition to INGOs like World Vision and Oxfam, this includes TNCs such as Exxon and IGOs such as WHO. Some INGOs may also choose to be accredited by the International Organization for Standardization (ISO). The One World Trust has identified more than 309 accountability initiatives worldwide. Given this veritable menagerie of accountability mechanisms, it is not surprising that one commentator has described the situation as "accountabalism" (Weinberger 2007).

INGOs therefore face multiple accountability mechanisms, all of which may increase administrative burden and costs and thereby reduce the amount of money available for project funding. They must carefully balance the legitimate needs of institutional and private donors with accountability to beneficiaries and do so in a way that does not undermine the entire enterprise. As Michael Hammer and Robert Lloyd of One World Trust emphasize, this will only occur when an organization recognizes the potential benefits of improved accountability to achieving the organization's mission and therefore drives the processes internally rather than having accountability' imposed externally.[13] This requires strong organizational leaders committed to the concept, an investment in skilled staff, a process of staff engagement that emphasizes the link between accountability, and staff's personal motivations for working in the sector, organizational structures that emphasize learning, accountability, and experimentation and a favorable external environment—progressive donors, open governments, and strong links to other INGOs.

Demonstrating Effectiveness and Efficiency

In 1996, Fowler and Biekart (1996, 132) argued that the hard truth for INGOs was that:

> the goals they set and aspire to are beyond them. The problems they address are too complex. The agencies' size and institutional position does not give sufficient leverage on the larger forces and systems which keep the poor poor; and their financial dependence on government does not allow them the autonomy to challenge the self interest of Northern countries that stand in the way of change . . . Through their existing development and relief projects on the ground they are not going to be the catalysts and force for poverty alleviation, inclusion, and social justice in the new world order.

On the other hand, one of the factors behind the growth in size of INGOs and a key source of INGOs' legitimacy and credibility for advocacy activities is their presumed effectiveness and efficiency in achieving development and humanitarian outcomes. The ACFID NGO Effectiveness Framework defines "effectiveness" as the promotion of "sustainable change that addresses the causes as well as the symptoms of poverty and marginalization—[that is] reduces poverty and builds capacity within communities, civil society, and government to address their own development priorities" (www.acfid.asn.au). INGOs' effectiveness is often compared with the perceived failures and high costs of bilateral and multilateral aid. However, the evidence for the effectiveness and efficiency of aid and development INGOs' work is poor. Certainly, the poor themselves are not pointing to the work of NGOs as the basis for them moving out of poverty:

> Nongovernmental organizations (NGOs) are hardly mentioned as a support in moving out of poverty. NGO assistance accounts for only 0.3 percent of the reasons cited for poverty escapes. . . . This does not mean that NGOs are not present or

doing important humanitarian work. It means either that NGOs affect only a small number of people or that their work is not perceived to have a direct effect on poverty. (Narayan 2009, 40)

Instead, "in country after country, when we asked movers to name the top three reasons for their move out of poverty, the answers most frequently emphasized people's own initiative in finding jobs and starting new businesses" (Narayan 2009, 19). Similarly, a number of studies undertaken by researchers at Tufts University suggest that from beneficiaries' points of view:

the provision of aid is a top-down, externally driven, and relatively rigid process that allows little space for local participation beyond formalistic consultation. Much of what happens escapes local scrutiny and control. The system is viewed as inflexible, arrogant, and culturally insensitive. This is sometimes exacerbated by inappropriate personal behavior, conspicuous consumption, and other manifestations of the "white car syndrome" (Donini et al. 1999, 11).

While there is solid evidence that most development projects implemented by INGOs deliver their key intended outputs (Riddell 2008, 270), it is far more difficult to assess whether these outputs result in positive impact on the lives of beneficiaries. The majority of INGO projects probably provide "tangible benefits but many have probably made only a small contribution to improving the lives and enhancing the well being of beneficiaries" (Riddell 2008, 272; see also Fowler 2000a, 13-19). However, in the face of growing demands from donors and other stakeholders for improved evidence of impact and efficiency, this is unlikely to be good enough, and INGOs will be left exposed to a loss of legitimacy, criticism, and increased competition from for-profit contractors unless they can improve this situation.

There are a number of reasons for the poor level of evidence to support the effectiveness of INGOs. First, the proportion of the budget of a government-funded project that can be spent on monitoring, evaluation, and research is often quite small, and despite donors' demand for increased effectiveness, they have seldom been willing to increase this amount. As a result, this part of INGOs' work has been seriously underfunded.

Second, there are a number of methodological limitations that must be addressed. These include measurement, attribution, aggregation, and ownership problems (Roche 2010). For example, indirect benefits are often a very important outcome of development projects, yet they can be extremely difficult to measure and can be easily overlooked by community members themselves.[14] In fact, according to a World Bank study, "the real benefit of poor people's collective action is to society. Working together in small groups creates unity, trust, social cohesion, and a sense of social belonging to units larger than the immediate family. It fosters a sense of citizenship essential to functioning, stable, and cohesive democratic societies. This is the beginning of civil society" (Narayan 2009, 38). While the importance of building such social capital is well-known, attributing the value of a particular development activity to its growth is extremely difficult. There is also the issue of time—the social change that INGOs are seeking often takes decades.

Third, there are cultural and governance problems. Too often, trustees and board members judge and reward management on the basis of the growth in income of the INGO rather than measuring performance by the positive impact that the INGO's activities have on the communities they serve (Ahmed and Potter 2006, 115). The aggregation problem is a particular challenge to providing trustees or board members with data to measure management's performance. While a number of INGOs disclose aggregated quantitative data at the input and output levels (e.g., funds invested, total number of people reached, or children sponsored), since more meaningful impact assessments are very difficult to convert into quantitative measures, they are not usually open to aggregation in any meaningful way (Roche 2010). As the large INGOs improve their accountability by increasing their transparency, this situation will become progressively less sustainable, and much more effort will need to be invested in overcoming the difficulties in demonstrating effectiveness. In this context, the recent Open Forum initiative by the European Confederation of NGOs for Aid and Development (CONCORD) is a welcome project. Through an NGO-led process over two years, the Open Forum aims to develop a vision for NGO development effectiveness, common principles and guidelines on how to apply these principles in preparation for the DAC's next High-Level Forum in Beijing in December 2011.

The extent to which INGOs are cost effective is also not clear. One recent macro-economic study by the IMF suggested that "[o]ur results show that NGO aid reduces infant mortality and does so more effectively than official bilateral aid. The impact on illiteracy is less significant" (Masud and Yontcheva 2005). Global Fund (2008) analysis also suggests that, on average, NGOs were more effective than government grantees. On the other hand, Roger Riddell (2007, 277–8) argues that assessing the cost-effectiveness of NGO projects is very difficult since there is insufficient data to form firm judgments in most cases. In addition, many development projects are not designed to be scalable. Very little attention is given in project design to how successful interventions might be sustainably spread through a community. For large INGOs with significant infrastructure to support, the return on investment of many activities is, therefore, too low. There are a number of possible solutions.

First, since they have both size and geographic spread, large INGOs should concentrate on interventions that have the potential to be increased in scale and that may be applicable in other contexts. As Kharas (2008, 70) argues, there are currently "too many 'success stories' with little follow up on scale." Provided INGOs also put in place information and other management systems that allow promising practices to be transferred, this should help them increase both effectiveness and efficiency. Such information management systems will also help the large INGOs avoid repeating mistakes made elsewhere.

Second, INGOs also need to find much better ways to measure the indirect benefits of their work, such as increased empowerment of local people or groups. Thirdly, they must become more adept at using successful interventions as a basis for advocacy for systemic changes that have far greater impact. Of course, even compared to INGO's development work, "the monitoring and evaluation of advocacy and influencing work is critically underdeveloped" and there is "very little systematic research on how successful INGOs are in influencing policy processes, especially from the point of view of those actually involved in the policymaking process in the South" (Chapman and Wameyo 2001; Chowdhury et al. 2006, vi). Since advocacy, campaigning, and policy work already account for a significant proportion of INGO expenditure, this lack of evidence of impact is a current problem that is only going to become more acute (see Case Study 6.1). For example, Riddell (2007, 264) estimates that advocacy activities now comprises around 15 percent of total development expenditure.

The poor evidence base for the effectiveness and efficiency of aid and development INGOs leaves them unable to respond to the demands of donors, open to attack by critics, and unable to counter competition from for-profit contractors who increasingly see business opportunities in the sector. If the largest aid and development INGOs are going to be prepared for the challenges of this century, it is clear that they will need to invest more in people, systems, and processes that respond to the demand for increased effectiveness and efficiency in a way that does not undermine accountability to beneficiaries. The organizational changes required to achieve this are considered in more detail in Chapter 6. INGOs will also need to be more upfront with private donors about the measurement challenges they face. Otherwise, in the long run, they risk undermining not only their own organization but also the increased public and private support for aid generated by Make Poverty History and other campaigns.

Finally, they will need to use emerging communication technologies in more creative ways. As terrifying as it may be to communication specialists, this could include "equipping partners and communities with the ability to self represent their achievements, challenges, and assessment of the support they receive" (Roche 2010), a real and perhaps not unwelcome erosion of the power INGOs have held in the past as gatekeepers between donors and beneficiaries.

Increasing Harmonization and Coordination

International pressure to improve humanitarian and development coordination has been growing for many years. While in the past, most of this pressure has been focused on bilateral agencies and the UN (see Chapter 2), as INGOs have grown in significance, they too have faced increased expectations that they will better coordinate their activities with one another and with those of other aid and development actors, particularly bilateral and multilateral donors. Better coordination between donors and agencies holds out the promise of improved resource allocation, increased impact, and reduced administrative burden on local governments and partners who often struggle to respond to the enormous variety of demands from different donors and agencies. To date, most responses by INGOs have been targeted at improving resource allocation and co-ordination in humanitarian situations. For example, in 1991, the Inter-Agency Standing Committee (IASC) was created to facilitate policy development and dialogue among the UN, the Red Cross movement and INGOs in humanitarian situations.[15] More recently, initiatives like the Principles of Partnership and a plethora of UN reforms have all sought to improve coordination and harmonization in humanitarian emergencies.[16] Although responding to the lead of the UN, INGOs have often been actively engaged in these reform proposals.[17] By comparison, coordination of development activities is much more ad hoc.[18]

While there are potential benefits from improved coordination and harmonization of aid and development work, this agenda also contains a number of difficulties and potential pitfalls for aid and development INGOs. First, it is extremely difficult to reach agreement among so many actors on what systems and processes will be followed, and INGOs risk having their interests ignored. For example, Mierop (2006) suggests that current humanitarian coordination is "UN-centric" and "out of touch with the field reality." Second, donor-driven pressure for coherence may lead to INGO activities becoming linked to the political agendas of bilateral or multilateral agencies. This may be particularly a problem, for example, in situations where the UN is involved in an integrated mission and humanitarian coordination is not sufficiently separated from its political and military structure (Mierop 2006). Such associations may not only undermine the effectiveness of their work but also compromise the security of INGO personnel (Donini et al. 2008, 24). For example, MSF's concern about the tensions between the UN reforms to improve coordination and harmonization and their humanitarian principles, has led it to decline the invitation to join the IASC both at headquarters and field level, to withdraw from the Steering Committee for Humanitarian Response, and not to join clusters in order to preserve the independence of its humanitarian activities.[19] Third, increased harmonization and coordination carries the risk of a loss of innovation, often seen as one of the competitive advantages of INGOs, homogenization, and even groupthink. Finally, it can be very difficult for Southern NGOs to meet the demands of the harmonization and coordination agenda potentially creating tensions between INGO and their partners or between different affiliates within INGO families.

The harmonization and coordination task has also been made more complex by the number of new actors. According to World Bank research, aid is now more fragmented than ever before. The average number of bilateral donors per recipient country rose from 12 in the 1960s to more than 33 in the 2001 to 2005 period (IDA 2007). The proliferation of other actors has been even more spectacular. This includes not only megaphilanthropists, such as the Bill and Melinda Gates Foundation, and public private partnerships, such as the GFATM, but also the development activities of corporations, such as mining companies, a growing number of small relief or development INGOs, faith-based groups, and even rock stars. As Mathew Bishop (2008, 43) argues, the traditional aid and development actors have now been joined by "billionaires, foundations, multinational companies, social entrepreneurs, NGOs, actors, rock stars, eccentrics, [and] preachers," and this "remarkable variety of voices and ideas" must be taken into account as part of the humanitarian cacophony.

Aid and development INGOs will need to respond to the challenges presented by the changes in the development industry and, in particular, the harmonization and coordination agenda in a number of ways. First, they must ensure their own houses are in order. Even among the affiliates of an INGO there are often significant challenges with coordination and harmonization (Simeant 2005). As Cathy Shutt makes clear (2009, 17) "everyday life in [big] INGOs is characterized by pressure to resolve, manage, or gloss over differences between the way different parts of the organization behave and the varied ways in which individuals work." Second, they must continue to invest in influencing the harmonization and coordination agenda at the international level and in understanding how it is impacting on their partners and affiliates at the country level. Third, they will need to carefully analyze the advantages and disadvantages of participating in this agenda and be prepared to withdraw from processes or in situations where they assess it does not improve outcomes on the ground. Of course, the coordination agenda may require agencies to put aside competition for resources and may reduce an agency's growth, something very difficult for management to do if their performance is being principally assessed on this basis.[20] Fourth, they must carefully manage the extent and nature of their interaction with the military and be much more active in developing policies and procedures to help staff engage with the military in humanitarian situations.[21] Finally, there must be much greater involvement in coordination of development activities on the ground.[22]

Responding to Great Expectations

At the beginning of Charles Dickens' famous novel, the young orphan, Philip Pirrip (Pip), is endowed with "great expectations" together with the necessary financial means by which to achieve them. In some ways, like Pip, globalization has endowed the largest aid and development INGOs with great expectations. Modern communication technologies, the ability to rapidly deploy people, money, and goods all around the world and global brands have created an enabling environment for INGOs to grow. On the other hand, these same factors, combined with INGOs' increased resources and capacity, have created great expectations about their ability to respond. These expectations take a number of different forms. The first is the international community's expectation that the large aid INGOs will, almost universally, respond to humanitarian emergencies.[23] Since neither of the UN's lead agencies for humanitarian emergencies (UNHCR and OCHA) have their own capacity, often the only means by which an international humanitarian response can be mounted is through the IFRC, INGOs, and local NGOs.[24] In addition to their dedicated emergency resources, INGOs like World Vision often also have large numbers of local staff involved in development work that can be quickly deployed to relief efforts. It is therefore not surprising that the largest aid and development INGOs routinely account for up to 75 percent of emergency aid flows (Slim 2007b).

However, it is not only their response capacity that raises expectations. Governments and international organizations also have growing expectations that the large INGOs will be able to engage with them in a sophisticated way. While large INGOs may have spent most of the twentieth century as outsiders detailing problems with the international system, in the twenty-first century they will more likely be insiders, expected to help develop the solutions to global problems (Sustainability 2003; Clarke 2003, 103). As argued in Chapter 3, their growing influence means that large INGOs are now regularly consulted and invited to provide input on proposals or reforms. These invitations provide opportunities for INGOs to have further influence in the international arena. Recognizing this, most of the large INGOs have permanent offices in major humanitarian capitals like Geneva, Brussels, and New York. Even smaller, Southern-based INGOs are seeking permanent presences to better influence IGOs. For example, CUTS International, an India-based NGO active in consumer advocacy and trade issues, has recently opened an office in Brussels (www.cuts-international.org). IGOs are also involved in the development of new norms and help to diffuse those norms across other international actors, that is, they have "productive power."

Therefore, it is critical that INGOs improve their policy skills and depth, that their information systems can provide appropriate data, and that their engagement is sophisticated and informed so that they are able to increase their influence over international institutions and thereby improve their effectiveness.[25] Poor sharing of existing technical resources and research within INGO families further undermines their capacity. For example, despite the presence of NGO representatives on the GFATM board and their role in implementing GFATM grants in the field, the large aid and development INGOs have little policy influence on the GFATM at the global level. Unlike more specialist agencies, they are perceived as lacking any specific technical skills of benefit to the GFATM, and their engagement is often seen as unsophisticated.[26] A study by the ODI confirms the lack of connection between policymaking and field data and the lack of effective communication of evidence to policy makers. Policy makers often questioned NGOs' "ability to provide an accurate, fair, and critical analysis" (Chowdhury et al. 2006). It also confirms the lack of technical or expert knowledge and skills among NGOs. These deficiencies are discussed further in Chapter 6. There are also growing expectations by policy makers that aid and development INGOs will make better use of their operations or partners in the South to facilitate increased Southern advocacy in the North and at international meetings. Not only will this improve their legitimacy, it is also likely to make their advocacy more effective.

Finally, in order to secure funds for their emergency response, these INGOs regularly seek media exposure that reinforces the expectations that are placed on them. Media attention is often crucial to increasing awareness of an emergency in order to raise public funds or place pressure on governments into providing public funds. Where an emergency cannot achieve significant media coverage ("forgotten emergencies"), prohibitive fundraising costs can prevent INGOs mounting an effective response. This creates a symbiotic relationship with the media—INGOs must create newsworthy stories and the media provides the basis for

INGOs undertaking appeals to government and the public. This symbiotic relationship with the media has a number of operational implications. Senior executives and field staff must be media savvy, and large INGOs need to employ large numbers of public relations and communication experts to help manage their relationship with the media.[27] It also requires well-developed global information management systems and communication protocols to provide updates and the latest facts and figures for press releases and interviews. Finally, the impact on operations in the field of public comments must also be carefully managed, particularly given the increased politicization of aid and development outlined above.

Charles Dickens wrote two different endings for *Great Expectations*, one hopeless and empty and one more expectant but still ambiguous. In many ways, this reflects the double-edged nature of the great expectations bestowed on large INGOs. The benefits of increased expectations hold out the possibility of even greater influence and impact. However, they also create additional challenges: the need for astute media management; more effective information management systems; better trained staff; global brand management; and a deep understanding of the complex political implications, particularly on field operations, of public engagement. There is also the possibility that these growing expectations could one day become more formal obligations under international human rights law.[28] Then there is the ambiguity that comes from closer relationships with governments and international organizations and the interdependent relationship with the media. INGOs need to be alert to the potential tradeoffs such engagement may entail, such as a loss of independence or the loss of control over agendas or issues. In the same ways as INGOs can shape public attitudes or the behavior of states and IGOs, they can be similarly shaped and influenced. Without careful discernment, rather than engagement being constructive, an INGO's mission can be undermined by the goals and objectives of other international actors.

Conclusion: The Future Is Not What it Used to Be

The French poet Paul Valery (1989) famously said, "the trouble with our times is that the future is not what it used to be." This observation, from a man who lived through the massive changes wrought by the first and second World Wars, captures well the enormous challenges that the rapidly changing strategic context presents for large INGOs. This external change has profound implications for the nature of activities they undertake, the types of staff they employ, the skills of the leaders they select, the nature of organizations they partner with, how they raise financial resources, and the types of systems and processes they invest in. Given the apparent inability of states and international organizations to effectively respond to the growing number of transnational problems without assistance, if the largest aid and development INGOs fail to adequately respond to their changed strategic context and help to influence the development of new solutions, it is not clear how these problems will be addressed, certainly not in a way that promotes the interests of some of the world's most vulnerable and at-risk people. The extent to which large INGOs are able or willing to rise to this challenge and make the organizational changes required by their changing strategic context and at the same time address the internal challenges of their growing size and influence is the subject of Chapter 6.

Notes

1. A threshold is a key tipping point: see Lenton et al. (2008). Rising temperatures caused by climate change that lead to polar ice melting and in turn result in further increases in temperature as less of the Sun's radiation is reflected by the Earth's surface is an example of positive feedback. "When a natural system is characterized by thresholds combined with positive feedbacks, it is also likely to be characterized by abrupt changes, meaning a dramatic change that occurs when the system crosses a threshold and then sets off a chain reaction of positive feedbacks." See Sachs (2008, 79).

2. London-based think tank, Chatham House has estimated that food production needed to increase by 50 percent by as early 2030 (Evans, 2009).

3. One of the reasons is that child sponsorship, a key source of financial resources for agencies like World Vision and Plan, requires regular contact with sponsored children. This is a much more difficult and expensive challenge in more transient urban environments compared to rural ones. Appropriate programmatic interventions in urban settings tend to require much greater levels of partnering, increased local advocacy, deeper technical capacity in economics, and more engagement in promoting rights, responsible citizenry, and good governance with community-based accountability for local government services.

4. According to the OECD DAC 2006 Peer Review of the United States Aid Program, the Department of Defense currently manages around 22 percent of the total US foreign aid budget.

5. For example, the *Economist* (2000, 129) asked "Who elected Oxfam" in an article prior to the annual meetings of the IMF and World Bank in September 2000. More recently the *New York Times* asked "do-gooders to prove they do good" (Christensen 2004). See also Slim (2002).

6. See also Oxfam's attempts at increasing bottom–up accountability in Roche (2007).

7. More than 300 agencies have now signed on to this code.

8. Sphere was launched in 1997 by a group of humanitarian NGOs and the Red Cross/Red Crescent Movement. A handbook has been developed which includes a Humanitarian Charter and a number of standards. The charter and standards are intended to provide a common language for humanitarian organizations. See www.sphereproject.org.

9. ALNAP was established in 1997 and is dedicated to improving the quality and accountability of humanitarian action by sharing lessons, identifying common problems, and, where appropriate, building consensus on approaches. ALNAP members include organizations and experts from across the humanitarian sector, including donors, INGOs, Red Cross/Red Crescent, UN, and independent academic organizations. See www.alnap.org

10. The Humanitarian Accountability Project was established in 2001, and like the Sphere Project was the result of a stated commitment by humanitarian NGOs to address concerns regarding their accountability. It became the Humanitarian Accountability Partnership in 2003 focusing on developing practice through a small network of members. HAP membership requires a formal commitment to uphold HAP's Principles of Accountability.

11. According to Roche (2010), "Sphere and HAP are seen as mutually supportive: HAP providing the accountability framework that strengthens the practice framework provided by Sphere and vice versa. HAP also complements, but differs from, other international initiatives including People in Aid, the Quality Compass, and the Active Learning Network (ALNAP). Where People in Aid focuses on improving human resources in emergency response, and has developed a code of good practice, the Quality Compass is an initiative that seeks to implement quality assurance during project management and evaluation stages."

12. A similar scheme is currently under consideration by the Australian Senate.

13. Discussions with the author, September 25, 2008, London.

14. For example, on a recent visit to a women's microcredit program in Tanzania, I asked the women who had started a business what difference the business had made to their family's lives. Some talked about the improved health of her family, another about being able to send her children to school. However, another member said, "I used to borrow salt from my neighbors. Now they borrow salt from me." It is difficult for formal evaluations to capture this sense of empowerment and improved self-esteem and almost impossible to aggregate it with other project outcomes.

15. The IASC's membership comprises 11 UN bodies and 5 non-UN positions—the ICRC, the IFRC, and 3 for NGOs. This UN-dominated membership does not reflect the operational capacity to respond, 80 percent of which lies with NGOs and the Red Cross Movement.

16. The Principles of Partnership were developed by the UN, Red Cross Movement, and major NGOs to advance a partnership-based and field-driven approach to humanitarian reform. See Principles of Partnership Statement of Commitment, July 2007. www.globalhumanitarianplatform.org. Other UN-based reforms in this area include the creation of nine thematic clusters for coordination at field and global levels, a relaunched CERF, and strengthening of the human coordinator role as the hub for both clusters and the CERF.

17. For example, see "The Humanitarian Coordinator System: Issues for discussion," Informal Paper prepared by ICVA Secretariat, IASC WG, September 4, 2005.

18. Some coordination may occur through the role of the UN's resident coordinator, the efforts by governments of individual countries, and ad hoc international initiatives such as the International Health Partnership, see http: //www.internationalhealthpartnership.net/ihp_plus_about.html

19. A field based study by MSF on these issues suggested that the "UN reforms foster an environment conducive to the breaching of humanitarian principles of independence, impartiality, and neutrality" and stand "in tension with the inherent diversity and complementarity of humanitarian action, based on independence of analysis and intervention." See Derderian et al. (2007).

20. As Gordenker and Weiss observe, there is a mixture of "conflict, competition, cooperation, and cooptation" characterizing state NGO relations in the development process (Gordenker and Weiss 1995, 551).

21. See, for example, Thompson (2008). The emergence of the R2P concept is likely to increase the number of situations in which humanitarian and military activities are cojoined.

22. A recent report commissioned by Swedish INGOs with activities in Kenya concluded that there was too little cooperation among international NGOs, even in times of crisis, and that they therefore needed their own aid effectiveness process (see Koch 2008).

23. Plan International does not generally become involved in responding to humanitarian emergencies.

24. In extreme situations such as the Asian tsunami of 2004, state militaries may also be permitted to respond by host governments but as cases like Cyclone Nargis in Myanmar demonstrate, their intervention often carries too many political implications to make this possible.

25. In discussions between the author and employees of IGOs, examples of ignorance and unsophisticated and ineffective engagement by INGOs are often diplomatically mentioned. Even in some of the successful global campaigns such as those discussed in Chapter 3, there were many examples of poor or ineffective engagement. See Mekata (2000) and McDonald (2004).

26. Unlike for example, the Clinton Foundation that has developed speciality expertise in forecasting ARV requirements.

27. However, one of the recommendations of a survey of press relations is greater training for field-based staff (Ross 2008).

28. Traditionally, non-state actors could not be duty holders under international human rights law. However, increasingly, scholars and activists are arguing that human rights obligations should be extended to such non-state actors, especially corporations. Part of the justification for this is the changing nature of international society and especially the growing relative power of non-state actors (See Uvin 2004, 15). As a result, it is not difficult to envisage a situation where the largest aid and development INGOs were legally found to be duty holders under international law.

CHAPTER 6

Key Organizational Challenges for INGOs

Introduction

The increasing size and influence of INGOs and the challenges generated by the rapidly changing international context create a vastly different strategic landscape for the largest aid and development INGOs compared to a decade ago. This new landscape has profound organizational implications for INGOs if they are to effectively respond. These implications are the focus of the next three chapters. This Chapter will consider six critical, interrelated, organizational challenges: the legitimacy challenge, the human resource challenge, the leverage challenge, the technical challenge, the learning challenge, and the fundraising challenge. Chapter 7 will examine the management and governance challenges of large INGOs in the current environment and what is required to better prepare INGOs for the future. Chapter 8 will examine the change dilemma—the challenge to create an adaptive, flexible, and responsive organization. While this is certainly not an exhaustive list of the organizational implications that the largest aid and development INGOs face, these are the ones that flow the most directly from the changed international landscape and therefore go to the heart of whether or not the largest aid and development INGOs will be equipped to be effective actors in the international environment of the twenty-first century.

The Legitimacy Challenge: Please Mind the Gap

Legitimacy is at the heart of an INGO's ability to raise funds from donors, to advocate to governments and international organizations, and to fulfill its mission in poor communities. Legitimacy can be defined as "the right to be and do something in society—a sense that an organization is lawful, admissible, and justified in its chosen course of action" (Edwards 2000).[1] As outlined in Chapter 4, the declining legitimacy of states and TNCs is one of the factors that has supported the growth in size and influence of INGOs. Given the role of INGOs in raising issues of transparency, legitimacy, and accountability with governments and businesses, INGOs should

```
┌──( KEY POINTS: )─────────────────────────────────────────┐
```

KEY POINTS:

To meet the challenges created by their rapidly changing external environment and to build internal capacity more appropriate to their new size and international influence, INGOs must make a range of organizational changes.

1. INGO leaders need to be more alert to the importance of legitimacy and ensure that the source of legitimacy for decision making is clear. Although the large INGOs each have strong global brands, their reputations and legitimacy are far more fragile than they seem to realize.
2. Large INGOs must find ways to significantly increase the impact they are having. This means they must make much more of their key comparative advantages: their access to community-level information and the credibility that their current reputation provides.
3. INGOs must invest more in technical skills and significantly improved information management systems. The changing international context also requires INGOs to make organizational learning a true strategic priority.
4. Large INGOs must face up to their human resource challenges. They must give human resource issues a much higher strategic priority within their organizations, creatively address remuneration constraints despite increasing competition from other aid and development actors, improve their poor human resource systems, and tackle the ingrained cultural limitations to successful human resource management.
5. INGOs need to invest more effort in educating donors. This will provide a more reliable basis for claiming representational legitimacy, allow donors to better understand the inherently political nature of much of an INGO's work, and may persuade donors to improve funding of organizational capacity building.

expect to be held to at least as high a standard in these areas and to be able to demonstrate their compliance. Yet, as critical as it is, in my experience few senior managers at INGOs can describe what they believe are the sources of an INGO's legitimacy, let alone are actively involved in protecting or enhancing those sources. This is a real challenge because INGO legitimacy is fragile. With the increased politicization of aid and development, the rising expectations of stakeholders and the greater demands for accountability, as outlined in Chapter 4, questions of legitimacy are likely to be raised more often and more forcefully than ever before, and INGOs need to be better prepared to respond.[2]

Various authors propose a number of different bases for INGO legitimacy (Atack 1999; Brown and Jagadanada 2007; Ellis 2010). Building on the work of Atack and others, I suggest five sources for INGO legitimacy: representativeness, distinctive values, effectiveness, empowerment, and knowledge and expertise.

Representativeness comprises the extent of an INGO's transparency, accountability, and participation. This means that even though INGOs are not democratic institutions in the usual sense, they can still obtain a measure of representativeness by "being accountable to and dealing transparently with their constituencies, partners, or beneficiaries in the South" (Atack 1999, 858). This important interrelationship between an INGO's legitimacy and its accountability is affirmed by many practitioners and academics and further supports the arguments made in Chapter 5 that INGOs must invest greater effort in improving their accountability.[3] Of course, since INGOs have multiple stakeholders with different and even sometimes contradictory interests, building positive stakeholder perceptions of an INGO's legitimacy is a very complex process. For example, increased donor accountability can undermine an INGO's legitimacy if it reduces "downward" accountability. One of the ways this can occur is if an INGO becomes overly dependent on one donor for funding or becomes a tool for the implementing of a foreign government's policy in a developing country. In this case, they are unlikely to be perceived to be representative of beneficiaries, and their legitimacy based on this source will be diminished.

An INGO's values can also be a source of legitimacy, especially their support for and promotion of the rights and moral claims of others. According to Rodney Hall (2005), the basis for INGOs' moral authority comes from INGOs' expertise, their role as referee, and their role representing a socially progressive or perhaps a morally transcendent position. He refers to this as "normative" moral authority. However, a significant problem for large INGOs is that this source of legitimacy becomes more difficult to sustain the larger they become (Korten 1990, 104). As they become larger and more bureaucratic, without a strong focus on stakeholder accountability, they can become inward focused, and decision-making can become dominated by internal political considerations rather than the best interests of beneficiaries. To guard against this, Edwards (2008, 39) suggests checking "the degree to which a strategy or mix of strategies compromises the logic by which legitimacy is claimed" in order to test whether self-interest is subordinating mission. This test places the question of legitimacy at the heart of strategy formulation. Formally adopting and implementing a rights-based approach to its work may also assist large INGOs in remaining focused on the interests of beneficiaries (Ronalds 2008a).

The third source of INGO legitimacy, according to Atack, is their effectiveness in achieving development outcomes. As argued in Chapter 5, compared to the perceived failures of state and multilateral aid, INGOs are presumed to be effective and efficient. Their operational success in turn adds to their credibility when they engage in advocacy.

The fourth source of legitimacy is the extent to which INGOs empower the poor that they purport to serve. As Keck and Sikkink argue, one of the important functions that INGOs can perform is to provide access to the international arena for domestic civil society. For INGOs, legitimacy is enhanced by this empowering of domestic actors (Keck and Sikkink 1998, 12-13). INGOs may also increase empowerment from, for example, the use of participatory methods in INGO programming and by adopting more inclusive governance structures. On the other hand, empowerment is reduced when INGO activities actually crowd out more legitimate local actors. For example, Hugo Slim (2007a) warns against the "substitution effect" of large INGOs who, through their financial and operational power "can act to replace the state in certain areas, challenge the state, or do a bit of both."

Although not expressly identified by Atack, the fifth source of INGO legitimacy is an INGO's knowledge and expertise, especially in relation to their advocacy activities. For example, Robert Hall (2005) argues that an INGO's expertise forms part of its moral authority and is therefore also a source of legitimacy. Similarly, Keck and Sikkink (1998, 21) argue that NGOs depend "on their access to information to help make them legitimate players." While knowledge and expertise is clearly required for an aid and development INGO to be operationally effective, its value to the organization goes far beyond this instrumental role. For example, knowledge and expertise are a key reason why INGOs are seen to have a right to comment in the media, to advocate on issues, to participate in international meetings, and lobby or advise governments. There is a strong interdependency at work here. Knowledge and expertise are a source of legitimacy, but legitimacy is also critical to INGOs being seen as credible sources of information.

The legitimacy of INGO advocacy requires particular attention. Of course, some critics deny that INGOs have any legitimate role in advocacy at all. According to Ellis (2010), the rationale of these critics is based on the view that "the only acceptable political engagement is by individuals and political parties" and "even privately funded groups . . . warp the public debate through emotive single-issue behavior and should not be allowed." This also reflects a more traditional view of international relations in which the public and private realms are separate, and INGOs as private actors have no role to play in public policy setting at the international level (Mills and Joyce 2006). However, disagreements about the legitimacy of INGO advocacy activities are more commonly about the circumstances in which INGOs may have legitimacy and the basis for that legitimacy. For example, INGOs sometimes claim legitimacy to undertake advocacy on the basis that they represent citizens or groups in a recipient country or citizens in a donor country. For example, as part of its efforts to secure increased commitments for Australian ODA in the lead up to the 2007 federal election, WVA sent letters to all members of the House of Representatives informing them of the number of WVA supporters who lived in their electorate, an implicit claim of representativeness. Of course, INGOs need to approach such claims cautiously. If the basis for this claim is not strong, an INGO risks a backlash from the people it claims to represent. For example, some campaigns by INGOs against World Bank projects suffered from this failure (Mallaby 2004).

An important source of legitimacy for INGO advocacy is their knowledge and expertise. For example, reliable information on the true scale of a humanitarian emergency or human rights abuses obtained through field activities is a critical basis for INGO lobbying of governments to take action. Similarly, legitimacy for advocacy may arise from an INGOs' moral authority (based on an INGOs' values for upholding the moral claim of others), its effectiveness in addressing the issues that are the subject of the advocacy activities or the extent to which it is empowering local NGOs to raise their issues at the international level. On the other hand, some of the most damaging incidents for INGO credibility have occurred where INGOs have allowed ideology or rhetoric to displace knowledge and expertise and have thereby supported causes or interventions that do not reflect local communities' priorities or actually do harm.

An example of the damage that can be done to an organization's credibility when it fails to sufficiently invest in technical skills is Greenpeace's involvement in a campaign on the disposal of the Brent Spar drilling rig in 1995. Although the campaign was ultimately successful from Greenpeace's perspective, it was severely criticized for distributing inaccurate information about the environmental impact that disposing the rig at sea could have (Clark 2003, 102). No wonder then that Hugo Slim (2002) claims that questions of "voice accountability," the veracity of what INGOs say, and the authority by which they say it will be a key twenty-first century issue for them.

The challenge of minding the gap between an INGO's rhetoric and activities has a number of implications for INGOs. INGO leaders need to be more alert to the importance of legitimacy and ensure that the source of legitimacy for decision-making is clear, at least within the INGO. They need to spend more effort educating donors, since this will make donors a more reliable basis for claiming representational legitimacy and allow them to better understand the inherently political nature of much of an INGO's work. Maintaining an INGO's legitimacy reinforces the importance of investing in technical resources, information collection, and management mechanisms and increased accountability. INGOs also need to clarify with donors, especially government donors, the basis upon which funds are accepted and the extent to which donors can influence an INGO's policies.[4] Finally, they need to actively support sector-wide initiatives at improving legitimacy. Even if the largest aid and development INGOs improve their performance in this area, they still suffer when there are scandals involving others in the sector.[5]

The Human Resource Challenge

One of World Vision's six global values is that it values people. Oxfam GB (2007, 14–16) states that "Oxfam is . . . committed to career development and succession planning, with a strong emphasis on 'growing our own.'" Save the Children's US website states, the "key to our mission is to attract, motivate, and retain the best people in the right positions." While each of these organizations correctly identifies the critical place that human resources play in their success, their operational reality appears to fall well short of their rhetoric. Global talent management and succession planning within World Vision does not exist yet in any significant form. Interviews with human resource staff at Oxfam GB confirm that, while there is a talent management system within Oxfam GB, it is relatively unsophisticated and is not coordinated with other affiliates of the Oxfam family. Discussions with executives at Save the Children also confirm that they do not have any global talent management system. While individual affiliates of any of these large INGO families may have well developed human resources management processes, if these organizations are to effectively compete with other actors for the best people and make the most of their existing talent, these processes will need to function globally.

The quality of INGO leaders and the professionalism of staff is undoubtedly the single most critical element in these organizations effectively responding to the increasingly complex and unpredictable challenges they face. While organizational strategy is important, it always lags the strategic context in fast changing environments and cannot, by definition, accommodate the unpredictable. If the large INGOs are going to successfully transform into twenty-first century organizations, they will need to focus far more on developing higher quality human resources and significantly upgrade their human resource systems.

The challenge of developing leaders of sufficient skill and knowledge to meet the needs of twenty-first century INGOs and for them to be able to effectively respond to the external challenges outlined in Chapter 4 is enormous. In one of the most eloquent summaries of the human resource challenge that INGOs face, Hugo Slim (2005) paints a daunting picture:

> Humanitarian agencies need more than managers and humanitarian scientists. In all their people, but especially in their front line leaders, they need . . . intuitive and creative realists. Steeped in humanitarian ideals, this kind of person is also a creature of context and a master or mistress of the possible in every situation and every relationship. She or he gauges the right moment, finds the right person, spots the right plan, and is able to take others with them. Such art is likely to be deeply innovative, highly tactical, and not a little cunning.

Similarly, Jim Collins (2005), a leading American management thinker, suggests that the complex governance and diffuse power structures that are common in INGOs create additional complexity for leaders compared to the business world. While in corporations leaders have at least a degree of executive leadership, that is, the power to simply make decisions, leadership in INGOs is characterized by legislative leadership. Legislative leadership relies on persuasion, political currency, and shared interests to create the conditions for the right decisions to be made (Collins 2005). As one NGO leader described it, "the only adhesive available to many nonprofit leaders is conversation and consultation" (Silverman and Taliento 2005). This means that INGOs require even more talented leaders (Collins describes them as "level 5" leaders—his highest categorization).

This style of leadership is much more people-centered. Like many professional services contexts, it is based on providing an enabling environment and can be contrasted with a scientific style of management that "stresses control, hierarchy, and instrumentality" (Lewis 2007, 18). Fowler (2000c, 173) argues that successful leaders of INGOs are also "driven by and committed to a conviction that self-development of people is possible and necessary." An effective leader is humble while maintaining an "inner self-confidence that is not dependent on possessing power but, in contradiction, is expressed by a willingness to share it" (Fowler 2000c, 173). They also need to be curious and adaptive. "Adaptiveness" is expressed as a "willingness to experiment and take calculated risks" (Fowler 2000c, 173). They have the capacity to communicate a new agenda or direction in a way that is, or appears, consistent with the organization's values in an inspiring way. They need "good political insights and contacts . . . without patronage or erosion of principle" (Fowler 2000c, 181). Finally, Fowler (2000c) argues that those people enjoying the privilege of leading INGOs should be at the "forefront of creating virtuous spirals of sustainability" by which he means organizations that display four elements—performance, reputation, learning, and adaptation.

This style of leadership is also consistent with the much greater role that employees' values play in NGOs.[6] Since values are so important to people who work in INGOs, the way in which something is done is often as important as the way it gets done (Lewis 2007, 18). While this can sometimes be frustrating, particularly in an environment where there is significantly increased pressure to demonstrate effectiveness and can be carried too far, a less balanced management approach can lead to alienation and de-motivation of INGO employees.

At the same time, the growth in the aid and development sector, the increase in bilateral and multilateral aid budgets, and the emergence of new actors such as GFATM and the Bill and Melinda Gates Foundation are increasing the demand for these types of leaders and, compared to INGOs, these other organizations are often able to pay higher salaries. As one study found, INGOs are themselves recognizing "the problem of retaining quality staff in an increasingly competitive job market, particularly where there seems to be a lack of clarity about roles, responsibilities, training, and opportunities, especially amongst researchers" (Chowdury et al. 2006, 17). As INGOs have grown and become more complex management challenges, they have increasingly turned to the corporate sector to find their next chief executive. While such people bring much needed experience in managing very large, geographically dispersed organizations, they do not necessarily have an appreciation for the difficulty of leading an organization dedicated to achieving complex social change, at both a global and national level, in many of the world's most difficult environments. They also often rely far too heavily on financial metrics, especially those related to income growth, as proxies for success (Clark 2003, 137). Silverman and Taliento (2005) of McKinsey & Company agree that business leaders lack "real understanding of what it takes to lead a nonprofit." They argue that "too many well-meaning business people who move into leadership roles in nonprofits end up frustrated and ineffective because they don't fully appreciate the challenges" (Silverman and Taliento 2005). This reinforces the enormous need for INGOs to invest more in growing more capable leaders that have the skills to lead a large, global organization with a social change mission. One way for large INGOs to recruit leaders who have the necessary breadth of experience is to more intentionally use board positions to develop future CEOs or presidents. In this way, experienced leaders can be recruited with the necessary skills from the corporate sector or elsewhere while still providing the opportunity to develop their understanding of the INGO before becoming CEO or president.

The choice of leader also sends powerful cultural messages about organizational change and operating styles. The boards of INGOs need to be careful to ensure that the way these signals are interpreted by staff are consistent with those they want to send.

However, the human resource challenge is not limited to INGO leaders. As discussed in Chapter 5 and in more detail in this Chapter, large INGOs need to significantly increase the technical skills at their disposal to meet many of the challenges they are facing. This will necessitate the recruitment of many more technical experts, requiring these organizations to adopt many of the characteristics of professional service organizations.[7] Adjusting to this change in organizational make-up presents another enormous human resource challenge for large INGOs. The good news for INGOs with stretched budgets is, while remuneration is important in professional service organizations, it is not the only factor that attracts high-quality staff. The bad news is that becoming more like a professional services organization will require some very significant organizational changes indeed. High-quality staff want to learn and develop professionally, they want their work with the INGO to enhance their career opportunities, and they want to be affiliated with like-minded professionals. They also value some autonomy of professional work—the opportunity to pursue professional interests. They expect that they will be consulted before any significant organizational or strategic changes that impact them are made and their views listened to. Finally, they value flexibility, especially over time (Lorsch and Tierney 2002). These characteristics are even more important to the "Internet generation," those people who have grown up with the Internet. They value freedom and choice even more strongly than their parents, they expect the workplace to be both meaningful and fun, they expect things to happen fast, and they expect constant innovation (Tapscott 2008).

These factors do not only apply in Northern contexts. They are equally important in attracting employees in developing countries. In addition to providing strong learning and development opportunities, such employees are attracted to the strong international brands of the large INGOs and their poverty alleviation mission, since many have experienced poverty first hand and have global citizenship values (Ready et al. 2008). Emphasizing these factors is useful to help counteract the lower financial remuneration that INGOs often offer in such places compared to the UN or TNCs. Investing in the quality of field staff is also likely to pay significant dividends in terms of the effectiveness of programs. Front line field staff can sometimes be the least educated, poorest paid, and least respected within an INGOs' organizational hierarchy. Yet they are the ones who are expected to deliver high-quality community development while simultaneously providing the myriad of donor reports, financial accounts, annual operating plans, progress reports, and funding requests required by all of the other layers of the organization. Addressing the tendency in some INGOs to transfer any talented field staff to head office and ensuring that they receive appropriate pay and other opportunities is critical to helping such staff cope with these manifold demands.

INGO leaders need to worry as much about missing out on or losing great talent as they do about missing out on or losing good donors. In successful professional service organizations in other industries, senior staff devote significant time and attention to activities such as recruiting, nurturing and mentoring staff, succession planning, and performance reviews, which lesser organizations will neglect or delegate to human resource departments (Lorsch and Tierney 2002). An organization's promotion process becomes a critical signal to aspiring employees about what they value in emerging leaders. Senior staff also need to ensure that the organization has a strong employment brand, especially in such a competitive market. Another characteristic of high-quality staff in professional service firms is that they do not work for less talented bosses for very long—they may put up with it in the short run but they will not remain indefinitely, a factor that poses another significant challenge for aid and development INGOs. As Charles Handy (1992, 64) says, "in an organization dominated by new professionals you cannot tell people what to do unless they respect you, agree with you, or both." Similarly the critical organizational characteristic of knowledge-sharing is more likely to occur in an environment where staff feel committed to the organization, value their colleagues, and respect their leaders (Britton 2005, 15).

The "vocational" nature of work in large INGOs, less competitive remuneration, and managers and board members poorly equipped or unwilling to deal with performance issues or to transfer managers to more suitable positions means that some senior staff in INGOs are employed for too long or in the wrong positions. For example, at World Vision's National Directors Conference in May 2006 (comprising around 200 of the organization's most senior leaders), the average tenure with World Vision of those attending was 13.3 years. Over 27 percent of attendants had been with World Vision more than 20 years and 43 percent more than 15 years. In particular, a majority of the most senior people present had been with WV for 20 or more years. Only 17 percent of attendees were female. Given the change in the complexity and strategic context for INGOs, the length of tenure of World Vision's most senior people means its senior leaders may not have the skills required or may place the organization at risk from a too-conservative or insulated culture. In comparison, in most professional service organizations, turnover runs at between 10 and 20 percent per annum. The result of staff turnover that is too low is that succession planning, where it occurs, becomes very difficult, and talented staff leave to pursue career development elsewhere.

Of course, this is not to suggest that length of tenure per se is a problem or that low staff turnover is always bad. Given the complexity of the issues faced by large INGOs and the number of relationships that are required for success, experience, and organizational history are important. In addition, since development culture is largely a relational and intuitive one, high turnover, especially at the community level, mitigates against understanding of culture and people, process, and ownership. However, maintaining perspective, remaining open to new ideas, and seeing that skills remain cutting edge can all be more difficult once employees (especially senior managers) have been in the organization for a long period of time. This is why there is such a strong emphasis on developing strong learning cultures in successful law and medical practices, an issue discussed further later. Without a strong learning culture to ensure that staff's skills and abilities continue to grow and develop, a professional services organization can quickly become introspective and out of touch with its strategic context and find itself without the necessary skills to effectively carry out its organizational mission. This is also why investing in professional development is so critical to an INGOs' success. Increased links between universities, think tanks, and INGOs may also help.[8] Yet, repeatedly in discussions with staff of INGOs, they confirm my own experience that one of the first items removed in any budget process is professional development. This lack of adequate investment in leadership development combined with the enormous growth in the aid and development sector means there is a massive shortage of competent people, particularly for large INGOs who are normally seeking to employ the most skilled and experienced staff. For example, Thomas Tierney (2006) estimates that just in the United States, not-for-profits will need to find almost 80,000 new senior managers every year (based on organizations with revenues of more than US$250,000 annually).

Accordingly, the human resource issues at the largest aid and development INGOs are perhaps the most significant internal challenges they face. Unfortunately, many seem ill prepared. While not all of the problems may apply to all of the largest aid and development INGOs, in interviews with senior managers of many INGOs, nearly all identify with at least some of them: the relatively low profile of human resources issues among INGOs' senior management; the low capacity of current leaders to manage human resource issues; remuneration constraints despite increasing competition from other aid and development actors; poor human resource systems;[9] and ingrained cultural limitations to effective human resource management. Nonetheless, it remains imperative that the huge gap between organizational practice and rhetoric in the area of human resources is closed if the largest aid and development INGOs are to be effective in the twenty-first century.

The Leverage Challenge: Advocacy, Partnering, and Harnessing Markets

Despite the dramatic increase in the size and influence of INGOs outlined in Chapter 3, they are still dwarfed by the magnitude of their mission. As a result, one of the key challenges for all aid and development INGOs is to find ways to leverage their still relatively small financial and other resources to achieve a much greater impact. In physics, leverage is defined as the mechanical advantage gained from using a lever (Grant and Catchfield 2007, 35). For INGOs, there are three main mechanisms, or "levers," for achieving leverage: more advocacy, more effective partnering, and harnessing markets. Although all of the large aid and development INGOs initially saw themselves as primarily service oriented

(Fitzduff and Church 2004, 4), Oxfam, in particular, has been actively engaged in advocacy for some time, and the other large aid and development INGOs have also recently been increasing the amount of advocacy work they are undertaking. However, much more needs to be done. Most of the large INGOs engage in rhetoric about collaboration and partnering but their relationships among one another more often resembles that of competitors. To date, successful INGO partnerships with organizations outside of the sector are few and far between. Finally, INGOs' use of markets to achieve social ends is even more nascent. Each of these three mechanisms for increasing an INGO's impact will be explored in this section, together with some of the organizational implications of investing more resources in these activities.

Advocacy

The first way for aid and development INGOs to increase their impact is to undertake more advocacy, defined broadly as "promoting the cause of others" (Bebbington et al. 2008, 310). However, advocacy is also important to INGOs for other reasons. As outlined in Chapter 5, advocacy is a vital component of INGOs' response to meeting the new development challenges of environmental degradation, rising food insecurity, and urbanization. Advocacy is also vital to the long-term sustainability of most development projects. While projects may be able to demonstrate progress in the short term, the external environment often does not provide the context for this success to be exploited or even sustained. It is not surprising then that the Grant and Crutchfield (2007) study of 12 high impact NGOs (domestic and international) found that high impact NGOs bridge the divide between service and advocacy and become good at both. This view is supported by Keck and Sikkink (1998) and Bebbington et al. (2008). This, then, is a critical twenty-first century challenge for aid and development INGOs: Can they become good at both implementing aid and development programs as well as advocacy?

There are three key advocacy modalities: policy change and implementation; citizen education or awareness building; and citizen mobilization.[10] Advocacy can also take place at the local level, the national level in both developed and developing countries, and at the international level. Of course, aid and development INGOs already undertake a significant amount of advocacy and, as outlined in Chapter 3, have a long history of very influential roles in many international advocacy campaigns. In fact, Riddell (2007, 264) estimates that advocacy comprises around 15 percent of total INGO development expenditure. Nonetheless, most aid and development INGOs still approach advocacy in a relatively unsophisticated way (Chowdhury et al. 2006). This will need to change if they are to meet the challenge of significantly increasing their effectiveness since advocacy, informed by an INGO's grass roots work, can "assist an INGO replicate its model, gain credibility, influence much larger systems and structures, and acquire funding for expansion" (Grant and Catchfield 2007: 35).

The leverage potential of advocacy is well illustrated by DATA (Debt, Aids, Trade, Africa). The Gates Foundation argues that their investment of US$1 million in DATA has led to US$50 billion in debt relief (Bishop 2008: 48). Putting to one side the attribution issues implicit in such a claim, it is clear that sophisticated global campaigns, especially where they are supported by celebrities, can have significant influence over government policy. It also illustrates that at least some large INGO donors are beginning to appreciate the value that advocacy can have in leveraging their philanthropic dollars. Despite their size, these donors realize that they too need to minimize the amount of direct resource transfer and maximize the involvement of other organizations with far deeper pockets (Bishop 2008: 49).

Nonetheless, there may be a number of reasons why increased advocacy may be difficult or even controversial for aid and development INGOs. First, advocacy is an inherently political activity. It seeks to change the systems, structures, institutions, and policies that either cause poverty or allow it to be perpetuated. Increased involvement of aid and development INGOs in advocacy, therefore, exacerbates the politicization of aid and development activities, as discussed in Chapter 5. Some commentators allege this is a breach of the traditional humanitarian value of neutrality, and they are probably correct. However, as argued above, aid and development has always been an inherently political activity, and the largest aid and development INGOs never sought to be strictly neutral, in comparison, for example, to the ICRC. Instead, aid and development INGOs have generally adopted a pragmatic view of neutrality. As the ODI (2007) argues in its recent review of advocacy in Darfur, neutrality should be "sufficiently nonpartisan to facilitate access to affected communities, while also sufficiently flexible to allow advocacy."

However, even such a pragmatic approach to advocacy may, in difficult political contexts, increase staff safety concerns, place an INGO's government registration under pressure, or lead to the withdrawal of government officials from involvement in the agency's activities. For example, statistics compiled by the ODI (2007) suggest a correlation between increased advocacy and decreased staff security, at least in Darfur. On the other hand, best practice in advocacy involves developing methods tailored to each unique environment in order to minimize these risks. For example, in difficult political contexts, aid and development INGO advocacy may involve less confrontational methods, such as the provision of

Case Study 6.1: The ROI of Advocacy

Calculating the "return on investment" (ROI) from advocacy is notoriously difficult. The Gates Foundation believes that it achieved an enormous return on its US$1million investment in DATA. However, the extent to which US$50 billion of debt relief can be attributed to DATA is unclear, and its impact on poverty indicators, while undoubtedly considerable, is difficult to calculate. Similarly, an evaluation of Make Poverty History's 2005 campaign identified a number of areas where the campaign significantly contributed to policy change in the UK and elsewhere without seeking to calculate an actual ROI (Martin et al. 2006).

Despite the difficulties, WVA has sought to calculate the ROI on the initial phase of its Don't Trade Lives campaign. Don't Trade Lives is an advocacy campaign to unite Australians against human trafficking and slavery. Don't Trade Lives examines the issue of labor exploitation in the contexts of Asia and West Africa and looks at how our purchasing behavior relates to these issues.

From Easter 2008, the campaign focused on convincing Australian manufacturers and retailers of chocolate to protect children working on cocoa farms through the purchase of fair-trade cocoa. For 17 months, more than 25,000 Australians participated in the campaign's action on the chocolate industry. This included visiting chocolate manufacturers and retailers, signing petitions, holding protests, and visiting members of parliament to demand change. The total investment by WVA in this aspect of the campaign over this period was AUD260,000 (approximately US$210,000).

On August 26, 2009, Australia's largest seller of chocolate, Cadbury Australia, announced it would use fair-trade cocoa in the production of their most popular product, Cadbury Dairy Milk Chocolate, in both Australia and New Zealand. Overnight, Cadbury's decision tripled the amount of fair-trade cocoa available in Australia. While it is likely that Cadbury would have adopted a fair-trade system of purchasing cocoa for the Australian market eventually due to global pressure, evidence from senior Cadbury executives themselves suggests that this decision was brought forward by at least two years due to the Australian campaign.

The direct benefit to cocoa farming communities in Ghana is the US$150-per-ton price premium achieved through the fair-trade system and a guaranteed minimum price. While the minimum price guarantee only applies when the world market price is below US$1500 per ton, for the 20 years to December 2008, the average monthly cocoa price was below the $1500 threshold for 139 out of 240 months.

By applying these price increases to the 3,900 tons of cocoa that will be purchased by Cadbury Australia through the fair-trade system, a net benefit of approximately US$1,181,700 will be achieved over the two years, benefiting 39,000 people (including 23,400 children) in a sustainable way.

In addition, there are the incalculable benefits to those children whose involvement in cocoa production came at the expense of their education or well-being. This ROI calculation also ignores the economic flow on effects to noncocoa growers in the community and the indirect benefit from increased community education in Australia. Finally, it is anticipated that other Australian chocolate manufactures will be forced to follow Cadbury's lead, resulting in a much larger impact over time.

information confidentially to third parties or advocating that influential foreign governments place pressure on the offending government. In these contexts, INGOs also need to undertake this advocacy as collaboratively as possible, building coalitions with other like-minded groups as often as possible. Of course, advocacy can also increase humanitarian access. Many people attribute increased humanitarian access to Darfur in 2004 to behind the scene advocacy activities and INGO advocacy was certainly a factor in increased humanitarian access in Myanmar after Cyclone Nagris (ODI 2007).

As outlined earlier in this chapter, more advocacy is also likely to mean that issues of accountability and legitimacy become more prominent. As Hugo Slim (2002) has made clear, "as groups who make it their business to demand accountability in others, it could be said that NGOs and human rights organizations have a particular responsibility to lead by example in this area and shine as beacons of legitimacy and accountability." There may also be internal barriers to an aid and development INGO undertaking more advocacy. For example, within some INGOs, local boards of INGO affiliates or of partners often represent interests associated with existing power structures and may therefore be reluctant to become associated with advocacy activities or suffer personal cost as a result of them.[11] Nonetheless, despite the effort that must be invested in addressing these serious issues, the potential leverage that advocacy provides to INGOs' impact means that this is an investment well worth making.

Partnering

The second way for aid and development INGOs to increase their impact is to become much more adept at partnering and collaboration. The term "partnering" is used to describe a large 'number of arrangements and has a long history in development practice. However, in this context, I use the term "partnering" to mean a relationship between two or more organizations that is more than transactional, is characterized by trust, common goals, and mutual benefit in the sense that the parties are able to achieve a greater result together than they could individually. Collaboration is a less formal or more ad hoc form of partnering.[12] While smaller INGOs approach partnering and collaboration in a more instinctive (if still not very sophisticated) way, the size of the largest aid and development INGOs sometimes encourages them to be more insular. The sheer number of internal stakeholders that senior managers must navigate to reach decisions means that there is little time, or energy, left for building external networks that may facilitate partnerships. Crutchfield and Grant (2008, 109) also claim that many

Case Study 6.2: Aid and Development INGOs and the US Government

Since the first debate on foreign aid took place in the US Congress in 1794, the United States' approach to aid has constantly swung between those who argued that the United States had a moral obligation to provide humanitarian assistance and those who argued that it was inappropriate or even illegal to use public funds for such purposes (Lancaster 2008, 94). Over time, this debate has led to considerable public skepticism about the value of aid, ignorance of the amount of aid actually provided and to the United States having the lowest level of public support for foreign aid of any DAC country (Stern 1998, 15). Many US aid and development NGOs have avoided criticizing their own government's attitudes toward aid for fear of being labeled political or unpatriotic or putting access to USAID funding at risk (Clark 2003, 196).

In this context, Barak Obama's view on the United States' responsibilities toward the world's poor is a significant break with the past. In his inauguration speech he said:

> To the people of poor nations, we pledge to work alongside you to make your farms flourish and let clean waters flow; to nourish starved bodies and feed hungry minds. And to those nations like ours that enjoy relative plenty, we say we can no longer afford indifference to suffering outside our borders; nor can we consume the world's resources without regard to effect. For the world has changed, and we must change with it.

The election of Barak Obama together with a growing understanding following the terrorist attacks of September 11, 2001, that in a globalized world, Americans' security and well-being are inextricably linked to that of Afghans, Kenyans, and Indonesians, could create the perfect opportunity for US-based offices of large aid and development INGOs to build a much stronger domestic constituency for aid in the twenty-first century. In fact, if the growing interest of the Christian Right in aid issues continues, this combination of factors could lead to one of the most important changes in US foreign aid policy in decades and to sustained higher levels of US ODA.

Changing US public opinion about the effectiveness of aid and building a pro-aid domestic constituency is critical for addressing global poverty—Hulme (2008) calls it the "dinosaur in the room." As Thomas Friedman (2008, 6) argues in his latest book, *Hot, Flat, and Crowded*, "Whether you love us or hate us, whether you believe in American power or you don't, the convergence of hot, flat, and crowded has created a challenge so daunting that it is impossible to imagine a meaningful solution without America really stepping up."

Changing US public opinion will require US-based offices of large aid and development INGOs to invest far more in their domestic advocacy capability. However, if such investments are successful, it could prove to generate the greatest return on investment for the world's poor of any of their activities.

large NGOs have a culture of organization orientation that "keeps them focused more on building their own enterprise at the expense of others." This tendency must be resisted at all costs. Partnering and collaboration generate a number of distinct advantages for INGOs. As Grant and Crutchfield (2007, 34) make clear, high-impact NGOs "work with and through organizations and individuals *outside of themselves* to create more impact than they ever could have achieved alone." Partnering with other INGOs can be a useful tactic to reduce the challenges of advocacy in difficult political contexts. However, partnering may also improve the effectiveness of advocacy. Since technical skills are limited, pooling resources reduces costs and can increase the amount of available data, thereby improving an INGO's policy credibility and reducing duplicated, contradictory, or misinterpreted research (Chowdhury et al. 2006). Improved collaboration can also encourage greater interagency learning.

Further, partnering is a key requirement for responding to some of the new development challenges faced by aid and development INGOs. For example, aid and development INGOs must work much more closely with environmental INGOs if they are to successfully meet the challenges posed by climate change (LaFleur 2008). Partnering with human rights INGOs can also be a good strategy to help aid and development INGOs manage the increased politicization of their work and balance the need to maintain operations with addressing human rights abuses. Many donors are also demanding that aid and development INGOs demonstrate their capacity to partner. For example, Henrietta Fore, the USAID Administrator, set a target for the organization to increase their Public Private Partnerships in 2009 by 40 percent. Large aid and development INGOs who wish to maintain their USAID funding will need to be increasingly prepared for such arrangements.

Of course, INGO partnerships must encompass a broader range of actors than just other INGOs, academic institutions, or international organizations. INGOs will need to become much better at engaging the corporate sector as well. As Jeffrey Sachs argues, "there are no solutions to the problems of poverty, population, and environment without the active engagement of the private sector" (Sachs 2008, 52). Large INGOs are increasingly recognizing the importance of the private sector in addressing global poverty. Together with a number of international organizations, they have launched a range of initiatives aimed at creating a corporate constituency for global poverty and promoting corporations' active involvement in developing solutions. Initiatives by IGOs include the World Business Council for Sustainable Development, the UNDP's Growing Inclusive Markets Initiative, and the International Business Leaders Forum. World Vision has launched a major cross-sector partnering initiative (the XSP Project) and in Australia was a founder of Business for Millennium Development (See www.b4md.com.au). Oxfam GB's work with Unilever on understanding the development impact of a TNC was pioneering (Clay 2005). Where a corporation's core business is harnessed, it can drive significant local economic and social development, whether through the employment generated by a company's local distribution network, the production of raw materials, or the provision of key infrastructure.

However, as discussed in Chapter 2, commentators like Simon Zadek argue that a more far-reaching revolution is taking place in the aid and development industry with the potential to challenge not only the role of large aid and development INGOs' but also that of other more traditional aid and development actors. He argues that the most important new actor in the aid and development industry is the complex combination of the old actors into a new, collaborative organization. Such collaborative organizations are not only involved in the delivery of aid and development activities but also global rule setting, or "collaborative standards initiatives," as Simon Zadek describes them. These include such diverse initiatives as the Equator Principles governing project finance, the Global Reporting Initiative (GRI), EITI, and the Forest Stewardship Council at the international level and many others at the national level. Large INGOs have been involved in the creation of many of these collaborative organizations and standards initiatives and continue to play a significant ongoing role (see Case Study 2.1). Such ongoing involvement is critical given the increasing resources that such organizations have at their disposal and the need to contribute to ensuring their accountability and shaping their policies as these organizations and initiatives mature.

However, like advocacy, partnering can create a number of potential pitfalls and generates a range of operational challenges for INGOs. For example, more sophisticated partnering is resource intensive and requires specialist expertise. Successful partnerships require INGOs to be very clear about what they want from the partnership, to understand what value each party brings to the table, and what is motivating the other party to invest in the relationship. It requires enthusiastic leadership who can support the partnership through the resolution of difficult issues. Good partners are also aware of power disparities in the relationship and are careful not to exploit them.[13] One particular downside to partnering, especially in a fast changing strategic context, can be its potential to slow down decision-making. Many corporate partners are also ill equipped to partner with INGOs. As Silverman and Taliento (2005) argue, "too many cross-sector partnerships—which are central to addressing society's most intractable problems—fail partly because business leaders don't cope well with the nonprofit sector's different culture and demands." Finally, partnering also requires a change of culture. Although not discussed openly to any great extent, there can be a sense of competition among the largest aid and development INGOs. While some competition is healthy and the differences among the largest INGOs contribute to the diversity and vibrancy of the sector, ultimately the largest aid and development INGOs share a common mission and will have the most impact by collectively helping one another to succeed. As Grant and Catchfield (2007, 38) explain, high impact NGOs "freely share wealth, expertise, talent, and power with other nonprofits not because they are saints, but because it's in their self-interest to do so."

Market Mechanisms

The third, and probably most controversial, way for aid and development INGOs to increase their impact is to harness the power of markets. There are a variety of ways that INGOs can become involved in markets to achieve their mission, and although still relatively limited, the largest aid and development INGOs are cautiously involved in most of them.[14] One of the most advanced is encouraging corporations to act in a more development-friendly way by influencing consumers' purchasing decisions. For example, Oxfam GB actively influences companies to source their products ethically and promotes fair trade goods.[15] Similarly, WVA seeks to leverage consumer choice as a key part of its anti–child trafficking and anti-slavery campaign.[16] The power of this form of leverage was well illustrated by Wal-Mart's decision in July 2009 to require all of its suppliers to include labeling disclosing the environmental costs of making products sold in Wal-Mart stores. Wal-Mart's sheer size—it has more than 100,000 suppliers—means the decision will have a beneficial ripple effect for the environment not just through the United States but overseas as well.

The use of markets in developing countries to help solve poverty by large INGOs is far more limited. This has led commentators such as Easterly (2008, 6–7) to criticize aid and development INGO's and other aid actors for an over-reliance on large-scale planning and insufficient support for "searchers"—local actors who are incentivized, especially through markets, to find case-by-case solutions to problems that meet their customers' needs. While writers such as Easterly underestimate the extent of market failure, especially in developing countries, and their approach can be overly polemical, the underlying argument that aid and development actors need to do more to empower searchers has validity and is a reminder to the largest aid and development INGOs that they need to do more to encourage innovation, accountability, and participation in their programs. One relatively new INGO that is dedicated to using social enterprises for social rehabilitation and economic empowerment is Swiss-based Hagar International (see www.hagarpro-ject.org). Hagar runs a number of businesses in the hospitality sector in Cambodia, for example, that employ abused and exploited women. Until its recent sale, Hagar Cambodia also ran a soymilk manufacturing business that produced 264 gallons per hour of nutritious drink at an affordable price and with a long shelf life. In total, in 2008, Hagar directly employed 466 people in its social enterprises.

The extent of the opportunities for INGOs to use markets for economic and social development in developing countries was demonstrated in a report by Boston Consulting Group (2009) for the World Economic Forum. The report emphasized the opportunities at the bottom of the pyramid for the simultaneous achievement of corporate economic benefit and social impact. Similarly, a recent World Bank (2009) report called for "liberalization from below." According to the World Bank (2009, 42), "actions should seek to transform markets so that poor people can access and participate in them fairly." The bank outlines several ways to achieve this: "[S]caling up and linking poor people's livelihood activities; providing connectedness through roads, telephones, electricity, and irrigation; easing access to loans that can be used for production; and providing information, business know-how, and skills to connect to mainstream markets." To assist in this, the largest aid and development INGOs will need to become more adept at understanding how markets work and when market interventions can and cannot solve some of the problems they are engaged with. Of course, this will also help the largest aid and development INGOs better understand how their own activities can negatively impact markets, thereby undermining their own mission (Barber and Bowie, 2008).[17]

Finally, least developed is INGOs' involvement in finding mechanisms that make markets in both developed and developing countries work better or using market opportunities to generate new ways to fund their aid and development activities. Unlike other nonprofit sectors that raise a significant proportion of their funds through commercial or semicommercial activities, the aid and development sector raises almost none.[18] While there are a number of operational and cultural challenges that would need to be addressed to change this situation, the opportunities to raise new sources of financial resources for INGOs are significant. An interesting precedent is the International Finance Facility for Immunization, a global bond issue developed by the Global Alliances for Vaccines and Immunization (see Case Study 6.3). Another important future source of new funds for development purposes is the sale of carbon credits generated by community development projects. For example, WVA recently sold carbon credits generated by a community forest in Ethiopia to the World Bank. The funds generated were, with the community's consent,

Case Study 6.3: International Finance Facility for Immunization

The International Finance Facility for Immunization (IFFIm), launched in 2006 and championed by the UK government, uses capital markets to convert long-term government pledges into immediately available cash resources. As governments honor their pledges, the IFFIm bonds are repaid.

IFFIm's initial offering in November 2006 raised US$1 billion among institutional investors. It is anticipated that, over time, up to US$4 billion in bonds may be issued using this mechanism. The funds raised by IFFIm are used by the GAVI Alliance, a public–private partnership working to reduce vaccine-preventable deaths and illnesses among children under five.

By March 2008, GAVI had disbursed 90 percent of IFFIm's initial US$1 billion. Not only does this approach mean that programs could be implemented much faster, it also means that costly up-front investments were adequately financed and long-term funding predictable.

While there are risks that such large up-front funds may not be used effectively by developing countries' governments, this risk appears to be outweighed by the social and economic returns from the long-term health benefits from increased child immunization. From a donor's perspective, the overall costs do not change but the benefits to beneficiaries and developing countries should be higher.

For more information, see http://www.iff-immunisation.org

---

used to partially fund a range of development projects in the community. The potential possibilities of such market-based fundraising have become even more important in the face of the reduced prospects for global economic growth over the next few years.

To greater and lesser extents, the largest aid and development INGOs are already involved in advocacy, in partnering, and in harnessing markets, and some of their early initiatives have had a significant positive impact. Oxfam GB's promotion of Fair Trade in the United Kingdom is a good example. However, all three of these activities still face some cultural or ideological resistance within the largest aid and development INGOs. They are also areas that require new skills and the management of new risks (see Crutchfield and Grant 2008, 73–78). On the other hand, increased partnering and use of markets has the potential to unlock new sources of funds and, through increased collaboration with other development actors, improved access to technical skills. Nonetheless, it remains critical that the largest aid and development INGOs find ways to significantly magnify their impact. To achieve this, advocacy, partnering and harnessing markets will need to become a much more standard part of their armory in the twenty-first century.

The Technical Challenge: More Sophisticated Political, Economic and Social Analysis

In "The Hubbert Peak," an episode of season six of the NBC's *The West Wing*, legislation to impose fuel mileage standards is discussed by White House staffers, and a likely global food crisis is predicted when peak oil is reached. More than three years after this episode was first shown on US television, the largest aid and development INGOs scrambled to respond to this very scenario, seemingly caught off guard.[19] This highlights a real absurdity in the largest aid and development INGOs: A fictional television program can invest in research for the purposes of creating a more realistic script, yet such resources in the world's largest INGOs, operating in the real world where people's lives are at risk, are still considered a luxury. If INGOs accept that international relations is socially constructed then surely one of the key projects for INGOs is to develop what Hulme (2008, 343) calls an "owl:" a "theoretical body of knowledge that can be stripped down into a persuasive policy narrative." This will require more sophisticated political, economic, and social analysis supported by highly skilled communicators. It will also require some creative thinking to find ways to pay for access to these resources. However, it is vital that the largest aid and development INGOs meet this challenge if they are going to continue to be equipped to play an effective role in international relations into the twenty-first century.

There are a number of reasons why the largest aid and development INGOs need to increase their ability to undertake more sophisticated political, economic, and social analysis. First, increased technical skills are required for many of the new development challenges that aid and development INGOs face in the twenty-first century.

Second, increased technical specialization is also required for INGOs' advocacy work and to meet expectations of governments and international organizations that, because of INGOs' newfound size and influence, now expect INGOs to engage with them in a more sophisticated way. As Clark (2003, 103) argues, there are increasing expectations that large INGOs will shift from problem-focused advocacy to solution-focused advocacy. Similarly, Fitzduff and Church (2004, 1) argue, the "real test of NGOs policy usefulness now will be the quality of their policy contributions: How do they move from being critics of policy to playing the role of an informed and thoughtful source of viable policy alternatives[?]" Yet, both Clark (2003) and Chowdhury et al.'s (2006) research suggests that current INGO capacity is well below policy makers' expectations.

For example, Chowdhury et al.'s (2006, 16) research found that "one of the most frequently recurring lessons learned from the consultations was that in order to improve their interaction with policy makers, CSOs need to improve their own capacity. "Capacity" is a very broad term, covering many aspects, from policy advocacy skills to technical knowledge, research skills and resources." This lack of capacity is illustrated by INGOs' lack of impact on one of the most significant international policy changes of the last 20 years: the move to a post–Washington consensus (Hulme 2008).[20]

On the other hand, the extent to which many of the largest INGOs are seeking to influence international climate change negotiations is demonstrated by the number of policy, advocacy, and media staff that attended the UNFCCC Negotiations in Copenhagen from December 7 to 18, 2009 (see Figures 3.2 and 6.1). Greater technical skills are also required in developing world contexts. For example, a study in Malawi observed, "while the political space is opening for civil society participation in policy processes, the lack of capacity and policy advocacy skills among CSOs is the greatest drawback that requires urgent redress" (Chowdhury et al. 2006, 17). Increased technical capacity in this area is also required to engage with and sometimes counter the use of increasingly technical arguments by corporations in areas that impact their work. A good example of this type of sparring is provided by the climate change debate (see, for example, Hamilton 2007; and Union of Concerned Scientists 2007).

Third, increased technical skills are also required to ensure that INGOs do not do harm through indirect negative aspects of their work. For example, Mary Anderson's (1999) seminal work on aid and conflict argues that "when international assistance is given in the context of conflict it both affects and is affected by that conflict." She argues that this occurs in a number of ways, including the way stolen aid resources can support armies and buy weapons, the way aid resources can impact local markets, the way distribution of aid can either feed tensions or reinforce

Figure 6.1 NGO Attendance at the UNFCCC Negotiations in Copenhagen (Dec 7–18, 2009)

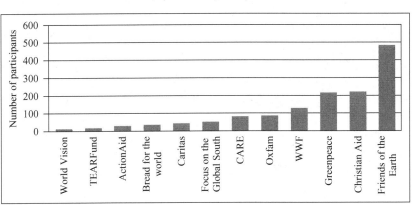

connections, and the way aid can legitimize people's actions or agendas, supporting the pursuit of either peace or war (Anderson 1999, 39). Their greater size and influence means that the largest aid and development INGOs now have a greater impact on markets and political affairs than in the past. There is, therefore, an increased risk of INGOs doing harm.

Of course, as Fiona Terry (2002) argues, humanitarian assistance always has some negative consequences, even if these are not immediately visible to aid organizations. Terry says that "pretending that aid can actually be given without causing any harm is utopian." Thus she argues that seeking to do no harm may be too high a standard and that it may be enough to understand the harm your actions may have (through better technical skills) and seek to ameliorate them while closely monitoring the net effect that your activities are having.

Fourth, where INGOs are involved in harnessing markets, they will need more sophisticated technical skills. The depth and breadth of new technical skills required by INGOs to engage in emerging carbon markets provide a strong demonstration of this point. Finally, increasing an INGO's technical knowledge and skills is one way to increase an INGO's legitimacy, since expertise contributes to their moral authority (Hall 2005).

On the other hand, there are a number of hurdles that make it difficult for the largest aid and development INGOs to effectively address this challenge. The first is how to find resources to pay for more sophisticated political, economic, and social analysis. There are a number of potential solutions. One is increased collaboration among INGOs on policy issues.[21] Some of the necessary resources can also be sourced through improved partnerships with academic institutions.[22] However, while some policy analysis can be outsourced, INGOs will still need to invest in more in-house resources. Despite some modest growth in technical resources over the past few years, the technical resources of the large INGOs are still extremely limited. The large INGOs are also not very good at sharing resources among affiliates (see Case Study 7.1). Without a certain threshold level of in-house expertise it is very difficult for an organization to even identify critical issues or to know where to begin seeking answers to the questions they generate. To fund these resources, INGOs will need to be prepared to either reduce direct project expenditure on the basis that they can demonstrate that it leads to a greater overall impact or find donors who are willing to provide specific funding for INGOs' technical resources, either on a subject by subject basis or more generally. Of course, in the longer run, more sophisticated engagement with international organizations and governments should also lead to increased funds. By demonstrating their depth of expertise through policy engagement, governments and international organizations will better appreciate the situations where the largest aid and development INGOs can add real value to their own aid and development work.

The second hurdle is attracting the professional technical resources that INGOs need. This can be particularly difficult in the area of economics (Keane 2008). High-quality technical staff want to learn and develop professionally, they want career options—will working at the INGO open doors in the future?—and they want to be affiliated with like-minded professionals. Traditionally, the largest aid and development INGOs have not provided this type of working environment.

The third hurdle is overcoming the lingering cultural aversion to "professionalization" that exists in some aid and development INGOs and their preference for "doing." For example, Peter Uvin (2004,19) claims that compared to some other INGOs, the development community "tends to develop multitudes of tools and practices for facing up to constantly changing operational challenges but typically gives these matters little theoretically informed or conceptually grounded thought." Similarly, Britton (2005, 6) describes it as an "adrenaline culture, where the delivery of outputs is seen as the main measure of success" (see also Goold 2006, 4; Lewis 2007, 20). While the action-oriented culture of the largest aid and development INGOs must be retained, it must be balanced with shrewdness and intelligence if they are to meet the challenges of the twenty-first century. This requires significantly enhanced institutional learning, a process that integrates thinking and doing and is the next challenge for large INGOs that this book will focus on.

There is also sometimes seen to be a trade-off between being professional and "walking with the poor." According to Anheier (2000, 2), even the term "management" was "often regarded as a 'bad word' in the non-profit world, as a practice at odds with what some regard as the essence of the sector: voluntarism, philanthropy, compassion, and a concern for the public good" (see also Korten 1990, 156). Unfortunately, the term "professional" appears little understood in the sector, and there is a widespread view that it is somehow inconsistent with values-based cultures (Lewis 2007, 20–21). Quite the contrary. Traditionally, a profession was a highly skilled occupation—even a vocation or calling—closely linked to specialized university faculties that provided independent advice, served a broader public interest, and was regulated by a code of ethics. From this perspective, the professionalization of the aid and development sector is not something to be avoided but embraced as highly consistent with the sector's values.

The Learning Challenge: Power in the Information Age

Since at least the early 1990s, development literature has emphasized the strong correlation between organizational effectiveness and an organization's ability to learn from experience.[23] Learning is central to improving program quality and should be a key motivation for gathering and analyzing monitoring data, since it is from such data that small but important improvements in project effectiveness are developed (Britton 2005, 9). However, it is important for two other equally critical reasons.

First, aid and development INGO access to community-level information and data should be one of their most important comparative advantages over other development actors and a key source of their international power in the Information Age. Other aid and development actors have already recognized this. Both the UNDP and World Bank have emphasized their roles as knowledge brokers (see Boas and McNeill 2004; McNeill and St Clair 2009).

Second, in the midst of the current strategic revolution, organizational learning becomes essential to assist the largest aid and development INGOs anticipate, react, and respond to the change occurring around them. As Britton (2005, 5) argues, it is critical to INGOs' "organizational adaptability, innovation, and sustainability." Similarly, Sachs (2008, 326) identifies learning, "its investment in knowledge and its capacity to identify crucial needs," as key to the Rockefeller Foundation's success. The importance of aid and development INGOs becoming "learning organizations" is therefore not contested. Yet, as recent research among British INGOs by the INGO umbrella group BOND (Goold 2006) found, the sector appears "stuck." It understands its importance but is seemingly unable to respond. The study found that "over 50 percent of NGOs and donors surveyed felt that a radical departure was needed to overcome the 'stuckness' of the sector on the issues of learning" (Goold 2006). Similarly, Lewis and Wallace (2000, xiv) argue that "finding ways to become learning organizations . . . largely continues to evade NGOs." The scale of the problem is reflected in the use of terms such as an "NGO disease" or "clinical amnesia" to describe the failure of INGOs to learn from their experience (Britton 2005). This section will examine the reasons why large INGOs are finding it so difficult to become learning organizations despite the dire need for such change and propose some operational changes that may begin to remedy the situation.

There seem to be a number of reasons why the largest aid and development INGOs are not good at learning. First, there is significant evidence that the use of logical frameworks (usually referred to as "log frames"), required by most donors and widely used within the largest aid and development INGOs, "acts as a constraint to learning, at least at the project and program level," although this may be as much the result of a too-rigid application of the tool rather than the tool itself (Britton 2005, 6). Project funding also discourages "innovative learning, initiatives outside the project box, or facilitation of organization-wide or inter-organizational learning processes" (Goold 2006, 9).

In addition, while there is considerable literature on organizational learning, nearly all of it is based on Western models. However, since we know that learning is "understood differently across cultures and contexts" and that so many aid and development INGO staff are from non-Western backgrounds, this is an important limitation (Britton 2005, 4). The way that information technology often embeds cultural and institutional practices into the technology itself undoubtedly exacerbates this problem.

Organizational structure probably also plays a role in an organization's ability to learn, although organizational culture is undoubtedly a much more significant factor. While orthodox thinking suggests that flat organizational structures with fewer management layers and increased delegation of decision-making provides a more supportive environment for the lateral exchange of knowledge, "the evidence from some larger NGOs is that decentralization creates disconnected 'silos' which have little lateral contact and no longer have the channels of exchange once provided through specialist advisers based at head office" (Britton 2005, 6).

However, the most critical factor is leadership. Organizational leaders need to be passionate advocates for learning, model it, and encourage a culture of critical thinking. This means that if leaders wish the organization to take learning seriously, they must ensure they "provide the motive, the means, and the opportunity for learning" (Britton 2005, 14). In practice, INGO leaders often fail to provide the motive for staff to invest in learning and do not object when operational pressures crowd out time for reflection. Staff training and professional development budgets are nearly always one of the first to be reduced in any budget process, and the largest INGOs have chronically failed to invest in creating the organization-wide systems that support organizational learning. While this is seldom a result of an intentional undermining of learning on the part of organizational leaders, "small but significant decisions about priorities and resource allocation taken independently form a pattern that communicates a clear message" (Britton 2005, 14). On the other hand, since learning is ultimately about organizational change, in an environment where the organization may have outgrown the capacity of its current leadership, it may be those with overall responsibility for the organization that have the most to lose from encouraging learning (Britton 2005, 16).

Finally, competition between aid and development INGOs makes them reluctant to highlight organizational failures. Edwards (2008, 47) argues that the "institutional imperative of growth and market share still dominate over the development imperatives of individual, organizational, and social transformation." Competition based on overhead ratios also creates disincentives to invest in learning infrastructure.

The failure to become learning organizations is made even more stark by the potential value of knowledge to the largest aid and development

INGOs in the Information Age (see Chapter 2). Their access to community-level information combined with the "international seal of approval" that the credibility of their global brands can provide should be one of their most important comparative advantages over other development actors. According to Keohane and Nye (1998), "information power flows to those who can edit and credibly validate information to sort out what is both correct and important." To maintain their credibility, INGOs must develop a reputation for providing correct information, even when it may reflect badly on them. They must also ensure they sufficiently manage issues of legitimacy and accountability since, in this context, credibility becomes a crucial resource and key source of power. In the Information Age, then, organizations with high levels of credibility that can collect data, synthesize and analyze it, and distribute it widely are in a very powerful position On the other hand, organizations that fail to take advantage of their comparative advantages quickly become irrelevant. In fact, Senge's (1990, 349) research suggests "[T]he rate at which organizations learn may become the only sustainable source of competitive advantage."

If the largest aid and development INGOs are going to realize their comparative advantage in information and begin to use it more strategically in international relations, they need to make a number of key operational changes. First, organizational learning needs to become a leadership priority with the requisite changes in leadership behavior and organizational budgeting. Second, there needs to be a change in organizational culture to one that values reflection, nurtures wisdom, and transforms knowledge and experience into improved action. While "knowledge is information that individuals have reflected on, understood, internalized and are able to use . . . wisdom requires knowledge but wisdom is much more; it is 'the ability to think and act utilizing knowledge, experience, understanding, common sense, and insight' (Britton 2005, 9). Third, the largest aid and development INGOs need to address their massive underinvestment in the key enablers of organizational learning—namely information technologies (IT). While people are the key to developing strong organizational learning, information management systems are crucial to providing a conducive environment. Machine-based systems help share data, information, and even knowledge. They are also particularly important when organizations are involved in complex systems, since there are such large information requirements due to the intricate flow of connections across processes.

Improved information management systems are required by INGOs to respond to the increased complexity of their organizations and the demands to improve accountability and demonstrate effectiveness. Yet, actual investment in information technologies is well below those of comparable organizations. For example, a NetHope member survey determined that information technology spending in large INGOs as a percent of revenues ranged from 0.5 percent to 2.4 percent, with the largest number clustering around 2 percent.[24] A similar study of like-sized public and private sector organizations in the developed world determined that IT spending ranged from 2.9 percent to 8.5 percent with an average in the 4 percent range (Schott and Brindley 2008). The situation at World Vision provides a dramatic example. According to a survey conducted for World Vision in 2007, technology costs per employee were 82 percent lower than world-class organizations.[25] This resulted in business automation levels that were "far below world-class levels." Yet World Vision had many more operating locations than comparably sized companies, suggesting that its costs should have been higher. This under investment is even more dramatic if one accepts that a large proportion of an INGO's activities should be seen as analogous to a professional services firm, which usually has higher information technology demands. While this allows INGOs to demonstrate to donors that the proportion of its income spent on administration is low, it is clear from the research that this does not result in the most effective results. This, then, is a key problem for the largest aid and development INGOs. In the absence of alternative measures of effectiveness and efficiency, they have encouraged donors to compare their ratios of administrative costs to total revenue. Yet, even putting aside the way this ratio can be distorted by accounting definitions and noncash income, the ratio actually undermines INGO effectiveness and makes it far harder for them to access one of their key comparative advantages (reinforcing of donor expectations about overheads is discussed further later). The lack of investment in information technology and its low strategic priority also makes it more difficult for the largest aid and development INGOs to see the potential benefits of a range of new informational technologies to their work in communities and incorporate them into their programs. Not only is the diffusion of technology a key requirement for economic growth, it also supports local poverty alleviation in a number of other ways. Information technology can "be used as leverage for development in strengthening education, improving public services and governance as well as supporting agriculture and the service industry" (Geldof 2005). The use of technology in this way is often described as Information and Communication Technology for Development or ICT4D.

Creating a learning organization is a key internal challenge for the largest aid and development INGOs. It is a challenge that will require new leadership, new strategic thinking, new skills and capabilities, and a new culture of critical reflection and learning. Donors will also need to see the value in INGO investment in information technology. This requires the largest aid and development INGOs to be more honest about measures of effectiveness and to work consistently and transparently to build donor appreciation for the strong correlation between organizational effectiveness and an organization's ability to learn from experience.

Case Study 6.4: Does IT Matter?

In a May 2003 article in the *Harvard Business Review*, Nicholas Carr argued that as information technology's power and ubiquity has grown, its strategic importance has diminished. As a result, he argues that IT investments should be managed defensively, watching costs and avoiding risks.

His article sparked a heated debate in the pages of subsequent issues of the *Harvard Business Review*. Some people misinterpreted his article as saying that IT is no longer a source of dramatic organizational change. This is not the case. As one letter to the *Harvard Business Review* made clear, the value of IT should not be judged by its intrinsic value but by the opportunities that it creates for innovation that did not previously exist. The failure to appreciate this is one of the reasons a large customer relationship–management implementation project undertaken by WVA some years ago went wrong. Instead of using the IT implementation as an opportunity to review and improve business processes, it institutionalized the poor practice of the past in the new system.

Large INGOs also face other challenges. While access to information technology may be widespread, the insights required to harness its potential in new ways is still relatively rare. Further, the ability to adapt organizational processes to take advantage of the strategic possibilities that IT creates is even rarer (see Chapter 8). As a result, the gap between the organizational potential from IT and its realization has widened rather than narrowed.

This has been exacerbated by the way that IT innovation has continued at a rapid and sustained pace over time, quite unlike previous technological breakthroughs where innovation diminished as the technology matured.

Another limitation is that IT is often viewed by large INGOs merely as a more cost effective way of sharing data. While IT does help to achieve this, it can facilitate much broader benefits, including building trust across a dispersed global organization, making possible new partnerships and collaborations, and, most critically, developing and disseminating knowledge.

IT does not itself generate organizational change. Rather, it creates opportunities for innovation and improvement that organizations with the capacity to change and adapt can turn into significant strategic advantage. This is one of the factors that helped to propel Wal-Mart's success. They innovated continuously around new generations of IT, keeping ahead of competitors and creating a significant productivity advantage.

In the not-for-profit world, IT-aided innovation gives large aid and development INGOs the potential to leverage their community-based information for the purposes of systemic change in the structures that help to perpetuate poverty. It also provides them with the opportunity to leverage global knowledge and skills to dramatically improve their local effectiveness. Those large INGOs that can harness this potential will certainly be among the actors that are best positioned to contribute the most to the complex task of alleviating global poverty.

The Funding Challenge: Financing a Twenty-First Century INGO

The final challenge to be discussed in this Chapter is how the largest aid and development INGOs find the necessary resources to finance the organizational investments that they need to make to become next generation INGOs.

Of course, meeting some of the challenges outlined in this book will, of themselves, generate new financial resources. For example, INGOs who become involved in projects that have a positive impact on climate change may have the opportunity to sell Certified Emission Reduction (CER) credits generated by the project. The funds raised may not only meet the costs of the project but also cover the costs of other development activities in the same community. In 2007, WVA brokered the sale of CER credits to the World Bank generated through the regeneration of 2,728 hectares of degraded native forests in Humbo, Ethiopia. While this project was undertaken in accordance with the requirements of the clean development mechanism of the Kyoto Protocol, there are also a number of voluntary markets where customers who are not obligated to purchase credits can still do so to offset their environmental impact. As discussed above, there are also other market-based mechanisms that have the potential to provide significant new sources of income or to enhance existing sources of income (for example, see Case Study 6.2 on the International Finance Facility for Immunization).

More sophisticated engagement with international organizations and governments will also generate new resources. While there can certainly be tension between advocacy and fundraising goals, policy engagement with bilateral agencies can demonstrate an INGO's capabilities in an area and may lead to the INGO becoming the organization of choice for programming related to that area. Many multilateral organizations are also increasing civil society involvement in their programs. For example, under the newly introduced dual track financing, a civil society organization must normally be a principal recipient of GFATM grants alongside government.

The new international context and increased global focus on poverty issues is also generating new donors. The emergence of megaphilanthropists such as the Bill and Melinda Gates Foundation is the most obvious example, but the growing interest in global poverty issues combined with the increased recognition of the strong relationship between poverty and a state's security and stability has given rise to a number of other positive trends for resource generation. More than twenty new bilateral agencies have been established, not only by emerging powers such as India and China but also newly industrialized countries such as

Taiwan. It is estimated that these new bilateral agencies provided approximately US$8 billion in support of long-term development projects in 2005 (Kharas 2008, 59).[26] A growing middle class in emerging and developing economies also represents a significant private fundraising opportunity for INGOs. For example, Bussolo et al. (2008) estimate that by 2030 the number of middle-class people in the developing world will be 1.2 billion, larger than the total, combined populations of Europe, Japan, and the United States. As a result, the emerging economies of Asia and other newly industrialized countries such as Brazil, Mexico, and Turkey should be seriously considered as potential states in which to develop new fundraising offices. MSF has already established a fundraising office in Dubai in response to these changes (see www.msfuae.ae). For World Vision, the funds it raises in Asia are now greater than those it raises in Europe. New development actors such as the GFATM and GAVI and a significant increase in corporate funding also provides new sources of financial resources. While the global financial crisis is likely to make things difficult in the short term, the longer-term prospects for private giving, supported by high profile celebrities such as Bono and Angelina Jolie, also remain positive.

Another example of the positive impact of globalization on INGO fundraising is the increasing wealth of diasporas and their willingness to support development in their countries of origin. Extensive emigration over recent years has created diasporas around the world, and many emigrants have taken advantage of economic opportunities in their host countries to generate considerable wealth. Many members of such diasporas are organizing to assist the social and economic development of their countries of origin. For example, Jane Nelson (2008, 156) estimates that about US$240 billion was remitted by emigrant workers to developing countries in 2007. This is roughly twice the size of total ODA. If INGOs can tap into the desire of many emigrants to support their countries of origin, these diasporas could represent significant new sources of funding. However, given their understanding and links to their countries of origin, emigrants are also likely to demand that INGOs better demonstrate their "value add" compared to direct resource transfers to justify the administration costs that INGOs will ask emigrants to pay.

However, aside from these potential new sources of revenue, the ongoing issue of funding overhead remains a constant problem for INGOs. Increased investment in information systems and human resources, improved strategy development and context analysis, higher security costs from operating in difficult contexts, and the increased workload from the plethora of accountability mechanisms are all likely to increase an INGO's overhead—the proportion of revenue spent on ongoing administrative expenses that cannot be attributed to any specific program. Yet, both public and private donors have a very strong aversion to contributing to nonprofits' overhead. According to Dan Pollotta (2008), nonprofits are run according to an ideology that starves them of the money, techniques, and talents they need to succeed—things that are taken for granted in the business world. They are also too risk averse and short term, leading them to avoid bold new revenue generating ideas, particularly those that may require multiyear investments.

This ideology is reinforced by the media, donors, and even nonprofits themselves. Donors have an overwhelming preference for funding programs and often judge the effectiveness of a nonprofit not by its impact, but by its administration ratio. This approach to assessing nonprofits is constantly reinforced by the media. However, nonprofits have contributed to this situation by failing to educate donors about the relationship between the investment in an organization's underlying capacity and its long-term effectiveness or by providing alternative measurements of performance. In fact, even many aid and development INGOs positively reinforce donor's aversion to overheads by using them as a basis for competition. For example, Save the Children's US website not only boasted that it spent 90 percent of its income on programs and only 4 percent on management and administration in the 2007 fiscal year, it encouraged donors to see this as a key measure of its accountability (see www.savethechildren.org/about/financial.html). The website of World Vision Hong Kong goes even further. On the home page is a graph showing that only 2.4 percent of the funds allocated in 2007 were used for administration. In relation to relief funding, an incredible 98.2 percent was allocated to programming (www.worldvision.org.hk). At these levels, it becomes patently impossible for an organization to make the necessary investments required to develop and sustain organizational infrastructure, professionally develop staff, or meet their reasonable contributions to global advocacy and engagement activities.

Of course, the most appropriate level of overhead for an INGO will vary according to its operating model's context. If an INGO is more focused on merely financing aid and development in developing countries, one would expect its overhead to be lower. Such an INGO may, for example, have overhead more like the GFATM—GFATM's overhead in 2007 was 4 percent of total income or 4.5 percent of grants. By comparison, offices of large INGOs in developed countries are seeking not only to fund aid and development programs in developing countries, they also seek to achieve a range of social change goals in their own countries, contribute to domestic debates about aid policy and practice and support with technical and other nonfinancial resources those entities they fund. This multipronged strategy (see Figure 1.2) is far more complex and expensive than a pure program financing model. The problem that aid and development INGOs have encountered is that they have moved from a lower-cost program financing model to a high-cost model without bringing their donor base along with them. Government and some other donors do not value the broader organizational goals and INGOs have failed to convince other donors that they are more effective by adopting the multipronged approach. This has placed pressure on INGOs to keep overhead low despite their increasingly complex business model.

The result is that many INGOs are far less efficient and effective than they could be. While it is critical that INGOs display good stewardship and do not waste resources, the crude use of administration ratios by both INGOs and donors severely undermines INGOs' ability to invest in the people and processes that are necessary to be more effective (Bradach et al. 2008). As McKinsey consultants, Silverman and Taliento (2005) point out, "Donors should realize that an organization's programs are only as good as its management, and they should be willing to fund an adequate level of administrative overhead." This too will need to change. The largest INGOs in particular have a responsibility to better demonstrate the benefits of capacity building investments to an organization's impact. Similarly, donors must be prepared to fund overhead that provides the organizational capacity necessary for the complex task that INGOs are seeking to perform. INGOs must also stop reinforcing external expectations about overhead— and competing with one another on that basis—and learn to engage with donors in a more honest and sophisticated way than in the past.

Of course, such change is not easy. The fundraising environment is increasingly competitive. Not only are there many more INGOs than in the past, but INGOs face stiff competition from new aid and development actors and other organizations. For example, the (Red) campaign, championed by U2 front man, Bono, seeks to raise "awareness and money for the GFATM through the marketing and sale of (PRODUCT) RED branded products" (www.data.org). Similarly, Google.org and Omidyar Networks, the brainchild of eBay founder, Pierre Omidyar, were formed to invest in both for-profit and not-for-profit organizations that further their social missions (Dees 2008).

In addition, large aid and development INGOs must confront the challenge of developing new funding sources and then transitioning from an existing one to the new one. Organizations such as Plan and World Vision are concerned about their reliance on child sponsorship as the main source of their funding. Child sponsorship has proven to be a largely unparalleled source of long-term, flexible funding for such agencies and therefore well-suited to supporting the time frames necessary to contribute to true transformational development. However, it also generates relatively high administrative burdens and is sometimes implemented in a way that does not support rights-based, empowerment-oriented approaches to development (Pettit and Shutt 2008). Child sponsorship can also be an unsuitable funding source for the most unstable contexts. Nonetheless, finding an alternative, equally reliable source of funding and then transitioning to this new source is an enormous challenge. It is a challenge that will certainly require a much greater preparedness to take risks to develop the next generation of fundraising products.

Conclusion

In most organizations, budget planning normally involves management forecasting forward current activities, taking into account some basic economic data such as inflation and overall economic growth. If changes are made, it is usually based on changing conditions in the broader economy rather than any significant re-allocation of resources in response to more fundamental changes in the organization strategic context. In stable operating contexts, this business-as-usual approach may not place the organization in jeopardy. In comparison, as this Chapter has argued, the challenges facing the largest aid and development INGOs require a much more radical change in their strategy, culture, and operations. However, achieving the extent of change now required of them will not be easy. There are a number of obstacles to change within large INGOs, including a culture that does not merely produce inertia but often significant resistance to genuine change. Nonetheless, if they do not successfully take on the six challenges discussed in this Chapter, it is likely they will grow increasingly ill equipped to be effective actors in the international arena, dangerously out of step with their stakeholders, and ultimately fail to achieve their mission. As one commentator said, "the age of innocence is over for INGOs" and they had better start preparing (Gordenker and Weiss 1995, 555).

Notes

1. Alternatively, Atack (1999, 855) defines legitimacy as the "moral justifications for political and social action."

2. For example, a 2004 survey of press relations in relief situations suggested growing "criticism and skepticism in the press about relief organizations: " Ross (2008). See also Lewis (2007, 10–11).

3. For example, Edwards and Hulme (1995a, 14) argue, "NGOs do not need to be member-controlled to be legitimate but they do have to be accountable for what they do if their claims to legitimacy are to be sustained." Similarly, Brown and Jagadananda (2007) suggest that improving accountability to "appropriate stakeholders can strengthen . . . legitimacy by clarifying the interests they serve and how abuses can be controlled."

4. For example, the New Zealand Strategic Framework for Relations between NZAID and New Zealand INGOs provides inter alia "recognition of and support for the independence of the NGO sector, including its right within law to comment on government policy and work for change in that policy, irrespective of any funding relationship that might exist" (Ellis 2010).

5. For a study of NGO wrongdoing and its organizational implications, see Gibelman and Gelman (2004).

6. Handy (1988) "suggests that third sector organizations are essentially value driven organizations and that this poses distinctive management challenges because people work in these voluntary organizations for a variety of public and private motivations" (see also Lewis 2007, 29).

7. One might expect that the extent to which a large aid and development INGO can be characterized as a professional services organization will depend on the INGOs operating model. For example, it might be argued that organizations like Oxfam that work predominantly through partners and those affiliates of INGO families based in developed countries will most resemble professional service organizations.

8. While such links do exist, particularly with specialist organizations like ODI, Tufts University, and IDS, they need to be more strongly fostered. Further, as Alan Fowler (2000c, 177) says, "links between NGDOs and schools, colleges, and universities are weak or non-existent" and as a result "knowledge about and interest in NGDOs or voluntarism is not being nurtured in young people."

9. For example, a 2007 study found that "World Vision significantly under invests in human resource technology resulting in a multitude of human resource applications and little to no integration: "Achieving World-Class Performance, HR Benchmark Results, Executive Briefing, September 22, 2007, The Hackett Group.

10. Based on the work of Adil Najam, Lewis (2007, 130) describes three stages of the policy process: "agenda setting (the agreement of priorities and issues), policy development (making choices among possible alternatives and options), and policy implementation (undertaking actions to translate policies into practice)." Within this policy process, he then suggests that there are four roles that NGOs can play: service delivery (acting directly to do what needs to be done); advocacy (prodding governments to do the right thing); innovation (suggesting and showing how things can be done differently), and monitoring (trying to ensure that government and business do what they are supposed to be doing).

11. On the other hand, advocacy will be more effective where the INGO has strong links to the political elites of a country (He 2004, 235).

12. For a discussion of the broad nature of the partnership concept and some of the often inappropriate political or economic exigencies

that can lie behind the use of the concept, see Unwin (2005, 11). For a discussion of different forms of collaborative activities between NGOs based on their levels of formality, see Guo and Acar (2005).

13. The conduct of government donors and INGOs in relation to their developing world partners is often criticized in this regard. As Kelly (2007), says, "While the intention may be to characterize the relationship as one of equal partners, the reality is that the money, power and control largely reside with the rich country NGOs." See also Unwin (2005).

14. For a useful categorization of different types of engagement with markets, see Sustainability (2003) and Chapter 3 of Crutchfield and Grant (2008).

15. Oxfam was one of the pioneers of fair trade more than forty years ago and in 1991 co-founded fair trade Cafedirect, the United Kingdom's sixth largest coffee brand (Oxfam 2007). Oxfam GB's activities in this area contributed to Marks and Spencer, a major UK retailer, deciding to exclusively sell fair trade tea and coffee in April 2006. The result was a 6 percent increase in sales (Fry 2007).

16. WVA's campaign is called "Don't Trade Lives," see www.donttradelives .com.au and Case Study 6.1.

17. For example, CARE recently decided to cease monetizing US food aid grants over concerns that they did more harm than good (Dugger 2007).

18. Some INGOs are accessing small amounts of commercial or semicommercial sources of funding. This includes Opportunity International, who recently established a guarantee fund in the Balkans and Vision Fund International, World Vision's microfinance arm that has taken a revolving line of credit from Bank of America for US$25m.

19. The exception was ActionAid, which identified food and hunger as critical issues to campaign on in 2004 (see ActionAid 2007, 4).

20. Some INGOs criticized the impact of neoliberal policies but none had sufficient economic policy depth to provide viable alternatives. Essentially, in the 1980s and early 1990s, all serious development economists could ignore INGOs.

21. A good example of this is the collaboration among a number of INGOs to commission the Tufts University to produce *Ambiguity and Change:* Feinstein International Famine Centre (2004).

22. For example, WVA has formal partnership relationships with both Monash University and Australian National University that comprise, among other things, joint research projects, support for PhD students, shared technical resources, and collaboration on joint applications for federal government funding for relevant issues.

23. The importance of learning was a key theme in the Manchester Conferences of the early 1990s, referred to in the Review of Literature

on INGOs in Chapter 1. See also the literary review undertaken by Pasteur (2004). Organizational learning is defined as "the intentional use of collective and individual learning processes to continuously transform organizational behavior in a direction that is increasingly satisfying to its stakeholders" (Britton 2005, 8). A "learning organization" can be defined as "[An] organization with an ingrained philosophy for anticipating, reacting, and responding to change, complexity, and uncertainty" (Malhotra 1996).

24. The survey was conducted in October 2006 and involved 22 leading INGOs ranging in annual revenues from US$50 million to US$2 billion. NetHope is a nonprofit IT consortium of leading international NGOs. See www.nethope.org.

25. The report found that World Vision's IT cost per end user is US$1,564 compared with an average of US$9,443 for the peer group. Similarly, Oxfam GB spent just over 2,000 pounds per end users considerably lower than the industry average for an organization of Oxfam's size.

26. For an overview of emerging donors' policies and approaches, see Rowlands (2008).

CHAPTER 7

The Governance and Management of INGOs

Introduction

The largest aid and development INGOs are deeply contradictory and ambiguous organizations. They are accountable to donors in developed countries and to the communities in which they work in developing countries. They seek radical social change and often challenge state sovereignty, yet they receive substantial funding from governments and need to partner with them in developing countries for their work to be effective. Their activities are deeply political, but they aim to be nonpartisan or even neutral. To be legitimate, INGOs seek to do both service delivery as well as advocacy, despite the fact that they require different organizational structures, skills, and time frames. To achieve international influence and leverage, they need to be seen as a global organization. Yet the effectiveness of their development work is closely related to their local knowledge and the contextualization of their programming. As a result, the largest aid and development INGOs present vastly different and far more complex governance and management challenges than either for-profit or government organizations. This challenge is compounded by their exponential growth and the rapidly changing international environment.

In this context, therefore, this Chapter will consider four issues: the appropriateness of the global structures adopted by the six largest aid and development INGOs and some governance, management, and strategy issues that are particular to large aid and development INGOs. It will argue that while there is no "one-size-fits-all" solution, the different choices that the largest aid and development INGOs have made do impact their ability to respond to the changing international context. While devolved governance structures such as federations are very useful for encouraging a network culture that is a key element of success in the twenty-first century, sufficient decision-making power must be retained centrally in one form or another to ensure that large INGOs are able to implement organization-wide change in response to the external environment.

KEY POINTS:

- There is no one type of global structure that is most suited to INGOs. More and less decentralized forms both have advantages and disadvantages, depending on the context. There are, therefore, significant benefits in the diversity of approaches adopted by the largest aid and development INGOs.
- All of the largest aid and development INGOs must develop more flexible internal operational structures that enhance information flow, networking, and the ability to effectively respond to the greater number of large-impact, hard-to-predict events. These structures will have shorter life cycles than in the past.
- INGOs must begin to take management seriously and invest in developing highly effective and context-appropriate leaders and managers. They must also be able to overcome internal tensions to allow for the flexible deployment of these leaders and managers.
- Diffuse governance structures and the pace of change in a globalized world require leadership and management approaches that emphasize process, flexibility, and participation rather than command and control.
- While strategic planning remains important for communicating organizational vision and setting goals, a pragmatic, highly flexible approach will need to be adopted in this area. The strategic context is simply too complex for strategic planning to accurately encapsulate and the environment too unpredictable to forecast.
- Large INGOs need to ensure they sufficiently emphasize creativity, immediacy, experimentation, and initiative. Otherwise, they risk their growing size and bureaucracy leading to them prioritizing predictability over improvisation, constraints rather than opportunities and accounting over goal flexibility.

The Organizational Structures of Large INGOs

Each of the six largest aid and development INGOs have adopted different global governance and operating structures. World Vision is a federation comprised of locally incorporated organizations, with most national bodies having the right to send delegates to the Triennial Council, the highest decision-making body in World Vision. The World Vision board comprises 24 members. In 2009, the Board had members from 19 countries—both developed and developing countries with equal male and female representation. It is, therefore, a large, highly internationalized INGO, although members providing a large proportion of total funds— the United States, Canadian, and Australian offices, for example—continue to have significant influence and may, in practice, be perceived as first among equals. The implementation of World Vision–funded activities in a country must be managed by the local national office. Most offices in developing countries are supported by multiple World Vision support offices in rich countries. This usually means each local national office will have a variety of reporting requirements based on the needs of the support office and the sources of funding. The decentralized approach to programming allows for considerable innovation in approach between entities, as well as varying quality in implementation.

The federalist principles upon which World Vision is based seek to provide affiliates with considerable autonomy and authority to make their own decisions to advance the achievement of the global mission, vision, and values in accordance with the federalist principle of subsidiarity. This authority is vested in the national office governing board and local management. ActionAid adopts a similar approach to their local offices. However, control of the World Vision brand, the hiring or firing of national CEOs, commencing activities in new countries, or closing existing country operations are examples of reserve powers—decisions retained by the global center. World Vision has also recently reviewed and expanded the options available to the global center should a local office no longer comply with the criteria of membership. The "nuclear" option of dissociating a noncompliant office has now been complemented by a range of other options, including loss of voting rights at the Triennial Council. All offices are also subject to local and international audits and a peer review every three to five years.

At the time of writing, Plan International has 18 members, plus additional fundraising offices in Switzerland and Hong Kong. The recently reconfigured board consists of up to eleven directors, four of whom are entirely independent members and three of whom are from the South. This reduced board size, made up of volunteers from a broad range of sectors, backgrounds, and skill sets, is elected by the members' assembly and is accountable to it for all the decisions made by the international board. The Plan Members Assembly is the body that provides representation, with delegates appointed on the basis of an affiliate's relative size. Plan undertakes all development programs in developing countries and certain other common activities through Plan International, and most of Plan's country offices are branch offices of this entity. Since all Plan projects are collectively funded, Plan has had to develop a common approach to development across all affiliates. While this has been a difficult process, it has produced a high degree of alignment in development approaches. This can be compared with the far greater disparity of development approaches within Oxfam and even within World Vision. Global resource allocation and a number of finance, information technology, human resources, and global assurance systems are also managed centrally.

The Save the Children Alliance comprises 29 members, mostly based in developed countries. Of late, Save the Children has moved to an operating model where all aid and development activities in a country are managed by only one lead member and expects that by 2020 it will have a unified presence in every country in which it operates. However, Save the Children is now moving from a confederation of independent entities to a more interdependent model. In late 2009, the Save the Children Alliance board recommended that the organization adopt a single international program delivery unit (IPU) similar to Plan's model. The IPU will employ all of Save the Children's 12,000 field-based staff. This will also require Save the Children to develop a common programming framework and global indicators of success. Save the Children is forecasting that this change will result in cost savings of US$10 to 15 million. As part of these changes it is also proposed that a new international board be constituted comprising 14 people—9 appointed based on large members' contribution to revenue (each contribution of 8 percent to global revenue will entitle an office to one board seat), 3 appointed from among the smaller members, and 2 independents.

The number of Oxfam affiliates rose to 14 in December 2008, when Rostros y Voces, the Mexican Oxfam joined the confederation. At the time of writing, Oxfam India was not yet a full member of the Oxfam International Confederation but was proceeding in that direction. The other affiliates are Australia, Belgium, Canada, France, Great Britain, Germany, Hong Kong, Intermon (Spain), Ireland, New Zealand, Novib (Netherlands), Quebec, and the United States. Oxfam generally operates through local partners, although the practice varies slightly between affiliates. Oxfam Novib has a strict policy of only working through partners, while Oxfam GB has a significant number of international staff. Multiple Oxfam offices are often present in the same country. However, in large emergencies—affecting more than two million people—Oxfam GB will take over as lead agency (Webster and Walker 2009). Given the high level of sovereignty retained by Oxfam members, its current model can best be characterized as a confederation.

CARE is an international confederation currently consisting of 12 national members, including CARE Thailand. Each CARE country office presence is the responsibility of one of four lead members—either CARE US, CARE UK, CARE Canada, or CARE Australia—and all operations in that country are managed by the relevant lead member (Webster and Walker 2009, 4). CARE International's board of directors consists of the 12 national directors and a representative from each of the 12 member boards, usually the board chair, and the chairperson of CARE International.[1] This body usually meets twice a year. There is also an executive committee of the board that meets three to four times a year. Finally, the board has a number of working groups, such as a finance working group that considers the secretariat budget prior to it being considered by the board. CARE is aware of the need to boost its legitimacy by increasing representation from developing countries, and in 2010 both CARE India and CARE Peru are expected to become members.[2] Not surprisingly for a confederation, CARE's international secretariat has a relatively limited remit: to manage global governance, to manage CARE's global emergency response team, to oversee staff safety and security, and to undertake advocacy to multilateral and other international organizations and forums.

Médecins Sans Frontières (MSF) has 19 members, all in developed countries. Since MSF's work is focused exclusively on humanitarian emergencies, it does not seek to establish permanent offices in developing countries.[3] MSF's international secretariat performs very limited functions as individual members retain a high level of sovereignty. Nonetheless, MSF has created a number of specialized organizations called "satellites" to take charge of specific activities, such as humanitarian relief supplies, epidemiological and medical research studies, and research on humanitarian and social action. They include MSF-Supply in Belgium, MSF-Logistique, Epicentre, Fondation MSF, Etat d'Urgence Production, MSF Assistance, SCI MSF, SCI Sabin in France, Artze Ohne Grenzem Foundation in Germany, and MSF Enterprises Limited in the United Kingdom.

Table 7.1 Comparative Organizational Data of Large Aid and Development INGOs

	NUMBER OF MEMBERS	NUMBER OF COUNTRY OPERATIONS	STAFF IN SECRETARIAT OR GLOBAL CENTER	GLOBAL ORGANIZATIONAL FORM
World Vision	65	98	Approx. 550	Federation
Plan	18[i]	66	Approx. 200	Federation
SAVE	29[ii]	120	Approx. 30	Confederation
Oxfam	14	100	Approx. 60	Confederation
CARE	12	70	37	Confederation
MSF	19	84	6	Loose Confederation

Source: INGO websites, annual reports, and interviews

[i]The 18 member offices are Australia, Belgium, Canada, Colombia, Denmark, Finland, France, Germany, India, Ireland, Japan, Korea, Netherlands, Norway, Spain, Sweden, United Kingdom, and the United States. In addition, there are fundraising offices in Hong Kong and Switzerland.

[ii]As at December 2009, Save the Children had member offices in Australia, Jordan, Brazil, Korea, Canada, Lithuania, Denmark, Mexico, the Dominican Republic, Netherlands, Fiji, New Zealand, Finland, Norway, Germany, Romania, Guatemala, Honduras, Spain, Swaziland, Sweden, Hong Kong, Switzerland, Iceland, United Kingdom, United States, Italy, India, and Japan.

As this brief review demonstrates, the governance and operating structures of the six largest aid and development INGOs varies from the highly interdependent forms of World Vision and Plan to the more independent approach of MSF. This diversity is well illustrated by the vastly different number of people employed by their respective international secretariats. MSF International has six salaried staff, Save the Children's international secretariat approximately thirty—although this will massively increase as Save the Children adopts an IPU. CARE's international secretariat has 37 employees, Plan International around 200, and World Vision has around 550. Since there are advantages and disadvantages to each of these different governance and operating structures, each INGO must consider how their particular structure impacts their ability to meet the challenges they face in the twenty-first century.

The federal structure adopted by World Vision and Plan should, in theory, be well placed to deal with the constant change and complex interdependencies of our world. According to Charles Handy (1992, 59), federalist structures are useful because they deal with paradoxes of power and control, "the need to make things big by keeping them small, to encourage autonomy but within bounds, to combine variety and shared purpose, individuality and partnership, local and global."[4] Another benefit is that their high level of interdependence means they are more naturally networked than other structures. This is a critical attribute for a twenty-first century organization. In a world where influence is increasingly derived from one's position within a dense global web of connections, the more central one is able to make oneself or one's organization, the greater your power to orchestrate outcomes that serve your ends (Slaughter 2009). The significance of such networking is illustrated, as David Rothkopf (2008) suggests, by its increasing importance as a source of power for the global elite. He argues that, "such linkages are as distinguishing a characteristic of the super-class as wealth or individual position." Large, federated INGOs should be well placed to harness the power of networks.

The extent to which decision-making is centralized also impacts on large INGO's ability to meet the challenges outlined in this book. For example, while there are always a number of factors that are relevant, more centralized global structures should be more effective at activities that benefit from increasing economies of scale. As a result, INGOs with more centralized decision-making should, all things being equal, be more effective at engaging with IGOs such as the UN (Martens 2006). They should also be able to more effectively and efficiently develop global information management systems. This will allow them to leverage the power that accrues to credible international organizations able to collect, analyze, and distribute information. Conversely, the more autonomous

INGO affiliates are, the fewer resources are likely to be available for such purposes. On the other hand, less centralized structures may better facilitate those activities that need to be highly tailored to their context. Public fundraising and, of course, local development are good examples.

However, in practice, federations face a number of limitations, some of which are very significant in the context of INGOs. Federalist structures must be underpinned by people who are well informed, well intentioned, and well educated. This requires strong organizational values, robust information sharing, and a commitment to investment in people development. Without the people base, federalist structures will not succeed. Given the human resource challenges outlined in Chapter 6, this may be why INGOs like World Vision are struggling with federalist structures. Federalist structures also work best in a period of growth. When resources are scarcer and tough decisions are required, the lack of authority at the center can create problems for thinking globally. A federalist structure can also be "exhausting to govern since it relies as much on influence, trust, and empathy as on formal power and explicit controls" (Handy 1992, 60). As the global financial crisis slows INGO revenue growth, at least in the short term, it will be interesting to see the extent to which a shared sense of identity and values among family members allows their federalist structures to effectively respond.

A further critical issue for INGOs that have adopted federal systems is the extent to which they support or hinder significant organization change. Where power is highly decentralized, individual members retain the ability to be more entrepreneurial and innovative. On the other hand, an organization with highly dispersed decision-making and a large number of members runs the very real risk of being unable to obtain agreement to significant organization-wide change. This situation is exacerbated where a strong culture of consensus-based decision-making exists or where some members have an actual or effective veto. The problems of achieving change within the European Union and reform of the United Nations are both examples of these limitations. Such highly decentralized organizations will also be less likely to enjoy some of the advantages of a global organization—economies of scale in procurement and system development, international policy impact, and access to global human resources. As a result, depending on their decision-making model, the prevalent culture, and the powers of persuasion of key leaders, INGOs risk losing their ability to change and adapt as they become more centralized (see Chapter 8). So, the key issue for organizations such as World Vision and Plan is how to enjoy the benefits of a federated model without suffering from its potential for undermining the capacity for organization-wide change.

In comparison, Clark (2003, 110) argues that less centralized, more networked organizational forms are better suited to the twenty-first century.

He compares the multidivisional form (M-Form) of many large INGOs with the network form (N-Form) where organizations "delegate more power to the unit level, develop more fluid matrix ways of working, and view information as their most powerful tool." In Clark's (2003, 110) opinion, "networks have clear advantages of adaptability and problem solving" (see also Anheier 2005, 157). However, in my opinion, they also have significant weaknesses.

Highly decentralized, networked organizations find it hard to manage their brands, extract the benefits of scale, or act in a coordinated way, diminishing their impact when dealing with governments or IGOs. For example, Save the Children believes that it was only through unifying its multiple offices in Myanmar that it was able to recently win a large DFID grant. From an industry perspective, it is therefore advantageous that there is significant diversity in the global structures adopted by the largest aid and development INGOs. While I agree with criticisms by Michael Edwards (2008, 47) that there has been far too little innovation in the form and nature of INGO organizational structures, I do not believe that the solution is a one-size-fits-all approach. There are significant benefits in the large aid and development INGO adopting different approaches to global structure. For example, it may be that one or two of the INGOs can become truly multinational—World Vision is the most advanced in this respect—while others seek to remain "Northern" INGOs dedicated to building local partners, and still others adopt even looser structures, such as Jubilee 2000 or ICBL.

Large INGOs also need to develop more flexible internal operational structures that encourage rather than hinder the exchange of knowledge within the organization. For example, if INGOs are to be prepared for the uncertainty of the Information Age and to truly become learning organizations, their internal organization must be flexible and able to adapt and change according to learning and new information. This will most likely require increased investments in formal networks—organizationally supported groups of self directed people linked by common professional interest—and greater use of matrix management structures. While such matrix structures can require a greater investment in organizational coordination, the return from this investment is high since it tends to encourage "networking, connections, relationships, and the flow of information" (Sorgenfrei and Wrigley 2005, 36). A matrix organizational model provides a way to break down the barriers between specialists in different divisions of an organization and allows employees from different functional backgrounds to combine their skills and abilities to solve a common problem.[5] Organizational structures will also inevitably have shorter life cycles than in the past. Senior leadership should not seek to identify the perfect organizational design but rather be prepared to regularly review organizational structure to ensure that it is most suited to the rapidly changing strategic context. They will also all benefit from promoting global information management and human resource practices. This will maximize the value of field information and policy resources wherever they are located. It will also create an organization that is more attractive to critically needed technical professionals.

Governance Issues

The largest aid and development INGOs are also facing a number of governance challenges. First, given the complexity of their work, many find it difficult to recruit independent and volunteer board members with sufficient experience, knowledge, and time to provide appropriate governance. Unlike in the business world where there is an industry pool of retired senior executives that may be recruited to the board, this type of cross-fertilization is rare among INGOs. The large aid and development INGOs have sought to meet this challenge in different ways. Plan now has a wholly volunteer international board but some executives are concerned that there is a lack of connection and understanding of the business of Plan on the board. There are also concerns that the current structure does not allow for easy executive input from fundraising offices (international executives are the principal source of executive input).[6] While the chair of Plan's national director's team (an executive) is invited to international board meetings, this is not a practice that is formally supported by the organization's constituent documents. On the other hand, CARE has recently reconstituted its international board by combing the previous nonexecutive board with its national director committee to create a new 25-member board composed of executives and nonexecutives. In comparison, only one member of World Vision's international board is an executive, creating an important check and balance on executive activity. However, World Vision's board has responded to this knowledge issue by creating the Partnership Representative Committee (PRC), a body of senior executives from across the World Vision Partnership, which advises the president on matters of policy. While technically an advisory body, the PRC provides a pragmatic way for senior affiliate executives to provide high-level input. Oxfam is currently undertaking a review to determine how it will respond.[7]

Second, there is the challenge of finding ways for individual members and donors to have a voice in the governance of the organization and to balance that voice with the governance demands of a large, global organization. Participation by donors and other stakeholders in the governance of an INGO helps to improve legitimacy, although NGOs do not need to be member-controlled to be legitimate, provided they are accountable for what they do (Edwards and Hulme 1995a, 14). It can also significantly improve the effectiveness of advocacy. Where an organization does have a large member base with rights to elect directors or trustees, balancing the voting rights of members with the need to ensure a board with an appropriate mix of skills and geographical representation can be very difficult. To address this issue, the British Red Cross (2007), for example, has developed a hybrid model. "The board of trustees comprises nine trustees elected from the four UK territories and up to eight trustees co-opted by the board itself."

Another hybrid solution that some northern INGOs adopt is having a selected membership body appoint board members. For example, both Oxfam GB and World Vision Canada appoint trustees or board members in this way. According to Oxfam GB's *2007/8 Accountability Report*, Oxfam GB is governed by 12 volunteer, nonexecutive trustees. These trustees are appointed by the 32 members of the company's association. The 32 members are not only responsible for appointment of trustees but also the approval of the annual report and accounts, and agreeing to any changes to Oxfam GB's constitution. There is a joint trustee–member recruitment advisory group, which makes recommendations for new trustees and association members to the association annually. In comparison, the boards of most World Vision affiliates are self-appointing. They therefore lack a sufficiently incentivized constituency equivalent to shareholders to provide a check and balance on the exercise of board authority. Instead, a process of peer review has been adopted across all World Vision affiliates to review board performance (discussed later).

The third issue is the challenge of developing country representation on an INGO's board. As a federation, World Vision solves this issue by having an approximately equal number of international board members drawn from both northern and southern members. Plan's newly constituted international board must now have three members from developing countries. In comparison, the international boards of CARE, Oxfam, and Save the Children have more limited southern representation. Of course, board representation is only one way in which an INGO can ensure it is accountable to its constituencies, partners, or beneficiaries in the South. And merely being domiciled in a developing country does not ensure that a given board member will empathize with the poor that the organization seeks to serve. Board members from developing countries can often be more closely associated with the powerful elites than the poor. Nonetheless, there does need to be much more reflection by all six of the largest aid and development INGOs on how they can make their organizational structures more inclusive and thereby contribute to better empowerment of civil society in both developed and developing countries. This will not only improve their effectiveness, it will significantly add to their legitimacy at the international level.

Given their diffuse global structures, the fourth governance issue that large INGOs confront is the challenge of achieving global alignment of vision, mission and values. In companies, a global vision, mission, and values are prescribed, and any significant divergence would soon be rectified by the holding company removing local executives or board members. In an organization like the UN, each country is generally expected to pursue its own national interest, and there is only very limited—although arguably increasing—expectations about shared values. INGOs are therefore unique in seeking to both empower local affiliates while maintaining a cohesive global identity. This task is made even more difficult by the amalgamations of quite disparate entities that helped to create many of the largest INGOs. Many of these entities have a unique history, organizational culture, and values, often reflecting national culture and the foreign policy of their respective governments. The various INGO affiliates in a European country often have more common organizational culture than an affiliate of the same INGO in, say, the United States. It is, then, not surprising that it has taken some time to develop strong global values to assist global strategic decision-making. After all, while World Vision internationalized in 1978, Oxfam International was only created in 1995.

There are a number of mechanisms that can help INGOs improve their governance and overcome some of their inherent governance challenges. One mechanism is a stand-alone accountability report such as those produced by Oxfam GB and WVA. While such reports are at present more common in the corporate sector, they are arguably even more important to INGOs. Both reports were produced with reference to the Global Reporting Initiative's G3 Reporting Guidelines (see www.globalreporting .org). The GRI is currently developing an NGO Sector Supplement, which is expected to be finalized in mid-2010 following public consultations. Once this sector specific supplement is available, it is likely to be an important tool for improving NGO transparency. Another useful tool to improve alignment is World Vision's peer review. The peer review process complements finance and operations audits that together provide a basis for appraisal and accreditation of World Vision affiliates. Each World Vision affiliate undertakes a peer review every three to five years. The peer review is conducted by four senior World Vision leaders, one of whom should be an affiliate board member, one a representative from a developed country affiliate, one a representative from a developing country affiliate, and one a member of the Global Centre's Governance Department. Since all World Vision entities are reviewed using the same criteria, it promotes a sense of fairness across the federation.

Management Challenges

In a world characterized by almost instantaneous global communication, the sheer pace of change creates new management challenges for all types of organizations. This situation is well illustrated by the speed at which the 2008 global financial crisis impacted organizations around the world and just how little time senior managers had to position their organizations for a radically different environment (see Case Study 8.1). As a result, the context encountered by modern organizations could not be further removed from the stable operating environment dominated by routine tasks upon which sociologist Max Weber based his famous 1978 essay on bureaucratic management. A top-down management approach "which stresses control, hierarchy, and instrumentality" (Lewis 2007, 103) and that has characterized most bureaucracies is therefore poorly suited to today's organizational context. Instead, modern managers, particularly those operating within the diffuse governance structures common in so many INGOs must adopt enabling management approaches that emphasize process, flexibility, and participation (Lewis 2007, 103). Such an approach is probably better informed by chaos and complexity theory with organizational success derived from "an ability to manage the 'chaotic edge' between disintegration and ossification" (Lewis 2007, 17). Yet too many managers still adopt an approach to management that assumes it is a purely rational science. Rather, successful leadership in modern organizations requires a clever mix of art and science, and managers must be able to exercise both elements to ensure effective decision-making in a rapidly changing environment.

Compounding this difficulty is the distinctive management challenges posed by NGOs that generate significant additional complexity. The underlying source of this added complexity has been discussed by many commentators, with little agreement among them. Some argue they arise from NGOs' value-driven nature (Handy 1988), others point to the lack of a clear bottom line (Drucker 1990), some emphasize the disconnect between the providers of funds and the users of services (Hudson 1995) while still others highlight the inherent complexity of achieving and measuring social goals (Silverman and Taliento 2005). Whatever their source, responding to the management challenges that NGOs face has been made more difficult by the lack of suitable theoretical frameworks and models. Management models based on either companies or government are not necessarily suitable, and it is only relatively recently that a body of work focused on NGO management has emerged. For INGOs, there is also the added difficulty that what literature exists is generally based on Western ideas and models, a real limitation given the extent to which INGOs work cross culturally.

The lack of NGO specific management thinking has been exacerbated by NGOs themselves—they have often failed to take management seriously as a distinct discipline. Lewis (2007, 20) identifies five reasons for this lack of interest by NGOs in management: a culture of action; the pressure from donors to minimize overhead; an ideological aversion to an area seen as belonging to business; a sense that it is an agenda driven by donors and other outsiders; and a lack of awareness of the benefits that improved management can provide. However, as the management challenges faced by large NGOs have grown, this lack of interest in management theory and poor management capacity has seriously undermined organizational effectiveness. This must change. INGOs need to abandon their aversion to management and invest far more in encouraging individuals with aptitude in this area to develop their skills.

For large aid and development INGOs like World Vision, Save, Oxfam, and CARE, it is not merely their diffuse governance structures that create particular management challenges. While Korten (1990) and others may have argued that INGOs follow a common organizational evolution from the provision of relief, through increasing involvement in development activities and advocacy, to finally seeking to engender broader social movement to achieve structural change, the reality is far less linear. As they have evolved and better understood the interrelationships between programming, advocacy, and donor transformation (see Figure 1.1), aid and development INGOs have sought to combine activities with fundamentally different management requirements within the one organization. While simultaneously undertaking aid, development, and advocacy activities has allowed them to maximize income opportunities, meet stakeholder expectations, build powerful global brands, and potentially maximize impact, it has massively complicated their business model.

Effective responses to rapid onset emergencies require INGOs to place greater emphasis on top-down decision-making. The short time frames do not allow for staff capacity gaps to be easily solved from within. Funding sources are highly unpredictable, and the size of the organization must remain highly flexible to cope. Specialist skills such as logistics management are also required. As a result, most of the large aid and development INGOs have developed specific operating models to cope with large-scale emergencies (Webster and Walker 2009). By comparison, long-term development projects rely on high degrees of community empowerment and participation, although managers must balance this with instrumental dimensions of management. As Fowler (1997, 61) argues, management of development activities must be sufficiently consultative for shared ownership while directive enough to be timely. The task of managers in this context is to facilitate community decision-making and capacity building rather than direct it. Funding sources such as child sponsorship are predictable and long-term, facilitating the requisite long-term vision but also allowing for stagnation and reducing pressure for innovation. Advocacy and social mobilization have quite different needs. They must be managed more flexibly, remain highly tactical, must be exceptionally responsive to the political environment, and be very effective at building and leveraging networks. If large aid and development INGOs are to remain conglomerate-like, they must ensure they have managers capable of leading these different functions and the flexibility to shift them between countries as contexts and circumstances change.

World Vision's response to the 2004 Asian tsunami vividly illustrates the impact that combining these different functions within the same organization can have. Prior to the disaster, World Vision's offices in the effected countries were well established, primarily focused on long-term development activities. These offices were largely governed by indigenous boards and enjoyed a high degree of ownership and control by local management and staff. Almost overnight, they were required to shift staff from long term development to emergency response work, controlled by the World Vision Global Centre emergency response team. Large numbers of expatriates were flown in to boost capacity. The level of media scrutiny skyrocketed, requiring far greater communication and public relations skills. The offices were required to manage huge volumes of goods, creating massive logistical challenges. Within months, the total level of funding and staff had increased many times over. There was also an extremely high turnover of management and programming staff.

In this environment, there was significant tension over decision-making authority between office directors, local boards, international leaders, and leaders of the emergency response in country. Despite the scale of the disaster, the local boards and management resented the loss of control. This uncertainty and reduced trust significantly slowed decision-making. The friction also prevented World Vision responding flexibly to the management requirements of the context. For example, World Vision elected to maintain the national leadership in place prior to the disaster rather than replace it with alternative leadership more suited to managing such a humanitarian disaster. The result was that significant time and energy were used managing internal differences. As Webster and Walker (2009) demonstrates, these types of challenges are widespread among the largest aid and development INGOs.[8]

Another significant management challenge for large INGOs is managing global risks. These come in a number of different forms. One of the most important is managing a global brand. In a highly connected world, the conduct of any one member can easily affect the perception of the entire organization, and an adverse media story in one jurisdiction can quickly spread around the world. It is also not always clear whether an issue is merely domestic or whether it might have international implications. This creates tensions around decision rights—who decides policy positions and advocacy campaigns?—quality—how does one ensure minimum levels of quality across large numbers of affiliates?—consistency of brand values—has everyone made the same strategic choices?

The issue becomes even more complex the more involved an INGO becomes in creating a social movement, which by their nature are not amenable to top down control. The decision taken by most of the large aid and development INGOs is to require all affiliates to use the same brand and to specify the conditions under which it is used. By comparison, more informal networks such as Jubilee 2000 allowed national groups to decide whether or not they would use the brand and what that meant. Clark (2003, 113) argues that this allowed a strong network to emerge, and most members welcomed the coordinating role played by Jubilee 2000 UK. However, the lack of global governance and brand control allowed a more radical platform to be adopted by some southern members, which "significantly split the movement, eroding both its legitimacy and dynamism" (Clark 2003, 114).

Another global risk is foreign exchange risk. Plan International addresses this issue by managing foreign exchange risk centrally, and all Plan affiliates are guaranteed an exchange rate at the beginning of each annual planning cycle. In contrast, World Vision has a central treasury function that provides exchange rate guidance but does not yet guarantee a rate—although following the currency fluctuations caused by the 2008 global financial crisis, there was some pooling of currency gains and losses. There is unlikely to be one-size-fits-all approach to manage global risks. However, INGOs do need to become far more intentional about managing these risks and carefully weighing the advantages and disadvantages of more centralized control.

In the section dealing with the human resource challenge faced by INGOs in Chapter 6, the importance of investing in the professional development of staff was highlighted. This must include a real commitment, rather than merely rhetoric, from the large INGOs to develop highly effective leaders suited to the context and types of activities being conducted. It will not be appropriate to simply rely on recruiting managers from the government or corporate sectors. As a study by McKinsey & Company found, ". . . too many well meaning business people move into the leadership roles in nonprofits end up frustrated and ineffective because they don't fully appreciate the challenges" (Silverman and Taliento 2005). Similarly, while management approaches from the private sector may sometimes provide important insights—for example, a number of private sector case studies and research are used to support arguments contained in this book—they do need to be tested critically.

Success in reaching NGO goals is both harder to achieve and harder to measure than in the private sector. In particular, an overreliance on financial management approaches in some INGOs has arguably undermined their effectiveness rather than enhanced it. On the other hand, this does not mean that INGOs should avoid trying to identify suitable alternative measures of success. Too often, the difficulty of measuring progress toward a social goal has been used as an excuse for poor performance. Instead, managers of NGOs need to invest more time and effort in developing an appropriate mix of quantitative and qualitative goals and identifying ways to measure intangible goals.

In addition, INGOs must be prepared to use modern tools to help solve modern management problems. For example, an enabling style of management is being facilitated by a range of new Web 2.0 technologies. They include online forums, blogs, wikis, podcasts, videocasts, and social networks like Facebook and MySpace. These technologies have a strong bottom-up element, ideal for the values-driven environment in INGOs, allowing staff to collaborate more effectively and managers to easily engage a broad base of staff. In fact, they require a high degree of participation to be effective. Given the resource poor environment of INGOs and the reluctance of donors to support overhead, such technologies have the added benefit of not being technically complex to implement. Rather, "they are a relatively lightweight overlay to the existing infrastructure and do not necessarily require complex technology integration" (Chiu et al. 2009, 2). On the other hand, they are "inherently disruptive and often challenge an organization and its culture" (Chiu et al. 2009, 2). Managers, therefore, need to be prepared to lead in different ways, through informal channels, and by modeling the potential of this new technology. However, effectively deployed, these technologies will drive the next wave of improvements in organizational productivity and permit large, global organizations to be far more nimble than ever before.

Strategy Development in INGOs

Periods of enormous change provide extraordinary opportunities. For example, the recessions of the 1870s allowed Rockefeller and Carnegie to build dominant positions in the emerging oil and steel industries by taking advantage of the emerging technologies and weak competitors (Bryan and Farrell 2008). However, periods of immense change also create far more pressure for insightful strategic thinking. In the past, a range of factors has led the largest aid and development INGOs to largely avoid rigorous strategic thinking. One such factor is that their strong financial growth over the past ten years has crowded out strategic thinking as operational demands have been allowed to take precedence. Another reason for the lack of strategic thinking is that most managers in the largest INGO invest too little time in developing external networks. The internal complexity of INGOs means that the number of operational networks that a manager needs to succeed are quite large. Since operational networks are usually geared to meeting operational objectives, they do not help these managers solve strategic questions like external networks do (Ibarra and Hunter 2007).[9] This situation is compounded by a low capacity for strategic thinking and networking skills among existing managers and by the low senior management turnover.

The diffuse global governance structures and still relatively limited internal coordination among affiliates has also made collective global strategic thinking more difficult, although this has recently began to change. While the usual implications of such a perilous course have so far been avoided by the largest INGOs, as continued growth has provided the appearance of organizational health, it has nonetheless led to increasing organizational tensions as resource allocation becomes increasingly out of step with organizational needs. This deficiency has begun to be addressed by the largest aid and development INGOs. World Vision has had two major global strategic planning exercises since 2003 (see Case Study 8.3) and has begun to develop a framework for a global strategy. There are also now four emerging regional strategies that must be followed by the relevant national and funding offices. Similarly, Save the Children is currently preparing for the second five-year phase of its global strategy, which began in 2005. In 2007, Oxfam International's new five-year strategic plan commenced. However, despite these efforts they may still prove insufficient to meet the demands of the changing and unpredictable strategic context.

Traditional strategic planning may not be the most appropriate process for INGOs in the current rapidly changing strategic environment. In fact, there is considerable debate about the suitability of strategic planning at all in rapidly changing strategic environments, since it is "too reliant on pre-determined outcomes, a 'knowable' environment, and a predictable future" (Sorgenfrei and Wrigley 2005).[10] In addition, many strategic planning tools and processes are unsuited to highly unstable contexts. While they may provide "deep insight into untapped strategic opportunities in relatively stable markets, they rarely generate deep foresight into the opportunities that may arise in rapidly changing ones" (Courtney 2001, 42). As a result, some commentators argue that an "entrepreneurial attitude and the mastering of key capabilities will provide the necessary agility and flexibility to succeed in dynamic and complex environments" (Wirtz et al. 2007). One of the key capabilities for such an approach is adaptation. According to Sorgenfrei and Wrigley (2005, 9–10), "adaptation is a process of adjusting to new conditions to become better suited to the context or environment" and adaptive capacity is the "capacity to strategically adjust thinking and actions in response to changing circumstances based on relevant knowledge and improved understanding." On the other hand, Michael Porter (2001) argues that companies who fail in rapidly changing environments have simply not embarked on a coherent long-term strategy. The truth undoubtedly lies somewhere between these two extremes.

Strategic Planning remains important, as much for the benefits that come from the process as the end product. Leaders still need a basis for communicating organizational vision, and managers need goals at which to aim. However, a pragmatic, highly flexible approach to strategic planning needs to be adopted. The strategic context is simply too complex for strategic planning to accurately encapsulate and the environment too unpredictable to forecast (Wirtz et al. 2007, 297). Large INGOs in particular need to ensure they sufficiently emphasize creativity, immediacy, experimentation, and initiative and keep a watch for their growing size and bureaucracy, emphasizing the importance of predictability over improvisation, constraints rather than opportunities, and accounting over goal flexibility (Anheier 2000). They also need to be aware that, regardless of how well something may be developed on paper, if resources do not follow, it is meaningless. It is ultimately the realized strategy, not the intended strategy, that is important.

Finally, the largest aid and development INGOs need to improve the coordination among affiliates and have more robust internal conversations about the strategic choices that they wish to make as global organizations. While this is no doubt part of their natural maturing process, it has been impeded at times by unhealthy internal conflict management practices. While the largest aid and development INGOs may have once been able to operate despite their internal differences, the same communication technologies that have assisted their growth combined with the increased expectation of the media, governments, and IGOs means that such differences are now much more visible. As emphasized above, whether they realize it or not, their brands are now global. An action or the position taken by one affiliate will be considered to be the action or position of the global organization. Information on any website can be accessed globally, and local media can be easily sourced anywhere. This requires not only much tighter global brand and communication management but also that genuine strategic differences are identified early and resolved internally before they impact the global organization externally.

Some positive steps to improve global coordination within INGOs can be identified. The most advanced is the coordination that takes place in relation to humanitarian disasters (see Webster and Walker 2009). Many of the largest INGOs have also developed a global advocacy campaign, and they are beginning to share resources across affiliates in a way that more effectively leverages their global expertise. For example, World Vision has recently approved a new global way of sharing technical resources across affiliates based on a capability assessment of individual constituent offices called the Federated Network or Fednet (see Case Study 7.1). While these initiatives are still largely nascent and face significant organizational barriers, they do hold out the hope of large INGOs becoming much more networked organizations and therefore far more suitable to operating in the twenty-first century.

Case Study 7.1: Sharing Technical Resources

If aid and development INGOs are going to respond in a cost-effective manner to the demand for improved program quality and more sophisticated policy engagement with governments and other actors, they will need to become much better at sharing technical resources, not only between INGOs but also among affiliates of the same INGO.

At present, there are significant differences in technical resources among different affiliates of the same aid and development INGOs. For example, at Oxfam, Oxfam GB has a much greater technical capacity that the other Oxfam affiliates. This can result in programs receiving significantly different levels of technical input depending on the funding office.

This is certainly the case at World Vision where, to date, technical assistance for programs has been primarily resourced and allocated within bilateral relationships. It has been argued that this has resulted in duplication of capacity, inequitable, inefficient, and ad hoc allocation, as well as underutilization of capacity.

To address this weakness, World Vision is testing a new way to share technical resources through a Global Technical Resources Network (GTRN). The model is expected to be fully deployed in 2011. The GTRN is part of FedNet—an initiative designed to improve program quality, provide mechanisms for improved use and management of technical experts, and knowledge and assist World Vision operate in a more multilateral, networked way. A key part of the FedNet Framework is a capability assessment of every World Vision affiliate, irrespective of type. The capability assessment is used to identify capacity-building needs and priorities for each affiliate to inform a capacity building plans, as part of the overall World Vision Partnership Planning Cycle (PPC).

The GTRN is administered through a database populated with Subject Matter Experts (SMEs) who meet specified World Vision standards. In FY2010, this will include only World Vision staff, but in the future, all technical resources including external consultants will be provided through the GTRN.

Technical resources will be allocated by a "managed market" mechanism that will be demand rather than supply driven. The cost of these technical resources will be allocated to project costs or to the relevant affiliate office costs.

Conclusion: Strategic Intent Always Exceeds Strategic Capacity

On the foot of all of the PowerPoint slides prepared during the strategic planning part of the "Our Future" process (see Case Study 8.3) was the claim that, for all humanitarian organizations, "their strategic intent always exceeds their strategic capacity." I am not sure the source of this insight but, in my view, it lies at the heart of some of the governance, management, and strategy challenges of INGOs. Despite the enormous growth that INGOs have enjoyed over the past ten years, they are still small compared to the magnitude of what they are seeking to achieve. They must therefore find ways to make strategic choices that maximize the impact of their relatively small resources. This requires governance and management systems that balance flexibility and agility with the strength that can come from a shared global mission and strategy.

To effectively respond to the governance and management challenge of the twenty-first century will also require far more reflection on the skills and attributes of the people who sit at the very top of the largest aid and development INGOs. More than anything else, they need to be ambassadors to the outside world, media savvy politician types who are able to motivate a global organization around its common purpose and lead change. Board members and trustees need to understand that such people seldom have the time—or often the skills—to also be good managers. They therefore need to ensure that such organizational leaders are effectively supported by others who can ensure that organizational strategy and human resource issues are being managed effectively. Policy and media expectations also require that there are externally-focused, sector-expert ambassadors in critical areas who can engage with governments, corporations, faith groups, and the media in their area of expertise. Most of all, this governance and management challenge requires an organization that is able to change. This is the subject of the final substantive chapter of this book.

Notes

1. This new structure was established in November 2008 and replaced the previous general assembly, international board, and national directors committee.

2. Interview with Robert Glassner, Secretary General, CARE International, March 31, 2009.

3. MSF will close a program when the humanitarian emergencies ceases, local actors, or national authorities have sufficient capacity themselves, or when their activities can be replaced by longer-term solutions

(MSF 2007, 13). Of course, this means some MSF programs can, in practice, result in a long term presence in countries.

4. Charles Handy's work on federalist structures formed the basis for World Vision's global governance structure.

5. For a critique of matrix structures and a more radical solution to the challenge of increasing internal collaboration and information sharing, see Bryan and Joyce (2005). They argue for a simplified line management structure and to promote collaboration, "organizational overlays in the form of markets and, networks that help professionals work horizontally" (Bryan and Joyce 2005, 30). However, it is not clear to me that the challenges that their proposals create are necessarily easier to overcome that the management challenges created by matrix structures. Ultimately, the goal is to develop structures that support rather than hinder the exchange of knowledge within an organization. The most effective way to achieve this may vary between organizations.

6. Interview with Ian Wishart, Plan International Australia, February 4, 2009.

7. Interview with Judy Mitchell, Oxfam Australia, January 22, 2009.

8. See also McPeak (2001) who discusses attempts at Plan International to build organizational unity of purpose and reduce conflict between different parts of the organization.

9. According to Ibarra and Hunter (2007, 5), the "key to a good strategic network is leverage: the ability to marshal information, support, and resources from one sector of a network to achieve results in another."

10. Strategic planning was originally developed for military purposes. It deals with "the overall identity, direction, goals, and objectives of an organization" (Sorgenfrei and Wrigley 2005, 8).

CHAPTER 8

The Change Imperative: Can Large INGOs Adapt to a Rapidly Changing International Environment?

Introduction

While the legacy of former US Secretary of Defense, Donald Rumsfeld, is rightly debatable, he did understand that one of the consequences of our increasingly interconnected and complex world is a growing number of large-impact, hard-to-predict events. The "new strategic landscape" was one of "manifest uncertainty, of fundamental and catastrophic surprise" (Kaplan 2008). Rumsfeld believed that the United States would need to be prepared for more "unknown unknowns," events like the fall of the Berlin Wall in 1989, the terrorist attack on September 11, 2001, and the Asian Tsunami of Boxing Day 2004.[1] His assessment is echoed by the US National Intelligence Council that argues that "the rapidly changing international order at a time of growing geopolitical challenges increases the likelihood of discontinuities, shocks, and surprises" (National Intelligence Council 2008, 3).

For INGOs, not only is the global political environment uncertain and unpredictable, their industry is in the midst of a period of rapid transformation, they face new development challenges like climate change, peak oil, and urbanization, and they must contend with significant shifts in public and government expectations. In addition, large INGOs can also expect new technologies to create significant disruptions. Since many new technologies such as the mobile phone and Internet are network technologies, that is, the benefits that flow from them increase as more people use them, we can also expect that these disruptions could be very significant (Sachs 2008, 205–6). As a result, large INGOs will need to be experts at responding to change and adapting to the unpredictable in the twenty-first century.

However, a survey of recent organizational change in large aid and development INGOs suggests that it will be a significant challenge for them to undertake the degree of change that is required by their new

┌─⎛ **KEY POINTS:** ⎞─────────────────────────────────┐

The greatest challenge facing large aid and development INGOs is to change and adapt faster than their strategic context.

Achieving significant organizational change in any type of large organization is difficult, and most attempts usually fail. However, large aid and development INGOs face a number of additional, interrelated challenges.

Nonetheless, significant organizational change in INGOs is possible. The most critical factors for achieving success are

1. A compelling motivation for change that creates a high degree of shared worldview and a mutual commitment to change across the organization and its stakeholders;
2. The presence of internal change agents who are able to present their change objectives in a manner that is compatible with the organization's current culture and thereby leverage it to achieve change;
3. A compensation and reward structure that reinforces the desired behaviors;
4. Accurate data that supports the case for change and institutionalized analytical capability;
5. Genuinely committed leadership who continually reinforce the vision and the rationale for change; and
6. High-quality human resources.

└──┘

strategic context. This Chapter will use three categorizations of organizational change to analyze large INGOs' capacity to respond and adapt to their new strategic context. These three types of organizational change are strategic adjustments, strategic reorientation, and transformational organizational change. This Chapter will argue that, while there are examples of the first two types of organizational change, examples of transformational organizational change are becoming increasingly rare. Despite perceptions that INGOs are more innovative and less constrained by orthodox thinking or inflexible bureaucratic structures than some other international organizations, there is little evidence to support this. In fact, at a time when transformational organizational change is most required, it appears that large INGOs' capacity for such change is very low. This Chapter will consider the reasons why it appears so hard to achieve organizational change in large INGOs and conclude by proposing some recommendations for beginning to address this situation.

Organizational Change in Large INGOs

The constant pressure to respond to humanitarian crisis, meet urgent funding gaps, and deal with innumerable operational problems often leave staff of aid and development INGOs feeling that they are in a constant state of change. However, most of the change that occurs within large INGOs can best be described as strategic adjustments, the day-to-day tactical changes to an organization's activities that assist them to more effectively achieve the organization's strategic goals. Such change is very important for making incremental improvements to development and relief programs, advocacy campaigns, or operating systems and processes. Over time, such strategic adjustments can lead to INGOs making significant progress. For example, over recent decades, large aid and development INGOs have made enormous improvements in how they respond to humanitarian crises, particularly rapid-onset natural disasters such as hurricanes and earthquakes (see Webster and Walker 2009). Similarly, all of the largest aid and development INGOs are now undertaking more advocacy in a more professional way than in the past, and, as outlined in Chapter 5, all of the largest INGOs have taken a range of actions to improve their accountability. Many have also improved their global governance. However, such strategic adjustments, although very important, are unlikely to be sufficient to meet the demands of a radically changed strategic context.

Most large INGOs also undertake regular strategic reviews and identify new strategic goals for a future period of time, normally between three and five years. This type of process can be described as strategic reorientation (Lawler and Worley 2006, 9–10). While entailing a greater degree of change than strategic adjustments, a new strategic plan still normally builds off the base of the previous one increasing revenue or beneficiary targets, identifying new advocacy campaigns, or opening new field or fundraising offices. As such, it is rare that strategic reorientations lead to revolutionary change. Still, this process can lead to significant improvements in performance and impact. For example, this process has contributed to much of the growth in the size and influence of the largest aid and development INGOs over recent decades. It has also meant that large INGOs have contributed to the reform of international institutions like the World Bank, encouraged widespread debt relief for developing countries, positively impacted the conduct of war, and promoted human rights. Of perhaps even more significance is the way that large aid and development INGOs have helped change the development discourse on participation and successfully promoted the role of civil society and civic-driven development.

Far more rare is the type of radical organizational change that can be described as "transformational." An example of successful transformational organizational change is the 1976 decision by the four original founders of World Vision—the United States, Canada, Australia, and New Zealand—to relinquish significant power to an international secretariat, World Vision International, and create a global federalist structure. This was a revolutionary decision, one that has contributed to World Vision becoming the largest of the world's aid and development INGOs. As outlined in Chapter 7, since then, other INGOs have also undertaken an internationalization process of one type or another.

However, as significant as this change was for large aid and development INGOs, it has arguably not been as far-reaching and transformational as required by the vastly changed strategic context. Interviews with senior managers of many of the largest aid and development INGOs suggest that, for the most part, the internationalization that they have undertaken remains shallow, thereby severely limiting the potential benefits that may have otherwise flowed from this process. Edwards (2008, 47) goes even further, arguing that INGOs have failed to innovate "in any significant sense in the form and nature of their organizational relationships." While many of them have undertaken organization-wide international advocacy campaigns, technical resource sharing is still limited. There are no examples of effective global human resource management, and even World Vision still struggles to agree and implement organization-wide information technology platforms.

In addition, progress in other areas is far less than what might reasonably be expected given the dramatic changes in their strategic context. The largest aid and development INGOs struggle to respond to complex political or socio-economic emergencies. For example, they responded slowly to the global food crisis and found it difficult to employ alternative operating models after Cyclone Nagris devastated Myanmar. They have also, as Edwards argues, not been very innovative in finding ways to change the systems and structures that perpetuate poverty (Edwards 2008, 46). They have been very slow to respond to the increasing demands for improved effectiveness, and they are stuck with respect to becoming learning organizations.

This failure is seldom due to ignorance of the need for change but rather difficulty in successful execution of transformational organizational change. For example of the two significant global change processes undertaken by World Vision in the last ten years, very little real change resulted from the Big Goals process, and only marginal improvements have been achieved so far by the more comprehensive Our Future process (see Case Study 8.3). Such relatively unsuccessful reform can be compared with the quite radical changes World Vision has made in the past—the decision to internationalize in the 1970s, the adoption of new marketing techniques in the early 1980s, and a significant change to its development model at the beginning of the 1990s. Even the organization change undertaken by ActionAid, one large aid and development INGO that has been recognized for its organizational change in the past few years, while ambitious, is still yet to be cemented and may be insufficient to meet the demands of their changed strategic context.[2]

Perhaps one of the best examples of the difficulty for large INGOs of achieving transformational organizational change is in the way agencies such as Plan and World Vision conduct child sponsorship. (Save the Children's US affiliate and some ActionAid affiliates also offer child sponsorship). Both Plan and World Vision use child sponsorship to raise funds for broad-based development in specific geographic areas. The main advantage of child sponsorship is that it creates a strong link between an individual child and donor, resulting in a long-term, stable form of funding that is essential for development to be successful. In the case of Plan, child sponsorship constitutes 72 percent of global revenue; and in the case of World Vision, it accounts for around 60 percent. However, despite its benefits, there has also been considerable public debate about the potential weaknesses and shortcomings of child sponsorship. For example, it is sometimes criticized as paternalistic, perpetuating harmful stereotypes about poverty, and promoting dependence rather than empowerment.

Notwithstanding that these debates and shortcomings are well known to staff and that various policies have been adopted over many years by both agencies to address them, both have struggled to implement the organizational changes necessary to adequately address child sponsorships shortcomings. For example, in 2002, Plan launched its child-centered community development (CCCD) model to bring children to the center of its development process and address the shortcomings in their approach to child sponsorship. However, despite the conducive environment for introducing such changes created by Plan's centralized funding of all development projects, a recent detailed study of Plan's child sponsorship practices found that it still had a significant way to go in successfully implementing this transformational change (Pettit and Shutt 2008). Similarly, despite significant progress since the 1980s in improving World Vision's child sponsorship model, there is no reason to believe that if World Vision commissioned such a report, its findings would be radically different from the Plan report.

In some situations where significant organizational change has been attempted, it is begun too late or executed too slowly. An example is World Vision's re-organization of its microfinance activities. World Vision first became involved in microfinance in the 1970s. Since then, its activities have grown so that it is now one of the largest providers of micro-finance in the world. Micro-finance requires specialist skills and systems and benefits from economies of scale. However, despite the size of its activities, World Vision did not decide to create a specialist vehicle for its microfinance investments until 2003 (see www.visionfundinternational.org). Moreover, even when this decision was made, its progress in corralling its disparate microfinance activities has been executed too slowly. By 2009, only 4 of more than 47 microfinance institutions have been formally transferred to Vision

Fund. In the meantime, the microfinance sector has significantly matured and made revolutionary advances in the application of technologies, such as the use of mobile phones to facilitate financial transactions—led by M-PESA in Kenya, which, with more than seven million clients, has become the most widely adopted mobile money scheme in the world. As a result, like Yahoo's slow response to the threat that Google posed to its business (see Case Study 8.2), World Vision may have largely missed the market opportunity that its size, scale, and global reach could have provided. Over the next few years, commercial microfinance providers are likely to outcompete INGOs in lending to all but the poorest of the poor.

Even where a significant new direction has been successfully implemented, analysis suggests it did not reflect a systemic ability for organizational change. For example, Oxfam GB admits that one of its most significant recent changes, the decision to campaign strongly on climate change, was the result of dogged leadership by an internal advocate rather than systemic organizational capacity for change.

The inability of large aid and development INGOs to achieve transformational organizational change as they have grown has significant implications for their effectiveness and leaves them open to questions about their legitimacy and ongoing role in the contemporary world, let alone their fitness to continue to perform their role into the twenty-first century.

Facing up to the Change Imperative

Radical change is difficult for any organization. As Lawler and Worley (2006, xv) state in *Built to Change*, "most change efforts in established organizations fail to meet expectations because the internal barriers to change are so strong." They conclude, pessimistically, that most attempts at revolutionary organizational change are doomed to failure from the start. Similarly, in 2008, a McKinsey survey of 3,199 executives around the world found that only one transformation in three succeeds (Aiken and Keller 2009). This suggests that there has not been any real improvement in implementing organizational change since John Kotter's 1996 seminal work, *Leading Change*. Like the more recent McKinsey survey, Kotter's research revealed that only 30 percent of change programs succeed. However, as difficult as organizational change has been historically, globalization may well be making the situation even worse. As modern communication technology and transport has led to a dramatic increase in the speed at which information and ideas spread across the globe, the time that organizations now have to determine how they will adapt to a changing environment and implement that change has shrunk dramatically. Thus, globalization's compression of time and space has made organizational change even more difficult.

The reduced time that organizations have to respond to massive disruptive change is well illustrated by the 2008 global economic crisis. It took centuries for information about the smelting of ore to cross a single continent and bring about the Iron Age. In the age of sailing ships, it took years for knowledge to be shared. In comparison, each information update on the global financial crisis swept across the globe in seconds, and within less than three months from the collapse of the investment firm, Lehman Brothers, on September 14, 2008, the "contagion" had spread across Europe and Asia, resulting in the economy of one country after another falling into recession (see Case Study 8.1). While one needs to be careful making comparisons, in contrast the speed at which the Asian Economic Crisis spread just ten years earlier appears relatively leisurely—it took more than 12 months to eventually engulf Russia and Brazil and to lead to the collapse of the US hedge fund, Long-Term Capital Management.[3]

In addition to the inherent difficulty of radical organizational change, large aid and development INGOs face a number of additional, interrelated,

---

Case Study 8.1: Spread of the 2008 Global Financial Crisis

The collapse of the investment firm, Lehman Brothers on September 14, 2008, can be viewed as the beginning of the global financial crisis. On the same day, Merrill Lynch was sold to the Bank of America.

Within two days, the Federal Reserve had agreed to lend up to US$85 billion to American insurer AIG. On September 18, British bank Lloyds TSB had agreed to purchase rival bank HBOS. By September 20, the Bush administration was requesting US$700 billion from Congress to bail out firms drowning in bad debt. By September 21, the investment bank operating model had effectively been killed as both Goldman Sachs and Morgan Stanley had been granted approval to become bank holding companies. On September 26, the US government closed Washington Mutual and sold its assets. On September 29, European governments were scrambling to shore up financial institutions across the continent.

By October 7, Iceland was seeking a US$4 billion loan from Russia to shore up its currency. On October 10, Japan's stock market recorded its biggest one-day fall since 1987. On October 29, Hungary received a US$25.1 billion loan from the IMF. On November 9, China announced a US$600 billion stimulus package. By November 14, Europe was officially in recession and the United States recorded the largest ever fall in retail sales. Within a few days, Japan announced its economy had also slid into recession.

By the beginning of December, firms across the United States reacted to the crisis that had begun less than three months earlier in the financial sector by reducing employment in just one month by 533,000 as they sought to adapt to the new economic environment.

limitations. First, there has been considerable pressure from a number of both internal and external sources for alignment and conformity, which arguably have inhibited aid and development INGOs' ability to change and adapt. Pressure from donors, especially governments, to be more accountable and to harmonize programming with other development actors has encouraged aid and development INGOs to seek alignment, stability, and equilibrium to improve management control and coordination. The internationalization process that the largest INGOs have undertaken has also reinforced this trend.

As discussed in the previous Chapter, large INGOs have paid insufficient attention to how their global structures impact their ability to change and adapt, especially over time. As they have undertaken the internationalization process, global strategies and internal processes have undermined their ability to change. Unfortunately, it appears that the internationalization process has been too shallow to generate many of the potential benefits but sufficient to further reduce the ability of large aid and development INGOs to change and adapt. For the most part they retain complex and diffuse power structures that make organization-wide change very hard to achieve, as evidenced by the sad history of reform at the UN. This diffuse structure also creates a large number of stakeholders. As Silverman and Taliento (2005) argue the CEO of an INGO needs to "consult with his board, staff (and not just the senior team), important funders, and possible partners before making big changes in how the organization operates." The number of stakeholders inevitably results in slower decision-making.

Second, the large INGOs have developed an organizational culture that is not supportive of change and adaptation. As Nielson et al. (2006, 109–110) argue, consistent with constructivist theory, organizational culture of itself "inhibits the reform that necessitates the fundamental disruption of staff members' 'mental models.'" As new employees begin to learn the characteristics of an organization's culture, their strategies and choices become constrained, at first strategically and then, over time, habitually by those characteristics. However, in large INGOs, the inherent change inertia created by organizational culture is increased by a range of specific cultural factors that further inhibit organizational change. These include concerns over professionalization and corporatization, a strong bias for internal appointments in senior human resource recruitment—which has meant they have not accessed the external skills they need to help improve organizational practice or adopt new practices, unhealthy conflict management approaches—a tendency to be passive-aggressive and suppress conflict in favor of superficial agreement, for example; and a lack of institutional rewards for innovative thinking or planning beyond immediate problems.

In addition, as they have become subcontractors of government and grown, they have developed large bureaucratic organizations. As Nielson et al. (2006, 113) further argue, a bureaucratic culture, "once entrenched, can be highly stable and robust." As outlined in Chapter 3, INGOs have enjoyed exponential growth in revenue and influence, and this financial growth has been used as a key measure of executive success. This ongoing growth has not only provided the appearance of healthy organizations, it may have contributed to the dilemma of change. Since rapid growth can lead to managers feeling like they are losing control of the organization, they respond by putting in place control and accountability systems that further reduce flexibility and strangle innovation (Walker 2008b). On the other hand, the usual barriers to organizational change—concerns over loss of control, apprehension of the new, uncertainty, inconvenience, threats to the individual's status, and competency anxieties—all remain strong in INGOs.[4]

The result is an organizational culture that not only provides inertia to change but sometimes appears to strongly resist it. A conducive organizational culture is the key to organizational change, yet the culture of large INGOs has become increasingly unsupportive of such change, and changing a large INGO's existing culture can be very difficult indeed.

Third, their failure to become learning organizations has further reduced their ability to change, since learning is a key attribute that allows organizations to adapt to an uncertain future or, as Senge (1990, 13) says, "through learning we re-perceive the world and our relationship to it." INGOs' failure to invest in information technology also means that they have not developed the processes and systems that may help to offset the drag of an increasingly bureaucratic culture.

Making the situation worse, INGOs have generally lacked a sufficiently compelling motivation to overcome the internal barriers to change. While for-profit organizations have the discipline of markets and democratic governments the ballot box, due to the limited ability of donors to assess underlying performance, beneficiaries having little effective choice, and poor downward accountability, the largest INGOs do not face any similar external accountability mechanism. Anheier (2000, 13) argues that management of INGOs needs to be far more pro-active than in corporations because "performance signals from markets and electorates are incomplete, if not totally missing." The result is that despite widespread understanding about many of the problems facing INGOs, they continue to recur. For example, the Tsunami Evaluation Coalition's evaluation of the first two years of the Tsunami response concluded that, despite the quality measures that the sector has developed over recent years, the "lack of quality enforcement mechanisms means that the same problems keep reappearing in emergency responses" (Cosgrove 2007).

While they identified the potential for donor feedback to play a role as an external enforcement mechanism, since public knowledge is often limited and media coverage lacks detailed analysis, they were not seen as sufficient. The Tsunami Evaluation Coalition therefore recommended a "regulatory system . . . to oblige agencies to put the affected population at the center of measures of agency effectiveness and to provide detailed and accurate information to the donor public and taxpayers on the outcomes of assistance, including the affected populations' views of that assistance" (Cosgrove 2007). The recent investigation of Plan's child sponsorship practices mentioned here suggests that this problem is more widespread than just agencies' emergency responses. For example, the report suggested that "few if any of the critical findings reported here are new to Plan staff" (Pettit and Shutt 2008, 3).

Even INGOs' physical environment tends to conspire against change. INGOs often house themselves in pokey, poorly laid out buildings. While this may superficially appear to be good stewardship, INGOs need to take an evidence-based approach to the issue. For example, Becker (2007) argues that "in organizations faced with substantial change, high degrees of uncertainty and a need for agility, innovation, and rapid problem-solving, it is critical that the physical environment is one that facilitates multidisciplinary collaboration and speedy, free-flowing information sharing." He identifies five aspects that are important: the amount of variation in work settings; the spatial transparency—can they see one another? the degree of functional inconvenience—does the space promote chance encounters? the human scale of spaces; and the number of neutral zones.

In some ways, the leaders of large INGOs have successfully created organizations built to last rather than organizations built to change. Even if this was once an acceptable outcome, in the rapidly changing and chaotic environment that they now face, it is certainly not sufficient for facing the future. Accordingly, the next section will focus on ways that leaders of large INGOs can achieve radical organizational change.

Achieving Transformational Organizational Change

While change is difficult in any large organization and particularly hard in large INGOs, it is still possible. However, it will require that large INGOs not only face up to the critical need for radical organizational change but seek to learn from the experience of radical change in other organizations. Case studies from business, government, and nongovernment organizations point to a number of factors that are preconditions for any successful organizational change in large organizations and therefore provide very useful guidance for the largest INGOs.

First, the lack of a sufficiently compelling motivation for change must be overcome. While a plunging stock price or loss of market share often provides the motivation in for-profit organizations and the bureaucrats of democratic governments have the pressure of implementing the new policies of each incoming government, such external motivations are largely absent when it comes to INGOs. As a result, it must come from other sources. In the case of recent reform of the World Bank (see Case Study 3.1), the significant and sustained public criticism that the Bank received from former staff such as Joseph Stiglitz, advocacy networks such as *Jubilee* and *50 Years is Enough*, and the media combined to create a strong motivation for change—although there are mixed views on the overall success of the World Bank's recent reform (see Nielson et al. 2006). In large INGOs, it is possible that the loss of significant donor funding, the resignation of large numbers of staff, sustained operational stress, or an organization-wide recognition of a dramatically changed external environment may individually or collectively contribute to strong motivators for change. However, given large INGOs' demonstrated resistance to change, these factors are probably unlikely to be sufficient by themselves. Most of the leaders of the largest INGOs are, like the CEO of Yahoo (see Case Study 8.2), well aware of the threat posed by the changed strategic context, experience the pressure for improved performance from major donors, and are struggling to recruit the necessary talent. As Michael Edwards argues the "constant strategic reviews that you see now among international NGOs are a sign that they recognize the necessity of change, but most lack the intellectual clarity and courage to see what needs to be done and to do it" (Lewis 1998). In this context, the board of Plan are to be commended for their decision not only to commission a detailed review of their child sponsorship practices but to commit, ahead of time, to making it available on their website whatever the outcome (see Pettit and Shutt 2008). Commissioning such an independent report has the potential to create a broad and compelling case for transformational organizational change, and its publication contributes to creating an external compliance mechanism that will help to maintain reform momentum as the inevitable organizational barriers to change exert themselves.

Failing such an internally generated compelling case for change, one can envisage a situation where a difficult worldwide economic environment such as that generated by the global economic crisis combined with significant adverse media finally creates sufficient motivation for the necessary organizational change. While such a situation would be unfortunate and create additional transitional pain, it is preferable to the alternative of irrelevance. However, even where strong, multiple bases of motivation are present, it will not, by itself, be sufficient to enable significant organizational change.

Change managers also need to ensure that the motivation for change must be shared not only among an organization's senior management but also with employees, board members, and external stakeholders. In fact, some organizational change specialists argue that external stakeholders are the most critical audience to convince if the change is going to be successful. This can be extremely difficult and time consuming, since different stakeholders are often motivated to change by different drivers. In the case of INGOs, it is further compounded by the sheer number and variety of stakeholders. The benefits of change to poor communities, to donors and other supporters, to volunteers, and to employees all need to be carefully explained.

The second precondition for successful transformational organizational change is the presence of internal change agents who are able to articulate a coherent change agenda that is aligned with organizational values. This is especially the case in large INGOs where the personal values of staff are central to their professional motivations. If a new leader cannot identify such change agents among existing staff, then a key priority must be the recruitment of new staff who share the desired new world view and other attributes. In this regard, a major structural reorganization can also be useful. Not only does it allow a new leader to recruit the desired change agents, it can also serve to disrupt the underlying organizational culture and in its place create new structures of authority and incentives that help to realign staff expectations and behavior to the desired forms.

Once change agents are identified or recruited, it is important that they strategically engage the existing organizational culture toward their own ends. Nielson et al. (2006, 110) argue that this can be achieved by these reformers or "norm entrepreneurs," as they describe them, "couching change goals in ways that do not appear 'counter-hegemonic' but which are instead culturally compatible." In other words, these change agents must articulate the new "ideas and goals and fit new incentives to existing norms in ways that do not require current staff to wholly discard their pre-existing worldviews or behavioral habits" (Nielson et al. 2006, 110). In this way, organizational culture can be used to support broader organizational change rather than inhibit it.

Third, as the new organizational culture is being embedded, it is critical that organizational leaders and change agents are constantly aware of the signals that their decisions send about the way that new behavior will be rewarded. Not surprisingly, an organization's "people systems" have a significant influence over organizational behavior and outcomes (Taylor 2005).[5] This is one of the reasons why promotion decisions during a period of organizational change become so important. They signal to the organization that old organizational behaviors are no longer accepted

Case Study 8.2: Yahoo and Google

Yahoo was founded by Jerry Yang and David Filo in January 1994. By January 2000, at the height of the dot-com boom, Yahoo had one of, if not the leading online brand in the world. More Americans were using Yahoo as a portal to the Internet than any other website. Yahoo should have been set to become one of the leading companies of the Information Age.

However, Yahoo was operating in a highly fluid environment. Competitors were continuously appearing, consumer behavior was constantly changing, and the company's core source of revenue, search-driven advertising, was under relentless threat.

Of course, this was not news to the senior management of Yahoo. In 2002, Yahoo's CEO, Terry Semel, offered to buy a new competitor called Google for around US$3 billion, two years before Google's initial public offering. Semel's offer was rejected, and by 2004, just two months after it was publically listed, Google's market value had surpassed Yahoo.

Today, Google controls nearly 70 percent of the search-related advertising market, an industry worth more than $15 billion a year, is growing at roughly 50 percent a year and despite the global economic crisis had a market capitalization of around US$140 billion in July 2009.

On the other hand, Yahoo faces a very uncertain future. Semel resigned in June 2007, and his replacement, Jerry Yang, resigned in November 2008. In July 2009, after years of merger talks, Yahoo announced that it was turning over its search technology to Microsoft and would begin using its new search engine, Bing. The day after the deal was announced, Yahoo's share price declined by more than 10 percent, around 60 percent less than the price offered by Microsoft just a year earlier.

As is so often the case, it was not that Yahoo failed to appreciate that it was in a challenging strategic context. It also understood that Google's approach of placing text snippets in the margins of its search results was the way forward. Its downfall was that it failed to change as fast as its competitors and the external environment.

Although Yahoo purchased new search engine technology in 2002 and advertising placement technology in 2003, it took more than two years to integrate the search engine with Yahoo's other products. It was not until 2005 that Yahoo sought to integrate the advertising placement technology. By this stage, there were 10,000 employees, and any changes to the Yahoo homepage had to be negotiated across multiple departments. Moreover, integrating rather than building your own went against the entrenched culture and required the CEO to undertake a lot of internal politicking.

By the time Yahoo's senior management understood what was required to catch up to Google and how to overcome the internal impediments to change, it was too late.

and that new behavior will be rewarded. Promote members of the old guard and employees will interpret the change process as a façade and become cynical.

Similarly, if a change agenda is not funded, employees will rightly suspect that management is not committed to it. As a recent article in the

Harvard Business Review argued, "a theory of change that can't be funded isn't real" (Bradach et al. 2008, 94). Since the strategic intent of a humanitarian organization always exceeds its strategic capacity, hard prioritization decisions need to be made. If leaders avoid making the hard prioritization decisions, it is almost certain that the organizational reform will fail. On the other hand, if an organization's leadership demonstrates that it is willing to make such decisions, it reinforces to the organization that they are committed to the change agenda and that aligning with it will be rewarded, in this case, in the form of increased resources.

For example, as part of World Vision Australia's 2009 budgeting process, WVA created a multimillion-dollar strategic initiatives fund (SIF). This fund not only created a pool of resources for meeting new development challenges, for process re-engineering, and for the development of new fundraising products, it also helped management signal its strong commitment to the organizational change agenda. In fact, the difficult economic conditions that were being experienced at the time meant that the signal sent by reducing business-as-usual activities to create the SIF was even more significant than it would have otherwise been, underlining the transformative opportunity provided by a crisis. The message sent by the creation of the SIF was complemented by a strong commitment to invest in professional development despite the economic conditions; the re-allocation of resources to address new development challenges such as climate change, urbanization, and growing energy and food insecurity; and a strong emphasis on developing new fundraising products that would provide sustainable funding to the organization's new development priorities.

Fourth, it is critical that cultural change and new reward-and-incentive structures are supported by hard data. Such data will promote better decision-making, assist in building organization-wide consensus for the desired change, and help to more readily identify aligned and nonaligned behavior. As the Regis Debray quote at the beginning of this book succinctly encapsulates and as Sorgenfrei and Wrigley (2005) argue, "[O]rganizations, like individuals, observe and interpret reality according to previous experiences, which may then be fitted into received/accepted ways of viewing the world." To overcome this inherent bias against change will require a much greater focus by INGO leadership on their organization's analytical and adaptive capacity. While individuals within the large INGOs may have analytical and adaptive capacities, these capacities must become institutionalized for an organization to be able to effectively respond to change and adapt to the unpredictable.

Sorgenfrei and Wrigley (2005) suggest a number of ways to encourage this institutionalization process. Likewise, an investigation of reform at the World Bank demonstrated that organizational reform is more likely to succeed where the "desired behaviors and organizational outcomes are measurable ... and thus information is more symmetric and deviant behavior is easily identifiable" (Nielson et al. 2006, 110). This finding again reinforces the need for large INGOs to invest in human resource and information technology systems that are able to support such measurement.

The fifth factor is leadership. Not only must senior leaders be genuinely supportive of the change agenda, they must repeatedly communicate the vision and the rationale for change. They must also work toward creating a more supportive cultural environment, one that encourages experimentation, seeks to learn about new practices and technologies, monitors the environment, assesses performance, and is genuinely committed to continuously improving performance. However, this cultural change and its intended effects must be achieved without increasing the gap between the INGO and beneficiaries in communities.

Case Study 8.3: World Vision's "Big Goals" and "Our Future" Processes

In 2003, the World Vision National Directors Conference heard from national director after national director of the strain that many years of rapid growth was placing on World Vision's senior management and their staff. Like many other large INGOs, World Vision's systems, processes, and people were failing to keep pace with the demands created by years of double-digit growth. As a result, the World Vision president launched the "Big Goals" process to provide a hedgehog-like focus for the organization's myriad activities (the concept of the "hedgehog" was taken from Jim Collins' 2001 book, *Good to Great*).

However, despite the good intentions, the Big Goals process is generally perceived to have failed to achieve any major organizational change. This failure led to the launch of another major global change process in 2005 called "Our Future."

An analysis of the Big Goals process would appear to confirm that it failed to establish many of the preconditions for successful organizational change. Although organizational stress was a motivator, at the same time World Vision's growth was used to argue that the organization was generally on the right track—undermining the change message and reducing motivation to make the necessary 'tough' decisions. There were also insufficient internal advocates for change, and those that did exist were not able to build a narrative that resonated strongly enough with staff. Third, no behavior-changing signals were sent such as large restructures or improved performance management of nonperforming staff. Finally, there was insufficient senior leadership support for change within World Vision. It was even widely suspected by many staff that World Vision's international president was not genuinely committed to the proposed change agenda.

The extent to which the Our Future process avoids the mistakes of the Big Goals process and achieves major organizational change is yet to be seen.

This will also require that the leaders of the largest aid and development INGOs abandon the myth that because they are large or growing, they are necessarily being effective—as Grant and Crutchfield (2007) argue, NGO size does not necessarily correlate to impact. In the past, this has sometimes been used to undermine motivations for change. Organizational growth must be motivated by its relationship to increased impact rather than increased organizational or executive status.

Finally, the quality of an INGO's human capital is critical. This underlies once again the importance of creating a learning organization that promotes professional development.

Conclusion: Creating a Next-Generation INGO

Of course, successful organizational change is far easier to write about than to achieve. It is also becoming harder as globalization reduces the time to decide on and implement change. Nonetheless, as this Chapter demonstrates, transformational change is possible, and there are positive steps an organization's leaders can take to make such organizational change more likely to succeed. First, there must be a compelling motivation for change. As Peter Schwartz (1996: 223) argues, "getting a group to develop the capacity to change requires a high degree of shared worldview and a mutual commitment to change. The magnitude of the commitment is critical; without it, no one can hope to divert or even break the momentum of a large complex system." Second, internal change agents must build off the organization's existing culture, and they must be vigilant that the organization's compensation-and-reward structures and budgetary decisions reinforce the change they are seeking to achieve. Linking incentive-and-reward structures to measurable outcomes based on hard data makes both aligned and nonaligned behavior more evident. Third, senior leaders must continually reinforce the vision and the rationale for change.

Only those INGOs that can create an organizational culture that allows them to change at least as fast as their external environment can survive in the long run, and it will be those organizations that adapt the best that will be most successful.

Notes

1. At a Department of Defense news briefing on February 12, 2002, a linguistically challenged Rumsfeld said, "There are known knowns; there are things we know we know. We also know there are known unknowns; that is to say, we know there are some things we do not know. But there are also unknown unknowns—the ones we don't know we don't know."

2. Interview with Richard Miller, ActionAid UK, November 19, 2008.

3. The Asian financial crisis began in July 1997 and, by May 1998, had forced Indonesia's President Suharto to resign. However, an associated fall in oil prices and general investor concerns about lending to developing countries led to financial crisis in Brazil, Argentina, and other countries, including Russia. In August and September 1998, the Russian government defaulted on their government bonds, The Asian crisis also contributed to the collapse of Long-Term Capital Management in the United States in September 2008.

4. See also Fowler (1997, 204) for a long list of organizational, human, and relational sources of resistance to change in development NGOs.

5. People systems include the processes for the selection of employees, the promotion of employees, talent management, individual goal setting, evaluation, remuneration, and dismissal (Taylor 2005, 218–223).

CHAPTER 9

Conclusion: *Viva La Revolução*

Creating a Twenty-First Century INGO

This book has examined the revolution taking place around the largest aid and development INGOs. It has considered what critical organizational changes are necessary to allow INGOs to effectively respond to their changed context and continue to be important actors in international relations in the twenty-first century. While acknowledging that nation-states remain the principal actors, this book has argued that power in international relations has become less hierarchical and more diffuse than in the past; and the influence of states and some of their key functions are declining in relative importance to other actors and issues. Based on a constructivist approach, this book has also argued that the largest INGOs have been significant beneficiaries of this change and now wield considerable influence, both in domestic and international politics. This influence takes many forms, from formal positions on government delegations and IGO boards to critical, behind-the-scenes policy development and informal briefings. However, it is a complex relationship. The constitutive effects work both ways, and there are real limits to the power of INGOs. Theorists and practitioners of international relations, therefore, need to walk a careful line to ensure they neither ignore the effect of INGOs on international relations and thus impoverish our understanding of international politics nor place too much emphasis on them and run "the risk of assigning them functions they are not equipped to carry out" (Ahmed and Potter 2006, 253).

The international context is changing for INGOs in other ways as well. Climate change, reduced food security, peak oil, urbanization, and a more politicized operating environment present significant new development challenges for INGOs and make responding to humanitarian emergencies more difficult. In addition, there is now a much greater focus on INGO accountability, effectiveness, policy engagement, and coordination. This international context requires the largest aid and development INGOs not only to acquire new skills in order to meet the challenges of the changed international context but to approach their work in a much more sophisticated and politically sensitive way.

Their larger size, increased influence, the changed international environment, and new role as "insiders," has created significant organizational challenges for the largest aid and development INGOs. Although they each have strong global brands, their reputations and legitimacy are far more fragile than they seem to realize. Much more is now expected of them, and they must find ways to significantly increase the impact they are having. No longer can they simply "throw rocks," they must now be an informed and thoughtful source of viable policy alternatives.

These INGOs must also make much more of one of their key comparative advantages: their access to community-level information and the credibility that their current reputations provide. They must use their community-based information much more strategically to reframe international and domestic debates and influence states. Each of these challenges requires the largest aid and development INGOs to undertake a radical change in their strategy, culture, and operations. This includes the need to become much more flexible organizations in order to effectively respond to a greater number of large-impact, hard-to-predict events. It also requires them to focus far more on developing higher quality staff, to significantly upgrade their human resource systems, and to re-assess their approaches to governance, management, and strategy.

However, the evidence for the capacity of the largest aid and development INGOs to undertake such changes and remain relevant in the new international context is weak. There are strong internal barriers to change that accountability to donors and beneficiaries and other external enforcement mechanisms have not been able to overcome. Despite the obvious good intentions of so many people within the largest aid and development INGOs, these are not sufficient to drive the changes necessary for these INGOs to effectively fulfill their new role in international relations.

Instead, large INGOs must focus on six key factors that are critical for the effective transformational organizational change. These are

- a compelling motivation for change

- change agents who are able to articulate a coherent change agenda that is aligned with organizational values

- a compensation and reward structure that reinforces the desired behaviors

- hard data and institutionalized analytical capability

- genuinely committed leadership

- high quality human resources.

If large INGOs are not able to achieve the degree of change required of them by their changed context, there are other players willing, perhaps even eager, to take over their role. These include new philanthropists like Bill and Melinda Gates, entrepreneurs like Pierre Omidyar and Mo Ibrahim, new collaborative organizations like GFATM and GAVI and, of course, a range of for-profit corporations who see it as either a potentially profitable activity or necessary to support their core business operations. While they may bring a much-needed dose of innovation and help to improve the global aid system, the fall of large INGOs would nonetheless be a terrible loss. No other players are as dedicated to empowering people to be agents of their own destinies and to promoting the public good, even if their execution in this regard sometimes leaves much to be desired.

Unresolved Issues and Areas for Further Research

This book has sought to analyze key trends and events impacting INGOs and provide clear suggestions to the leaders of large INGOs on ways to better prepare their organization to be effective, pro-poor actors in the twenty-first century. Nonetheless, the size and complexity of the challenges facing the largest aid and development INGOs combined with an increasingly chaotic future makes the need for further research very clear. In my view, this research agenda could be approached at three levels: the international context, the industry context, and organizational context. Of course, while this may be a useful way to manage the breadth and depth of required research, one of the key characteristics of the issues facing INGOs is the way they cross so many boundaries, requiring us to approach such categorization carefully, not forgetting the dense interconnections that exist between issues in a globalized world. Nonetheless, this section will attempt to use this categorization to briefly highlight those issues that are likely to have the greatest impact on the future of INGOs yet are currently receiving insufficient attention from INGO managers and academics.

International Context

There are two standout issues at the international level that are likely to shape the strategic context for INGOs well into the twenty-first century. The first issue is the impact of the international security agenda on the goals and operations of INGOs. Terrorism and asymmetrical warfare featuring non-state actors and increasingly fought in the midst of noncombatants are likely to continue to cast a long shadow over international relations for the foreseeable future. While traditional conflict between states has been steadily decreasing, ongoing terrorist attacks and fears that individuals or small groups, often based in fragile or failed states, will access weapons of mass destruction, such as nuclear material or biological weapons, are having a profound impact on international security. Given that successful aid and development work is so impacted by government and intergovernmental approaches to international and domestic security, the international security agenda raises a number of significant issues for INGOs.

- How will the inter-relationships among the so-called triad of defense, diplomacy, and development progress, and how will it impact the relationship between states and INGOs?

- Will the personal security of INGO staff continue to deteriorate in many of the places where they are called to work? What are the best methods for providing for staff security while continuing to pursue an INGO's core mission? How does one, for example, balance increased concerns over staff security with ongoing community-based relationship building?

- Will donors support INGOs working in the most unstable and politicized contexts where operating costs are highest and sustainable impact often hardest to achieve? How do INGOs maintain sufficient independence in such operating environments when such a significant portion of their revenue often comes from bilateral agencies?

- How will INGOs strike a balance between participating in improved global aid harmonization and coordination with avoiding entanglement with bilateral agencies' security agenda? Should aid and development INGOs follow MSF's lead and withdraw from the process or should they remain engaged to improve aid quality?

- Will INGOs' freedom to operate and to constructively criticize government's domestic and foreign policy be compromised by the international security agenda, particularly given the recent decline in democracy and press freedoms?

The second key area for research at the international level is the nature and extent of the impact of climate change on the work of aid and development INGOs. While there are currently a plethora of reports and research papers that examine the impact of climate change on food security, migration, and the number and ferocity of natural disasters, there is very limited investigation of the potential impact of climate change on the organizations that are seeking to respond to these challenges, such as INGOs. For example, an analysis of World Vision's program expenditure suggests that the portion that has been spent on responding to humanitarian crises has increased from around 15 percent in 1998 to 35 percent in 2008. On some projections, the impact of climate change and increasing food insecurity could result in this proportion continuing to increase to more than 60 percent over the next decade. This scale of change raises a large number of significant operational issues for INGOs:

- Will sufficient funds and human resources be found to allow INGOs to adequately respond to this level of humanitarian need?

- How would a massive increase in food insecurity, migration, and conflict over resources impact the development work of INGOs? For example, what will be the political, social, and humanitarian implications if major rivers like the Ganges and the Brahmaputra cease to flow, either seasonally or permanently?

- How will donors respond? Will they be prepared to continue to increase aid levels in the face of slowing global economic growth, or will donor fatigue set in and domestic issues crowd out concern for the world's poor?[1]

Industry Context

Compared to a list of the world's largest corporations, the list of the largest aid and development actors has been incredibly stable for many decades. However, the last ten years in particular has seen an explosion in the number and diversity of actors engaged in addressing global poverty. A key industry issue for INGOs, therefore, is how they should interact with these new actors—are they new sources of funds, competitors, or collaborators? How will they impact the industry's structure and dynamics?

Bishop (2008) argues that in each great age of philanthropy, the government has ended up taking over the best of what new actors have brought to the social problem of the day and scaled it up, making such actors irrelevant in the long term. There is little doubt that the influx of new actors to the aid and development industry has brought much needed innovation and that even large INGOs have found scaling up successful interventions difficult. But will history repeat itself on this occasion? Will the new aid and development actors become an integral part of the aid and development sector or will governments supplant them? Or does the transnational nature of the problem combined with the failure of global governance discussed in Chapter 2 mean that this historical lesson does not apply? To date, many of the most significant new actors have not sought to become directly operational. However, if INGOs are unable to better demonstrate their effectiveness, will such new operational actors emerge? For example, given the size of its bank balance, it is likely that the Gates Foundation will continue to be a highly relevant aid and development actor in the future. However, what form will their engagement take? Will they remain primarily a funder and policy entrepreneur or will they develop an implementation capacity?

What about mergers? On the one hand, mergers between aid and development actors and environmental INGOs would make some sense in the face of climate change. However, mergers between NGOs are notoriously difficult to implement. Can the entrenched jealousies, territoriality, and pettiness that usually bedevil such activity, especially in the not-for-profit world, be overcome? Will a steep reduction in private fundraising brought about by the global financial crisis and especially impacting on smaller players provide a necessary incentive?

What is the future role of corporations and the military in aid and development work? Bilateral actors like AusAID already expend 65 percent of their budget through for-profit contractors. Is this proportion likely to change, or will new understandings of the development process drive for-profit contractors to seek partnerships with aid and development INGOs? Will INGOs be able to become more effective partners with corporations? Will corporations have the incentive to better understand the imperatives of INGOs, thereby becoming a better partner themselves? How do INGOs utilize the unparalleled capacity of the military, especially in disaster zones, without compromising their humanitarian principles?

Lastly, how will new technology impact on the industry's structure? For example, could new technologies allow disintermediation of the aid and development industry? Could mobile phones allow low-cost direct international transfer of funds to the poor, either as remittances from family members or from donors or lenders based in developed countries—bypassing even relative new industry entrants such as kiva.org?

Organizational Context

As discussed in Chapter 1, it is at the organizational level that there is the most obvious lack of INGO-specific research and thinking. Accordingly, the list of unresolved issues requiring more detailed investigation is most extensive in this area. First, there is ample scope for much greater investigation of the forces that are generating the growth in the size and influence of the aid and development INGOs, the development of what Ward (2007) calls a "political economy of INGOs."

Second, finding ways to address the organizational capacity gap in INGOs must be a key priority. The demands placed upon INGOs by the acceleration of change in the world, their own growth, and the increased expectations of stakeholders means that building organizational capacity must become one of the most important issues that INGO leaders grapple with. Yet, the constraints placed on INGO leaders by donors' aversion to funding overhead leaves many feeling a little like the Miller's daughter in the fairy tale *Rumpelstiltskin*—seeking to spin straw into gold. However, the already enormous gap between the demand for improved organizational efficiency and the supply of financial support and talented employees to drive improvements is only likely to be made worse by continued growth, rising expectations, and new challenges like climate change. As a result, key issues in this area that require urgent attention include:

- Finding ways to convince donors to change their perceptions about INGO administration costs and begin to increase investment in organizational capacity;

- Identifying ways to increase the pool of people who have sufficient experience and skill to lead INGOs in an uncertain and complex operating environment. For example, Thomas Tierney (2006) is forecasting an enormous NGO leadership deficit in the years ahead, leading to a talent war with the business and government sectors. He has estimated that just in the United States, not-for-profits will need to find almost 80,000 new senior managers every year (based on organizations with revenues of more than US$250,000 annually).

Part of the solution to addressing the organizational capacity gap should be better use of new technologies. Improved use of information technology will also assist INGOs exploit their comparative advantage over other aid and development actors. However, new technology brings with it significant challenges.

- Will INGOs be able to adapt to the opportunities and challenges presented by new technology? For example, computers are expected to be able to undertake 20,000 trillion calculations per second by 2011, estimated to be the speed of the human brain. How will this impact INGOs' operations?

- Can INGOs make the necessary IT investments to remain competitive and relevant?

- What types of systems will enable INGOs to manage digital data in a world where the total amount of information is increasing exponentially—it increased from 161 exabytes (161 quintillion bytes) in 2006 to an estimated 988 exabytes in 2007?

- Will large INGOs in particular be sufficiently savvy to adapt to a world where social media rather than newspapers has become the most important source of information? What changes will INGOs need to make to ensure they can effectively engage with potential donors, supporters and employees through social media sites such as Facebook, MySpace, and Orkut?

Third, more detailed research into the differences between and within each large INGO and how these differences impact on their ability to meet the challenges of their new international environment is required. This includes their different global structures, governance mechanisms, operating models, cultures, and strategies. In particular, there is a range of governance issues that INGOs must think much more deeply about:

- What type of INGO governance system will be best suited to the challenges of the twenty-first century? Most of the large INGOs have undergone periods of both centralization and decentralization. At present, there appears to be a tendency toward greater centralization. World Vision, Save the Children, and Plan are all currently becoming increasingly centralized. Is this change merely cyclical, or is it a result of these large INGOs adapting to the financial, social, political, and technological challenges in a globalized world?

- How do large federated and cofederated INGOs manage their global brands and manage organization wide risks?

- How do INGOs take advantage of their scale to reduce the cost of implementing new technologies?

- What does the growing economic power of emerging economies like India and China mean for the global governance of large INGOs? How does the governance of large INGOs need to adapt when a much larger proportion of their revenue will come from emerging economies such as China and India over the next few decades? Already, in 2008, World Vision's offices in emerging economies in Asia contributed US$324 million to total revenue, more than that contributed by its European offices.

Fourth, while it remains very difficult to make predictions about who of today's aid and development actors will continue to flourish into the future, what is clear is that if INGOs want to be among them they must become much better at demonstrating their effectiveness. Until they do, the overreliance on using inputs as INGO-performance metrics that currently pervades the industry will continue. The result is that INGOs will struggle to demonstrate the relationship between investing in organizational capacity and effectiveness and will under invest in areas such as advocacy. Accordingly, finding ways to communicate the impact of INGOs' work more effectively to a wide range of stakeholders must be a much higher priority in the future.

Finally, there needs to be much more focus on helping large INGOs change and adapt. Most organizational change models have been developed for the corporate sector and are of limited relevance to the much more complex organizational environment of large INGOs. And, as Chapter 8 argued, there is a range of factors that make organizational change particularly hard to achieve—large INGOs are currently built to last, not to change. This inability to change quickly, to be agile and adaptable organizations, is the greatest organizational risk facing large INGOs. As Nassim Taleb (2007) argues, it will be the rare, prospectively unpredictable but retrospectively predictable event that will create the greatest challenges for organizations in an uncertain and chaotic world. Finding ways to help large INGOs become much more organizationally prepared to respond to such events is the most critical unresolved issue of all.

The Final Word

The largest aid and development INGOs are important actors in international relations. Despite their shortcomings and failures, they remain some of the most powerful voices in the world for addressing key injustices and transnational problems such as global poverty, climate change, population growth, and income inequality. However, they could do much more by improving their current activities and leveraging them for greater impact using advocacy and other means. At the same time, they must address the valid concerns of donors, beneficiaries, and critics. This will require the largest INGOs, and particularly their leaders, to reflect more, reprioritize resources, and recommit to the age-old goal of putting themselves out of a job. If the turbulent strategic context that now confronts the largest aid and development INGOs becomes the catalyst for genuine and dramatic change in their strategies, cultures, and operations then *viva la revolución!*

Notes

1. The extent of the funding challenge is underscored by the record $4.8 billion funding gap for the UN's 2009 aid projects. The UN received only half of the $9.5 billion it sought for humanitarian work in 2009.

References

Abramson, P., and R. Inglehart. 1995. *Global Change in Global Perspective.* Ann Arbor: University of Michigan Press.

ActionAid. 2007. *ActionAid 2007 Annual Report: End Poverty Together.* Johannesburg: ActionAid International.

Ahmed, S., and D. Potter. 2006. *NGOs in International Politics.* Bloomfield, CT: Kumarian Press.

Aiken, C., and S. Keller. 2009. The Irrational Side of Change Management. *The McKinsey Quarterly*, April.

Allen, T., and A. Thomas. 2000. Agencies of Development. In *Poverty and Development in the 21st Century*, edited by T. Allen and A. Thomas, 189–216. Oxford: Oxford University Press.

Alston, P. 2005. Ships Passing in the Night: The Current State of the Human Rights and Development Debate Seen Through the Lens of the Millennium Development Goals. *Human Rights Quarterly* 27 (3): 755–829.

Anderson, K., and D. Rieff. 2005. Global Civil Society: A Sceptical View. In *Global Civil Society 2004/5*, edited by H. Anheier, M. Glasius, and M. Kaldor, 26–40. London: Sage.

Anderson, M. 1999. *Do No Harm: How Aid Can Support Peace—Or War.* Boulder, Colorado: Lynne Rienner Publishers.

Anheier, H. 2000. Managing Nonprofit Organisations: Towards a New Approach. *Civil Society Working Paper, no.* 1. London: Centre for Civil Society, London School of Economics.

Anheier, H. 2005. *Nonprofit Organisations: Theory, Management, Policy.* London: Routledge.

Anheier, H., M. Glasius, and M. Kaldor. 2001. Introducing Global Civil Society. In *Global Civil Society 2001*, edited by H. Anheier, M. Glasius, and M. Kaldor, 3–22. Oxford: Oxford University Press.

Annan, K. 2000. *We the Peoples: the Role of the UN in the 21st Century*, UN A/54/2000.

Annan, K. 2005. *In Larger Freedom: Towards Development, Security, and Human Rights for All*, Report of the Secretary General, UN General Assembly A/59/2005. March 31.

Armitage, R., and J. Nye. 2007. *CSIS Commission on Smart Power: A Smarter, More Secure America*. Washington, DC: Center for Strategic and International Studies.

Atack, I. 1999. Four Criteria of Development NGO Legitimacy. *World Development* 27 (5): 855–64.

Atkinson, R., and A. Eastwood. 2007. *Public Attitudes to Overseas Giving: Does Government Make a Difference?* Southhampton: Southampton Statistical Sciences Research Institute, University of Southampton.

Atwood, J, M., McPherson, and A. Natsios. 2008. Arrested Development: Making Foreign Aid a More Effective Tool. *Foreign Affairs* 87 (6):123–132.

AusAID. 2009. *Building on the 2010 Blueprint: A Reform Agenda for 2015*. Canberra: AusAID.

Barber, M., and C. Bowie. 2008. How International NGOs Could Do Less Harm and More Good. *Development in Practice* 18 (6): 748–754.

Barnett, M., and R. Duvall. 2005a. Power in Global Governance. In *Power in Global Governance*, edited by M. Barnett and R. Duvall, 1–32. Cambridge: Cambridge University Press.

Barnett, M., and R. Duvall. 2005b. Power in International Politics. *International Organization* 59: 39–75.

Beck, U. 1999. *What Is Globalization?* Cambridge: Polity Press.

Becker, F. 2007. Organizational Ecology and Knowledge Networks. *California Management Review* 49 (2): 42–61.

Beall, J., and S. Fox. 2006. Urban Poverty and Development in the Twenty-first Century. *Oxfam Research Report*. Oxford: Oxfam GB.

Bebbington, A., S. Hickey, and D. Mitlin. 2008. Can NGOs Make a Difference? The Challenge of Development Alternatives. In *Can NGOs Make a Difference? The Challenge of Development Alternatives*, edited by A. Bebbington, S. Hickey, and D. Mitlin, 3–37. London: Zed Books.

Bertini, C. and D. Glickman. 2009. *Renewing American Leadership in the Fight Against Global Hunger and Poverty*. Chicago: The Chicago Council on Global Affairs.

Bezanson, K. 2005. *Replenishing the Global Fund: An Independent Assessment*. Geneva: The Global Fund.

BHP Billiton Ltd. 2008. *Annual Report 2007*. Melbourne: BHP Billiton Ltd.

Bishop, M. 2008. Fighting Global Poverty: Who Will Be Relevant in 2020. In *Global development 2.0: Can philanthropists, the public, and the poor make poverty history?* edited by L. Brainard and D. Chollet, 42–52. Washington, DC: Brookings Institution Press.

Bishop, M., and M. Green. 2008. *Philantrocapitalism: How the Rich Can Save the World*. New York: Bloomsbury Press.

Bisley, N. 2007. *Rethinking Globalization*. Basingstoke: Palgrave Macmillan.

Boas, M., and D. McNeill, eds. 2004. *Global Institutions and Development: Framing the World?* London: Routledge.

Boston Consulting Group. 2009. *The Next Billions: Unleashing Business Potential in Untapped Markets.* Geneva: World Economic Forum.

Bradach, J., T. Tierney, and N. Stone. 2008. Delivering on the Promise of Nonprofits. *Harvard Business Review.* December: 88–97.

Brainard, L., and D. Chollet, eds. 2008. *Global Development 2.0: Can Philanthropists, the Public, and the Poor Make Poverty History?* Washington, DC: Brookings Institution Press.

Bangladesh Rural Advancement Committee. 2007. *Annual Report 2007.* Dhaka: Bangladesh Rural Advancement Committee.

British Red Cross. 2007. *Trustees' Report and Accounts, 2007.* London: British Red Cross.

Britton, B. 2005. Organisational Learning in NGOs: Creating the Motive, Means, and Opportunity. Praxis paper no. 3. Oxford: International NGO Training and Research Centre.

Brown, C. 2002. *Sovereignty, Rights, and Justice: International Political Theory Today.* Oxford: Blackwell Publishers.

Brown, L., and Jagadanada. 2007. Civil Society Legitimacy and Accountability: Issues and Challenges. Report for the Program on Civil Society Legitimacy and Accountability of CIVICUS and the Hauser Centre.

Brown, S., and R. Pomeroy. 2008. Food Summit Draws up Plan to "Eliminate Hunger." *Reuters,* June 3.

Bruhl, T., and V. Rittberger 2002. From International to Global Governance: Actors, Collective Decision-making, and the United Nations in the World of the Twenty-first Century. In *Global Governance and the United Nations System,* edited by V. Rittberger, 1–47. Tokyo: UNU Press.

Bryan, L., and D. Farrell. 2008. Leading Through Uncertainty. *The McKinsey Quarterly,* December.

Bryan, L., and C. Joyce. 2005. The 21st-Century Organization. *The McKinsey Quarterly* 3:25–33.

Burall, S., S. Maxwell, and A. Menocal. 2006. Reforming the International Aid Architecture: Options and ways forward. Working Paper 278. London: Overseas Development Institute.

Burke, M., E. Miguel, S.

Cantwell, N. 2008. Words that Speak Volumes. In *18 Candles: The Convention on the Rights of the Child Reaches Majority,* edited by J. Connors, J. Zermatten, and A. Panayotidis, 21–30. Sion: International Institute for the Rights of the Child.

CARE International. 2006. Cities on the Brink: Urban Poverty in the 21st Century. *CARE International Policy Update.* London: CARE International UK.

Carr, N. 2003. IT doesn't matter. *Harvard Business Review,* May: 41–49.

Chandhoke, N. 2002. The Limits of Global Civil Society. In *Global Civil Society 2002,* edited by M. Glasius, M. Kaldor, and H. Anheier, 35–53. Oxford: Oxford University Press.

Chapman, J., and A. Wameyo, A. 2001. *Monitoring and Evaluating Advocacy: A Scoping Study.* Johannesburg: ActionAid.

Chowdhury, N., C. Finlay-Notman, and I. Hovland. 2006. CSO Capacity For Policy Engagement: Lessons Learned from the CSPP Consultations in Africa, Asia and Latin America. Working Paper 272. London: Overseas Development Institute.

Christensen, J. 2004. Asking Do-gooders to Prove They Do Good. *New York Times,* January 3.

Chui, M., A. Miller, and R. Roberts. 2009. Six Ways to Make Web 2.0 Work. *The McKinsey Quarterly* February.

Clark, J. 2003. *Worlds Apart: Civil Society and the Battle For Ethical Globalization.* Sterling, Virginia: Kumarian Press.

Clay, J. 2005. *Exploring the Links Between International Business and Poverty Reduction: A Case Study of Unilever in Indonesia.* Oxford: Oxfam GB.

Cohen, M., M. Kupu, and P. Khanna. 2008. The New Colonialists. *Foreign Policy.* July/August.

Cohen, R. 2008. Cosmopolitan is Turned into a Slur. *Observer,* September 14.

Collier, P. 2007. *The Bottom Billion: Why the Poorest Countries are Failing and What Can Be Done About It.* New York: Oxford University Press.

Collins, J. 2005. *Good to Great and the Social Sectors: A Monograph to Accompany Good to Great.* London: Random House.

Commission on Global Governance. 1995. *Our Global Neighbourhood.* Oxford: Oxford University Press.

Cooley, A., and J. Ron. 2002. The NGO Scramble: Organizational Insecurity and the Political Economy of Transnational Action. *International Security* 27 (1): 5–39.

Cosgrove, J. 2007. *Synthesis Report Expanded Summary: Joint Evaluation of the International Response to the Indian Ocean Tsunami.* London: Tsunami Evaluation Coalition.

Council of the European Union. 2008. *Climate Change and International Security: Paper from the High Representative and the European Commission to the European Council.* S113/08, Brussels.

Courtney, H. 2001. Making the Most of Uncertainty. *The McKinsey Quarterly* 4: 38–47.

Crutchfield, L., and H. Grant. 2008. *Forces for Good: The Six Practices of High-impact Nonprofits.* San Francisco: Jossey-Bass.

Dasgupta, S., B. Laplante, C. Meisner, D. Wheeler, and J. Yan. 2007. The Impact of Sea Level Rise on Developing Countries: A Comparative Analysis. *Policy Research Working Paper No. 4136.* Washington, DC: World Bank.

David, R., and A. Manchini. 2004. Going Against the Flow: Making Organisational Systems Part of the Solution Rather Than Part of the Problem. *Lessons for Change in Policy and Organisations, No. 8.* Brighton: Institute of Development Studies.

Davies, A. 2009. Obama Struggles to Wed US Needs with the World's. *The Age*, April 4.

Davies, C. 2008. Cynicism Can Damage Democracy's Health. *Observer*, September 14.

Debray, R. 1967. *Revolution in the Revolution: Armed Struggle and Political Struggle in Latin America.* Penguin Books.

Dees, J. 2008. Philanthropy and Enterprise: Harnessing the Power of Business and Social Entrepreneurship for Development. In *Global Development 2.0: Can Philanthropists, the Public and the Poor Make Poverty History?* edited by L. Brainard and D. Chollet, 120–134. Washington, DC: Brookings Institution Press.

Derderian, K., E. Stobbaerts, L. Singh, S. Rocha, and D. Melody. 2007. UN Humanitarian Reforms: A View From the Field. *Humanitarian Practice Network* 39: 36–39.

Department for International Development. 2005. *Why We Need to Work More Effectively in Fragile States.* London: Department for International Development.

Deutsche Bank AG. 2009. Investing in Agriculture: Far-reaching Challenge, Significant Opportunity: An Asset Management Perspective. *Deutsche Bank White Paper.* New York: Deutsche Bank AG.

Development Initiatives. 2008. *GHD Indicators 2008.* Somerset: Development Initiatives International Limited.

Dichter, T. 1999. Globalisation and Its Effects on NGOs: Efflorescence or a Blurring of Roles and Relevance? *Nonprofit and Voluntary Sector Quarterly* 28 (4): 38–58.

Dichter, T. 2003. *Despite Good Intentions: Why Development Assistance to the Third World Has Failed.* Boston: University of Massachusetts Press.

Donini, A., L. Fast, G. Hansen, S. Harris, L. Minear, T. Mowjee, and A. Wilder. 2008. The State of the Humanitarian Enterprise. *Humanitarian Agenda 2015: Final Report.* Medford, MA: Feinstein International Centre, Tufts University.

Dugger, C. 2007. Charity Finds That US Food Did For Africa Hurts Instead of Helps. *International Herald Tribune*, August 14.

Drucker, P. 1990. *Managing the Nonprofit Organization.* New York: Collins.

Easterly, W. 2006. *The White Man's Burden: Why the West's Efforts to Aid the Rest Have Done So Much Ill and So Little Good.* New York: Penguin.

Easterly, W. ed. 2008. *Reinventing Foreign Aid.* Cambridge: MIT Press.

Ebrahim, A. 2003. *NGOs and Organizational Change: Discourse, Reporting, and Learning.* Cambridge: Cambridge University Press.

Edwards, M., and D. Hulme, eds. 1992. *Making a Difference: NGOs and Development in a Changing World.* London: Earthscan.

——— 1995a. "NGO Performance and Accountability: Introduction and Overview." Pp. 3–16 in *Non-Governmental Organisations—Performance and Accountability,* edited by M. Edwards and D. Hulme. London: Earthscan.

———— 1995b. "Beyond the Magic Bullet? Lessons and Conclusions." Pp. 219–228 in *Non-Governmental Organisations—Performance and Accountability,* edited by M. Edwards and D. Hulme. London: Earthscan.

————, eds. 1997. *Too Close For Comfort.* London: Macmillan/St. Martin's Press.

Edwards, M. 2000. *NGO Rights and Responsibilities: A New Deal for Global Governance.* London: The Foreign Policy Centre.

Edwards, M., and A. Fowler, eds. 2002. *The Earthscan Reader on NGO Management.* London: Earthscan.

Edwards, M. 2008. "Have NGOs Made a Difference? From Manchester to Birmingham with an Elephant in the Room." Pp. 38–52 in *Can NGOs Make a Difference? The Challenge of Development Alternatives,* edited by A. Bebbington, S. Hickey, D. and Mitlin. London: Zed Books.

Ellis, P. 2010. "The Ethics of Taking Sides." in *Ethical Questions and International NGOs,* edited by K. Horton and C. Roche, (forthcoming). New York: Springer.

Evans, A. 2009. *The Feeding of the Nine Billion: Global Food Security for the 21st Century.* London: Chatham House.

Falk, R. 2005. "Reforming the United Nations: Global Civil Society Perspectives and Initiatives." Pp. 150–186 in *Global Civil Society Year Book,* edited by M. Glasius, M. Kaldor and H. Anheimer. Los Angeles: Centre for the Study of Global Governance.

Feinstein International Famine Center. 2004. *Ambiguity and Change: Humanitarian NGOs Prepare for the Future.* Medford, MA: Tufts University.

Finnemore, M. 1996. *National Interests in International Politics.* New York: Cornell University Press.

Fitzduff, M., and C. Church. 2004. "Stepping up to the Table: NGO Strategies for Influencing Policies on Conflict Issues." Pp. 1–22 in *NGOs at the Table,* edited by M. Fitzduff and C. Church. Lanham: Rowman and Littlefield.

Florini, A., and P. Simmons. 2000. "What the World Needs Now?" Pp. 1–15 in *The Third Force: the Rise of Transnational Civil Society,* edited by A. Florini. Washington, DC: Carnegie Endowment for International Peace.

FAO. 2008. *Food Outlook, November.* Rome: FAO.

Foreign Policy Magazine. 2008. "The List: The World's Most Powerful Development NGOs." *Foreign Policy Magazine.* July. Washington: The Slate Group.

Fowler, A., and K. Biekart. 1996. "Do Private Aid Agencies Really Make a Difference?" In *Compassion and Calculation,* edited by D. Sogge,107–135. London: Pluto Press.

Fowler, A. 1997. *Striking a Balance. A Guide to Enhancing the Effectiveness of Non-Governmental Organisations in International Development.* London: Earthscan.

———. 2000a. "Civil Society, NGDOs, and Social Development: Changing the Rules of the Game." *Occasional Paper No. 1.* Geneva: United Nations Research Institute for Social Development.

———. 2000b. "NGO Futures: Beyond Aid: NGDO Values and the Fourth Position." *Third World Quarterly* 21 (4): 589–603.

———. 2000c. *The Virtous Spiral. A Guide to Sustainability for NGOs in International Development.* London: Earthscan.

———. 2000d. "Relevance in the 21st Century: The Case for Devolution and Global Association of International NGOs." Pp. 220–232 in *Development and Management.* Oxford: Oxfam GB.

———. 2008. "Development and the New Security Agenda: W(h)ither(ing) NGO Alternatives?" Pp. 111–130 in *Can NGOs Make a Difference? The Challenge of Development Alternatives,* edited by A. Bebbington, S. Hickey, and D. Mitlin. London: Zed Books.

Freiesleben, J. 2008a. "System-Wide Coherence." Pp. 37–53 in *Managing Change at the United Nations.* New York: Centre for UN Reform.

———. 2008b. *System-Wide Coherence – the 62nd GA Session and the Road Ahead.* New York: Centre for UN Reform.

Friedman, T. 2008. *Hot, Flat, and Crowded.* London: Allen Lane.

Fry, C. 2007. "Cottoning onto a Good Thing." *The Guardian,* April 13.

Fues, T. 2007. "Millennium development Goals and Streamlining the UN Development Architectures." *International Studies* 44 (1): 23–37.

Fukuda-Parr, S. 2004. "The Millennium Development Goals: Why They Matter." *Global Governance* 10: 395–402.

Garreau, J. 2008. "More Mobile, But Less Free." *The Age,* March 29.

Geldof, M. 2005. "Becoming an Information Society: The Role of New Information Technologies in Development." *Wilton Park Paper.* Steyning, West Sussex: Wilton Park.

German Advisory Council on Global Change (WBGU). 2007. *World in Transition—Climate Change as a Security Risk: Summary for Policy Makers.* Berlin: German Advisory Council on Global Change.

Ghani, A., and C. Lockhart. 2008. *Fixing Failed States: A Framework for Rebuilding a Fractured World.* New York: Oxford University Press.

Gibelman, M., and S. Gelman. 2004. "A Loss of Credibility: Patterns of Wrongdoing Among Nongovernmental Organizations." *Voluntas: International Journal of Voluntary and Nonprofit Organizations* 15 (4): 355–381.

Giddens, A. 1998. *The Third Way: The Renewal of Social Democracy.* Cambridge: Polity Press.

Glasius, M., M. Kaldor, and H. Anheimer. 2005. "Introduction." Pp. 1–34 in *Global Civil Society Year Book*, edited by M. Glasius, M. Kaldor, and H. Anheimer. Los Angeles: Centre for the Study of Global Governance.

Glasius, M. 2005. *The ICC: A Global Civil Society Achievement.* Oxford: Routeledge.

Global Fund. 2008. *Civil Society on the Ground: Community Systems Strengthening and Dual Track Financing: Nine illustrative Case Studies.* Geneva: Global Fund.

Gnaerig, B., and C. MacCormack. 1999. "The Challenges of Globalization: Save the Children." *Nonprofit and Voluntary Sector Quarterly* 28 (4) Supplement: 140–146.

Goold, L. 2006. "Working with barriers to organisational learning." *BOND Briefing Paper.* London: British Overseas NGOs for Development.

Gordenker, L., and T. Weiss. 1995. "NGO Participation in the International Policy Process." *Third World Quarterly* 16: 543–555.

Grant, H., and L. Crutchfield. 2007. "Creating High-Impact Nonprofits." *Stanford Social Innovation Review.* Fall: 32–41.

Greenpeace International. 2007. *Annual Report 07.* Amsterdam: Greenpeace International.

Grossman, L. 2009. "Iran Protests: Twitter, the Medium of the Movement." *Time,* June 17.

Guo, C., and M. Acar. 2005. "Understanding Collaboration Among Nonprofit Organizations: Combining Resource Dependency, Institutional and Network Perspectives." *Nonprofit and Voluntary Sector Quarterly* 34 (3): 340–361.

Hall, R. 2005. "Private Authority: Non-State Actors and Global Governance." *Harvard International Review* 27 (2).

Halonen, T., and M. Benjamin. 2004. *A Fair Globalization: Creating Opportunities For All.* Geneva: World Commission on the Social Dimensions of Globalization, International Labour Organisation.

Hamilton, C. 2007 *Scorcher: The Dirty Politics of Climate Change.* Melbourne: Black Inc. Agenda.

Handy, C. 1988. *Managing Voluntary Organisations.* Harmondsworth: Penguin.

Handy, C. 1992. "Balancing Corporate Power: A New Federalist Paper." *Harvard Business Review* Nov.–Dec : 59–67.

Hart, J., and S. Kim. 2000. "Power in the Information Age." Pp. 35–58 in *Of Fears and Foes: International Relations in an Evolving Global Economy,* edited by J. Ciprut. Westport: Praeger Publishing.

He, B. 2004. "Transnational Civil Society and the National Identity Question in East Asia." *Global Governance* 10: 227–246.

Held, D., A. McGrew, D. Goldblatt, and J. Perraton. 1999. *Global Transformation: Politics, Economics, and Culture.* Cambridge: Polity Press.

Held, D. and A. McGrew. 2002. *Globalisation/Anti-globalisation*. Cambridge: Polity Press.

Held, D. 2004. *Global Covenant: The Social Democratic Alternative to the Washington Consensus*. Cambridge: Polity Press.

Henry, K. 1999. "CARE International: Evolving to Meet the Challenges of the 21st Century." *Nonprofit and Voluntary Sector Quarterly* 28 (4) Supplement: 109–120.

Hillebrand, E. 2008. "Replay of Tragic Third Way." *The Weekend Australian*, April 26–7.

Hock, D. 1995. "The Chaordic Organization: Out Of Control and Into Order." *World Business Academy Perspectives* 9 (1).

Hudson, M. 1995. *Managing Without Profit: The Art of Managing Non-Profit Organizations*. Harmondsworth: Penguin.

Hulme, D. 2008. "Reflections on NGOs and Development: The Elephant, the Dinosaur, Several Tigers, but No Owl." Pp. 337–345 in *Can NGOs Make a Difference? The Challenge of Development Alternatives*, edited by A. Bebbington, S. Hickey, and D. Mitlin. London: Zed Books.

Hurell, A. 2005. "Power, Institutions and the Production on Inequality." Pp. 33–58 in *Power in Global Governance*, edited by M. Barnett and R. Duvall. Cambridge: Cambridge University Press.

Ibarra, H., and M. Hunter. 2007. "How Leaders Create and Use Networks." *Harvard Business Review*. January.

Institute for Global Policy. 2009. *Strengthening the Relationship Between ECOSOC and the Bretton Woods Institutions for a Coherent and Effective Financial and Economic Architecture*. New York: World Federalist Movement-Institute for Global Policy.

Interagency Standing Committee. 2008. "Climate Change, Migration, and Displacement: Who Will Be Affected?" *Working Paper* submitted by the informal group on Migration/ Displacement and Climate Change, October 31.

International Monetary Fund. 2009. *April World Economic Outlook*. Washington: International Monetary Fund.

Integrated Regional Information Networks. 2007. *Tomorrow's Crises Today: The Humanitarian Impact of Urbanisation*. Geneva: Office for the Coordination of Humanitarian Affairs.

Integrated Regional Information Networks. 2009. *Sudan: Aid Agencies React to Expulsions*. Geneva: Office for the Coordination of Humanitarian Affairs, March 5.

International Development Association. 2007. "Aid Architecture: An Overview of the Main Trends in Official Development Assistance Flows." *IDA* 15:19.

Ishay, M. 2004. *The History of Human Rights: From Ancient Times to the Globalization Era*. Berkeley: University of California.

Jolly, R., L. Emmerij, T. Weiss. 2005. *The Power of UN Ideas: Lessons from the First 60 Years*. Bloomington: Indiana University Press.

Kaldor, M., H. Anheier, and M. Glasius. 2003. "Global Civil Society in an Era of Regressive Globalisation." Pp. 3–17 in *Global Civil Society Year Book*, edited by Kaldor, M., H. Anheier, and M. Glasius. Los Angeles: Centre for the Study of Global Governance.

Kahler, M. 2004. "Defining Accountability Up: The Global Economic Multilaterals." *Government and Opposition* 39 (2):132–158.

Kaplan, R. 2008. "What Rumsfeld Got Right." *The Atlantic*, July/August.

Karns, M., and K. Mingst. 2004. *International Organizations: The Politics and Processes of Global Governance*. Boulder, CO: Lynne Rienner.

Katz, H, and H. Anheier. 2005. "Global Connectedness: The Structure of Transnational NGO Networks." Pp. 240–265 in *Global Civil Society 2005/6*, edited by M. Glasius, M. Kaldor, and H. Anheier. London: Sage.

Keane, B. 2008. "Climate Change 2: Enviro Groups Need to Talk Dollars and Cents." *Crikey*, October 17.

Keane, J. 2001. "Global Civil Society?" Pp. 23–47 in *Global Civil Society Year Book (2001)*, edited by H. Anheier, M. Glasius, and M. Kaldor. Los Angeles: Centre for the Study of Global Governance.

Keck, M., and K. Sikkink. 1998. *Activists Beyond Borders: Advocacy Networks in International Politics*. Cornell: Cornell University Press.

Kelly, L. 2010. "Ethical Behaviour in Nongovernment Organisations." In *Ethical Questions and International NGOs*, edited by K. Horton and C. Roche, [forthcoming]. New York: Springer.

Keohane, R., and J. Nye. 1998. "Power and Interdependence in the Information Age." *Foreign Affairs* 77 (5): 81–94.

———. 2000. "Introduction." Pp. 1–40 in *Governance in a Globalizing World*, edited by J. Nye and J. Donahue. Washington, DC: Brookings Institution Press.

Kharas, H. 2008. "The New Reality of Aid." Pp. 53–73 in *Global Development 2.0: Can Philanthropists, the Public, and the Poor Make Poverty History?*, edited by L. Brainard and D. Chollet. Washington, DC: Brookings Institution Press.

Kingsbury, D. 2007. *Political Development*. London: Routledge.

Koch, D. 2008. "A Paris Declaration for International NGOs?" *Policy Insights No. 73*. Paris: OECD Development Centre.

Korey, W. 2001. *NGOs and the Universal Declaration of Human Rights*. New York: Palgrave.

Korten, D. 1990. *Getting to the 21st Century: Voluntary Action and the Global Agenda*. West Hartford: Kumarian Press.

Kotter, J. 1996. *Leading Change*. Boston: Harvard Business Press.

Kramer, M. 2008. "Philanthropy, Aid, and Investment." Pp. 216–224 in *Global Development 2.0: Can Philanthropists, the Public, and the Poor Make Poverty History?* edited by L. Brainard and D. Chollet. Washington, DC: Brookings Institution Press.

Kupp, D. 2007. "Keys to the city." *Urban Working Group Report*. Monrovia, CA: World Vision International.

LaFleur, V., N. Purvis, and A. Jones. 2008. *Double Jeopardy: What the Climate Crisis Means for the Poor*. Washington: Brookings Institute Press.

Lancaster, C. 2007. *Foreign Aid: Diplomacy, Development, Domestic Politics*. Chicago: The University of Chicago Press.

Lawler, E., and C. Worley. 2006. *Built to Change: How to Achieve Sustained Organisational Effectiveness*. San Francisco: Jossey-Bass.

Lele, U., N. Sadik, A. Simmons. 2006. *The Changing Aid Architecture: Can Global Initiatives Eradicate Poverty?* Washington, DC: World Bank.

Lenton, T., H. Held, E. Kriegler, J. Hall, W. Lucht, S. Rahmstorf, and H. Schellnhuber. 2008. "Tipping Elements in the Earth's Climate System." *Proceedings of the National Academy of Sciences of the United States of America* 105 (6): 1786–1793.

Lewis, D., and T. Wallace. 2000. "Introduction." Pp. ix in *New Roles and Relevance: Development NGOs and the Challenge of Change*, edited by D. Lewis and T. Wallace. Bloomfield, CT: Kumarian Press.

Lewis, D. 1998. "Interview with Michael Edwards on the Future of NGOs." *Nonprofit Management and Leadership* 9 (1): 89–93.

Lewis, D. 2007. *The Management of Nongovernment Development Organisations* 2nd Ed.. London: Routledge.

Lindenberg, M., and C. Bryant. 2001. *Going Global: Transforming Aid and Development NGOs*. Bloomfield, CT: Kumarian Press.

Lipschutz, R. 2005. "Global Civil Society and Global Governance: or, the search for politics and the state amidst the capilliaries of social power." Pp. 229–248 in *Power in Global Governance*, edited by M. Barnett and R. Duvall. Cambridge: Cambridge University Press.

Litovsky, A., and A. MacGillivray. 2007. *Development as Accountability*. London: AccountAbility21.

Lorsch, J., and T. Tierney. 2002. *Aligning the Stars: How to Succeed When Professionals Drive Results*. Boston: Harvard Business School Press.

Macalister, T. 2008. "Energy agency sees oil price rising to $200 a barrel." *The Guardian*, November 7.

MacInnis, L. 2009. "U.N. says paralysed in Sudan without aid partners." *Alertnet*, March 10.

Malhotra, Y. 1996. *Organizational Learning and Learning Organizations: An Overview*. www.brint.com.

Mallaby, S. 2004. *The World's Banker*. Sydney: University of New South Wales.

Manning, R. 2006. *Will "Emerging Donors" Change the Face of International Cooperation?* Paris: OECD.

Martens J. 2006. "The future of NGO participation at the United Nations after the 2005 World Summit." *FES Briefing Papers*. Berlin: Friedrich Ebert Stiftung.

Martens, K. 2006. "Professionalised Representation of Human Rights NGOs to the United Nations." *The International Journal of Human Rights* 10 (1): 19–30.

Martin, A., C. Culey, And S. Evans. 2006. *Make Poverty History: 2005 Campaign Evaluation.* London: Firetail Limited.

Masud N., and B. Yontcheva. 2005. "Does foreign aid reduce poverty? Empirical evidence from nongovernmental and bilateral aid." *IMF Working Paper* WP/05/100. Washington, DC: International Monetary Fund.

Mathews, J. 1997. "Power Shift." *Foreign Affairs* 76 (1): 50–66.

Maxwell, S. 2006. *Review of The White Man's Burden: Why the West's Efforts to Aid the Rest Have Done So Much Ill and So Little Good.* London: Overseas Development Institute.

Médecins Sans Frontières. 2007. *MSF Activity Report 2007.* Paris: Médecins Sans Frontières.

McDonald, J. 2004. "Foreword: A View from Another World—The Policy Maker's Perspective." Pp. xi–xv in *NGOs at the Table: Strategies For Influencing Policies in Areas of Conflict,* edited by M. Fitzduff and C. Church. Lanham: Rowman and Littlefield.

McGann, J., and M. Johnston. 2005. "The Power Shift and the NGO Credibility Crisis." *Brown Journal of World Affairs* 11 (2).

McGrew, A. 2005. "Globalisation and Global Politics." Pp. 19–40 in *The Globilization of World Politics,* edited by J. Baylis and S. Smith, 3rd ed. Oxford: Oxford University Press.

McNeill, D., and A. St. Clair. 2009. *Global Poverty, Ethics, and Human Rights: The Role of Multilateral Organisations.* London: Routledge.

McPeak, M. 2001. "Tackling Fragmentation and Building Unity in an International Nongovernmental Organisation." *Nonprofit Management and Leadership* 11 (4): 477–491.

Mekata, M., 2000. "Building Partnerships Toward a Common Goal: Experiences of the International Campaign to Ban Landmines." Chapter 6 in *The Third Force: The Rise of Transnational Civil Society,* edited by A. Florini. Washington, DC: Carnegie Endowment for International Peace.

Mendelson, S. 2002. "The Power and Limits of Transnational Democracy Networks in Post-Communist Societies." Pp. 232–251 in *The Power and Limits of NGOs,* edited by S. Mendelson and J. Glenn. New York: Colombia University Press.

Mierop, E. 2006. "Putting Humanitarian Coordination in Touch with Reality." *Global Futures No. 2.* Monrovia, CA: World Vision International.

Mills, A., and D. Joyce. 2006. "Nongovernmental Organisations and International Norm Transmission on the Fault Lines of the International Order." *Cambridge Review of International Affairs* 19 (1): 11–19.

Monbiot, G. 2009. Bickering and Filibustering While the Biosphere Burns. *The Guardian*. December 19.

Moorehead, C. 1999. *Dunant's Dream: War, Switzerland, and the History of the Red Cross*. New York: Carroll and Graf.

Moya, D. 2009. *Dead Aid: Why Aid is Not Working and How there is Another Way for Africa*. London: Allen Lane.

National Intelligence Council. 2008. *Global Trends 2025: A Transformed World*. Washington, DC: US Government.

Narayan, D. 2009. *Moving Out of Poverty: Success from the Bottom Up*. Washington, DC: World Bank.

Natsios, A. 1996. Illusions of Influence: "The CNN Effect in Complex Emergencies." Pp. 149–168 in *From Massacres to Genocide: The Media, Public Policy and Humanitarian Crisis*, edited by R. Rotberg and T. Weiss. Washington, DC: Brookings Institution Press.

———. 2006. "Five Debates on International Development: The US Perspective." *Development Policy Review* 24 (2): 131–139.

Nelson, J. 2008. "Effecting Change Through Accountable Channels." Pp. 149–186 in *Global Development 2.0: Can Philanthropists, the Public and the Poor Make Poverty History?*, edited by L. Brainard and D. Chollet. Washington, DC: Brookings Institution Press.

Nielson, D., M. Tierney, and C. Weaver. 2006. "Bridging the rationalist–constructivist divide: Re-engineering the culture of the World Bank." *Journal of International Relations and Development* 9 (2): 107–139.

Nye, J. 2002. "Hard and Soft Power in a Global Information Age." Pp. 2–10 in *Re-Ordering the World*, edited by M. Leonard. London: Foreign Policy Centre.

OECD. 2009. *Development Aid at Its Highest Level Ever in 2008*. Paris: OECD.

Offenheiser, R., S. Holcombe, and N. Hopkins. 1999. "Grappling with Globalization, Partnership, and Learning: A Look Inside Oxfam America." *Nonprofit and Voluntary Sector Quarterly* 28 (4) Supplement: 121–139.

Overseas Development Institute. 2007. "Humanitarian Advocacy in Darfur: The Challenge of Neutrality." *HPG Policy Brief 28*. London: Overseas Development Institute.

Oxfam GB. 2007. *Accountability Report*. Oxford: Oxfam GB.

———. 2008. *IS Strategic Review: Benchmarking Extract*. Oxford: Oxfam GB.

———. 2009. *The Right to Survive: The Humanitarian Challenge for the 21st Century*. Oxford: Oxfam GB.

Oxfam International. 2007. *Oxfam International Annual Report 2007*. Oxford: Oxfam International.

Pallotta D. 2008. *Uncharitable: How Restraints on Nonprofits Undermine Their Potential*. Medford, MA: Tufts University Press.

Panyarachun, A. 2004. *A More Secure World: Our Shared Responsibility.* Report by the Secretary General's High Level Panel on Threats, Challenges, and Change. Geneva: United Nations.

Parker, K. 2009. "Too Much Information: the Bytes that Blow our Brains." *The Age,* April 5.

Parris, B. 2007. *World Vision Australia's Policy Position on Climate Change.* 2nd ed. Melbourne: World Vision Australia.

Pasteur, K. 2004. "Learning for Development: A Literature Review." *Lessons for Change in Policy and Organisations No 6.* Brighton: Institute of Development Studies.

Paul, J. 2003. *The Arria Formula.* New York: Global Policy Forum.

Pearlman, J., and B. Cubby. 2009. "Defence Warns of Climate Change." *The Sydney Morning Herald,* January 7.

Pettit, J., and C. Shutt. 2008. *The Development Impact of Child Sponsorship.* Brighton: Institute of Development Studies.

Pishchikova, K. 2006. "The Promise of Transnational NGO Dialogue: The Argument and the Challenges." *Cambridge Review of International Affairs* 19 (1): 49–61.

Plan International. 2009. *2008 Worldwide Annual Review.* Woking: Plan International.

Porter, M. 2001. Strategy and the Internet. *Harvard Business Review* 79 (3): 62–78.

Puchala, D., K. Verlin Laatikainen, and R. Coate. 2007. *United Nations Politics: International Organization in a Divided World.* New Jersey: Pearson.

Puddington, A. 2008. *Findings of Freedom in the World 2008—Freedom in Retreat: Is the Tide Turning?.* Washington, DC: Freedom House.

———. 2009. *Freedom In The World 2009: Setbacks and Resilience.* Washington, DC: Freedom House.

Rahman, S. 2006. Development, Democracy, and the NGO Sector: Theory and Evidence from Bangladesh. *Journal of Developing Societies* 22 (4): 451–473.

Ratha, D., S. Mohapatra, and Z. Xu. 2008. Outlook for Remittance Flows 2008–2010. *Migration and Development Brief No.8.* Washington, DC: World Bank.

Rieff, D. 2003. *A Bed for the Night: Humanitarianism in Crisis.* New York: Simon and Schuster.

Read, R. 2003. "Aid Agencies Reject Money Due to Strings." *Oregonian,* June 6.

Ready, D., L. Hill, and J. Conger 2008. "Winning the Race for Talent in Emerging Markets." *Harvard Business Review.* November: 63–70.

Reinmann, K. 2006. "A View from the Top: International Politics, Norms, and the Worldwide Growth of NGOs." *International Studies Quarterly* 50: 45–67.

Reus-Smit, C. 2001. "Constructivism." Pp. 209–230 in *Theories of International Relations,* edited by S. Burchill. Basingstoke: Palgrave.

Richard, J. 2002. *High Noon: 20 Global Problems and 20 Years to Solve Them.* New York: Basic Books.

Riddell, R. 2007. *Does Aid Really Work?* Oxford: Oxford University Press.

Risse, T. 2000. "The Power of Norms versus the Norms of Power: Transnational Civil Society and Human Rights." Chapter 7 in *The Third Force: the Rise of Transnational Civil Society,* edited by A. Florini. Washington, DC: Carnegie Endowment for International Peace.

Roche, C. 2007. *Conference on Active Citizenship, July 3, 2007: Oxfam Australia's Experience on Bottom–Up Accountability.* Melbourne: Monash University.

———. 2010. "The Seeming Simplicity of Measurement." In *Ethical Questions and International NGOs,* edited by K. Horton and C. Roche, [forthcoming]. New York: Springer.

Ronalds, P. 2008a. Do We Have to Choose? Implementing a Child Rights Based Approach at World Vision. Unpublished.

———. 2008b. "Human Rights, Aid and Development: A Complex Relationship in Complex Environments." *Human Rights Law Resource Centre Bulletin* 28: 1–2.

Ross, H., K. Verclas, and A. Levine, eds. 2009. *Managing Technology to Meet Your Mission: A Strategic Guide for Nonprofit Leaders.* San Francisco: Jossey-Bass.

Ross, S. 2008. *Towards New Understandings: Journalists and Humanitarian Relief Coverage.* San Francisco: Fritz Institute.

Rothkopf, D. 2008. *Superclass: The Global Power Elite and the World They Are Making.* New York: Farrar, Straus, and Giroux.

Rowlands, D. 2008. *Emerging Donors in International Development Assistance: A Synthesis Report.* Ottawa: International Development Research Centre.

Rudd, K. 2008. *First National Security Speech to the Australian Parliament.* December 4.

Ruggie, J. 2004. "Reconstituting the Global Public Domain—Issues, Actors, and Practices. *European Journal of International Relations* 10 (4): 499–531.

Sachs, J. 2005. *The End of Poverty.* London: Penguin Press.

———. 2008. *Common Wealth: Economics for a Crowded Planet.* New York: Penguin Press.

Salamon, L., W. Sokolowski, and R. List. 2003. *Global Civil Society: An Overview.* Baltimore: The Johns Hopkins Comparative Nonprofit Sector Project, John Hopkins University.

Sassen, S. 1999. *A New Geography of Power?* New York: Global Policy Forum.

Save the Children International. 2008. *Children Can't Wait: International Save the Children Alliance, 2008 Annual Review.* London: Save the Children International.

Schott, F. and W. Brindley. 2008. *Bridging the Humanitarian Productivity Gap*. McLean, VA: NetHope.

Schwab, K. 2007. *101st Annual Meeting of the American Jewish Committee May 1, 2007: Sticking To The Three B's—Binding, Bonding, and Building*. Washington, DC: American Jewish Committee.

Schwartz, P. 1996. *The Art of the Long View. Planning for the Future in an Uncertain World*. New York: Doubleday.

Sen, A. 1999. *Development as Freedom*. New York: Random House.

———. 2006. *Identity and Violence. The Illusion of Destiny*. London: Penguin Press.

Senge, P. 1990. *The Fifth Discipline: the Art and Practice of the Learning Organisation*. New York: Doubleday.

Shutt, C. 2009. Changing The World by Changing Ourselves: Reflections from a Bunch of BINGOs. *Practice Paper, No. 3*. Brighton: Institute of Development Studies.

Silverman, L., and L. Taliento. 2005 *What You Don't Know About Managing Nonprofits—And Why It Matters*. New York: McKinsey & Company.

Simeant, J. 2005. "What is going global? The internationalization of French NGOs 'without borders.'" *Review of International Political Economy* 12 (5): 851–883.

Singer, P. 2009. *The Life You Can Save: Acting Now to End World Poverty*. Melbourne: Text Publishing.

Slaughter, A. 2009. "America's Edge: Power in the Networked Century." *Foreign Affairs* 88 (1): 94–113.

Slim, H. 2002. *By What Authority? The Legitimacy and Accountability of Nongovernmental Organisations*. International Meeting on Global Trends and Human Rights—Before and After September 11: The International Council on Human Rights Policy. January 2002. Geneva.

———. 2005. *Idealism and Realism in Humanitarian Action*. Australian Council for International Development Humanitarian Forum. Australian Council for International Development. October 2005. Canberra.

———. 2007a. "What Happens to Government When Aid Agencies Are Around?" *Alert Net*, April 12.

———. 2007b. "White Toyota, White Aid." *Alert Net*, April 5.

Skidmore, P. 2008. "The Trouble with Politics." *The Australian Financial Review*, February 29.

Sorgenfrei, M., and R. Wrigley. 2005. "Building Analytical and Adaptive Capacities for Organisational Effectivenes." *Praxis Paper No. 7*. Oxford: International NGO Training Research Centre.

Stern, M. 1998. *Development Aid: What the Public Thinks*. New York: United Nations Development Program.

Stiglitz, J. 2002. *Globalization and Its Discontents*. London: Penguin Press.

Stoddard, A., A. Harmer, and V. DiDomenico. 2009. "Providing aid in insecure environments: 2009 update." *HPG Policy Brief 34*. London: Overseas Development Institute.

Strange, S. 1988. *State and Markets: An Introduction to International Political Economy*. New York: Basil Blackwell.

SustainAbility. 2003. *The 21st Century NGO: In The Market For Change*. Washington, DC: SustainAbility.

Tadjbakhsh, S. 2008. "Human Security." *Human Development Insights 17*. New York: United Nations Development Program.

Taleb, N. 2007. *The Black Swan: The Impact of the Highly Improbable*. London: Penguin Books.

Tapscott, D. 2008. *Grown Up Digital: How the Net Generation is Changing the World*. Columbus, OH: McGraw-Hill.

Taylor, C. 2005. *Walking the Talk: Building a Culture for Success*. London: Random House.

Terry, F. 2002. *Condemned to Repeat? The Paradox of Humanitarian Action*. New York: Cornell University Press.

Tierney, T. 2006. *The Nonprofit Sector's Leadership Deficit*. Boston: The Bridgespan Group.

The Economist. 2000. "Angry and Effective." *The Economist*. September 21.

———. 2008. "Survival of the Fittest: North Korean Society is Turbulent and in Flux." *The Economist*, September 27.

———. 2009a. "The Toxins Trickle Downward: A Downturn that Began in the Rich World is Hurting Those Who Can Least Afford It." *The Economist*, March 12.

———. 2009b. "Twitter 1, CNN 0: But the Real Winner was an Unusual Hybrid of Old and New Media." *The Economist*, June 20.

Thompson, E. 2008. *Principled Pragmatism: NGO Engagement with Armed Actors*. Monrovia, CA: World Vision International.

Union of Concerned Scientists. 2007. *Smoke, Mirrors & Hot Air: How ExxonMobil Uses Big Tobacco's Tactics to Manufacture Uncertainty on Climate Science*. Cambridge, MA: Union of Concerned Scientists.

United Nations Habitat. 2008. *State of the World's Cities 2008/9: Harmonious Cities*. London: United Nations Habitat.

United Nations News Service. 2008. "Global food crisis 'silent tsunami' threatening over 100 million people, warns UN." Geneva: United Nations.

United Nations Office for the Coordination of Humanitarian Affairs and the Internal Displacement Monitoring Centre. 2009. *Monitoring disaster displacement in the context of climate change*. Geneva: UN Office for the Coordination of Humanitarian Affairs and the Norwegian Refugee Council.

US Department of Defense. 2008. *National Defense Strategy*. Washington, DC: US Government.

Unwin, T. 2005. *Partnerships in Development Practice: Evidence from multistake-holder ICT4D partnership practice in Africa.* Paris: UNESCO.

Uvin, P. 2004. *Human Rights and Development.* Bloomfield, CT: Kumarian Press.

Valery, P. 1989. *The Outlook for Intelligence.* Princeton: Princeton University Press.

Walker, P. 2008a. "Short term life saving or long term change."*Getting Humanitarian Aid Right.* Medford, MA: Feinstein International Centre.

———. 2008b. "Complexity and Context as the Determinants of the Future." *Opinion Paper.* Medford, MA: Feinstein International Center Tufts University.

Walker, P, and D. Maxwell. 2009. *Shaping the Humanitarian World.* New York: Routledge.

Wallace, J. 2009. "The Security Dimension of Climate Change." Pp. 63–66 in *2009 State of the World: Into a Warmer World,* edited by the World Wide Institute. New York: W.W. Norton & Co.

Ward, T. 2007. "The Political Economy of NGOs and Human Security." *International Journal On World Peace* 24 (1): 43–64.

Waverman, L., M. Meschi, and M. Fuss. 2005. "The impact of telecoms on economic growth in developing countries. Africa: The impact of mobile phones." *The Vodafone Public Policy Papers Series.* 2: 10–23.

Weber, M. 1978. *Economy and Society.* Berkeley: University of California Press.

Webster, M., J. Ginnetti, P. Walker, D. Coppard, and R. Kent 2009. *The Humanitarian Costs Of Climate Change.* Medford, MA: Feinstein International Center.

Webster, M., and P. Walker 2009. *One For All and All For One, Intra-Organisational Dynamics in Humanitarian Action.* Medford, MA: Feinstein International Center Tufts University.

Weinberger, D. 2007. "The Folly of Accountabalism." *Harvard Business Review.* February 10.

Wheeler, N. 2002. *Saving Strangers. Humanitarian Intervention in International Society.* Oxford: Oxford University Press.

Williams, J., and S. Goose. 1998. "The International Campaign to Ban Landmines." Pp. 20–47 in *To Walk Without Fear. The Global Movement to Ban Landmines,* edited by M. Cameron, R. Lawson, and B. Tomlin. Oxford: Oxford University Press.

Wirtz, B., A. Mathieu, and O. Schilke. 2007. "Strategy in High-Velocity Environments." *Long Range Planning* 40: 295–313.

World Bank. 2006. *Making the New Indonesia Work For the Poor.* Washington, DC: World Bank.

World Bank. 2008. *The Growth Report: Strategies for Sustained Growth and Inclusive Development.* Commission on Growth and Development (the Spence Report). Washington, DC: World Bank.

————. 2009a. "The Global Financial Crisis: Assessing vulnerability for women and children." *Policy Brief.* Washington, DC: World Bank.

————. 2009b. *World Development Report 2010.* Washington, DC: World Bank.

World Vision Australia. 2007. *Annual Program Review: Responses to Poverty 2007.* Melbourne: World Vision Australia.

World Vision Australia. 2009. *Island Nation.* Melbourne: World Vision Australia.

World Vision International. 2006. "Humanitarianism Revisited: Issues for the Twenty-First Century." *Global Future* 2.

World Vision International. 2008. *HISS-CAM: A Decision Making Tool for Civil Military Police Engagement.* Monrovia, CA: World Vision International.

World Vision International. 2009. *World Vision International 2008 Review: Hope for the Most Vulnerable.* Monrovia, CA: World Vision International.

WWF International. 2008. *WWF Annual Review 2008.* Gland: World Wildlife Fund.

Zadek, S. 2008. "Collaborative Governance: The New Multilateralism for the Twenty-First Century." Pp. 187–200 in *Global Development 2.0: Can Philanthropists, the Public and the Poor Make Poverty History?* edited by L. Brainard and D. Chollet. Washington DC: Brookings Institution Press.

Zedillo, E., and T. Thiam. 2006. *Meeting Global Challenges: International Cooperation in the National Interest.* Stockholm: International Task Force on Global Public Goods.

Index

Note: Page numbers followed by an f, a t, or an n indicate the reference is to a figure, table, or note respectively.

About the Author

Paul Ronalds worked for World Vision Australia for six years—initially as director of policy and programs and then as deputy CEO and director of strategy. World Vision is Australia's largest INGO with an annual income of more than A$350 million, funding approximately 700 aid and development projects across 65 countries.

During his tenure at World Vision, Paul led a number of global initiatives on behalf of World Vision International, including acting as the global accountable executive for World Vision's response to the global food crisis and responsibility for World Vision's global strategy for engaging multilateral actors. Paul was also a team leader for a global strategy project designed to better position World Vision as a "next-generation NGO" and a key executive responsible for coordinating World Vision's response to climate change.

Paul has a background in law, business, and economics. Prior to World Vision, Paul worked in corporate law with Freehills, was cofounder of wishlist.com.au, one of Australia's most successful e-commerce companies, and chief operating officer of Urban Seed, an innovative and dynamic NGO that provides a range of services to marginalized people in Melbourne's inner city. Paul is a graduate of the St. James Ethics Center's Vincent Fairfax Fellowship in Ethics and Leadership and from 2006–8 was an industry representative on the Australian Council for International Development's (ACFID) code of conduct committee.

Paul has also held nonexecutive director roles at the First Step Limited, a rapid drug detoxification clinic in St Kilda, Melbourne, and the Christian Center for Socially Responsible Investment.

He has degrees in economics and law with honors from Monash University, a graduate diploma in applied finance from the Securities Institute of Australia, and a master's degree in international relations from Deakin University.

Paul is married with three children.